"(This) book is a wonderful and moving testimony to the strength and power of women as individuals and as sisters, to change themselves and their worlds."
> Marita Golden, author of *After, Migrations of the Heart: An Autobiography,* and *Saving Our Sons: Raising Black Children in a Turbulent World.*

"Barbara Morrison writes with insight and compassion about her plummet into poverty and her climb back up. The memoir is a story for now."
> Carol Brennan, author of *Headhunt, In the Dark,* and *Full Commission.*

"Ms. Morrison eloquently refutes the notion that there is a 'typical' welfare recipient. With compassion and moxie, she pulls back the curtain and shows us a more complex picture. Ms. Morrison's world includes gutsy women who find ways to move ahead with their lives despite demeaning bureaucratic and social attitudes, people who create communities of caring and sharing where they can laugh together, cry together, and hope together as they cope with their daily struggles. Her world also includes some whose hopes for a better life may not ever be realized and some who are on the brink of giving up. All are presented with a caring eye for the human details that link us together as a society."
> Mark Vidor, Assistant Director for Family Services, Department of Human Resources, Baltimore County Department of Social Services

Innocent

Confessions of a Welfare Mother

INNOCENT

Confessions of a Welfare Mother

B. Morrison

Baltimore, Maryland
www.apprenticehouse.com

ISBN: 978-1-934074-65-7

Portions of this book were previously published in *The Sun, Storyteller, Sin Fronteras, Scribble,* and *Tiny Lights.*

Printed in the United States of America

First Edition

Published by Apprentice House
The Future of Publishing…Today!

Apprentice House
Communication Department
Loyola University Maryland
4501 N. Charles Street
Baltimore, MD 21210

410.617.5265
410.617.2198 (fax)
www.ApprenticeHouse.com
info@ApprenticeHouse.com

Dedication

For Jill

TABLE OF CONTENTS

PROLOGUE

Why don't they pick that trash up? The thought skittered across my mind, almost as though someone else were speaking. Then I heard myself and—appalled—braked the car and pulled over, even before my mind caught up with my hands and feet.

Trash littered the sidewalk on both sides of Monroe Street: soda bottles, chicken boxes and newspaper pages caught between the front stoops. The sun, low in the afternoon sky, threw a shadow over one side of the street. On the other side, the sunny side, the harsh lines of the brick rowhouses and stone steps shimmered in the heat of a Baltimore August. The flat face of the houses boasted no ornamentation, merely crumbling mortar and discolored brick. Four were boarded up, one still stained by smoke.

On the shaded side of the street, a few people sat on the stoops, not moving, not even talking, simply sitting as though hypnotized by the heat. A heavyset white woman in shorts and a sleeveless blouse rested on one stoop, a thin woman dressed in dark blue on another. Down the block, an elderly African-American man with a dark baseball cap pulled low over his forehead roosted on a step.

They just sat there. They didn't read, didn't look at the passing cars. Just sat. Leaning forward with his elbows on his knees, the man looked down at his clasped hands. The heavy woman sat with her legs apart, her hands braced on her thighs. She looked across the street and up, head back, as though looking at the roofline. The other woman, the one in dark blue, twisted in upon herself: right knee crossed over left, right elbow on her knee, her right hand supporting her head while she gazed at the sidewalk. Too far apart on that long block to take any notice of each other, they just sat there in the heat, faces as blank as the unadorned brick rowhouses behind them.

Locked in my car, protected from the smells and sounds of the street by the sealed windows, I closed my eyes briefly and then looked around. On the house nearest me, the dirty white paint on the door was cracked and chipped. A drooping bedsheet hung inside the front window, while the upper two windows were covered by shades that were curled and brown at the edges.

Monroe Street steamed in the sun only a few blocks from the gentrified rowhouses of Federal Hill and the expensive tourist attractions of Baltimore's Inner Harbor. The streets there had been full of summer crowds, bustling between the Aquarium and the Science Center, the Convention Center and the shops at Harborplace, baseball caps tipped against the sun. But here no one moved.

A few cars went by. The streetlight changed and changed again. In my Honda, visor angled against the sun, air conditioning still blowing on my fingers as they gripped the steering wheel, I felt like a voyeur. The French language tape in the cassette player continued to roll out phrases: *C'est loin d'ici . . . Je suis perdu . . .*

No matter how isolated I was, sitting there in the artificial chill, I could not believe that I had even for a moment thought that the only problem with the people who lived on this street was laziness. It wasn't very long ago that I too sat on a front stoop, no job to go to, no money in my pocket, staring at the sidewalk.

Those years on welfare should have taught me once and forever to look beyond the stereotypes of poverty, but here I was, like any tourist who got lost looking for the Inner Harbor and ended up on Monroe Street, with my windows shut and doors locked, safe in my middle-class world, looking out and seeing only the trash and the stoop-sitting.

Why don't they pick that trash up?

It was the sort of comment anyone might make, the sort of comment I heard all the time from people around me. But I knew better. I knew about the inertia that kept people like the man and two women sitting there on Monroe

Street from getting up off the stoop and cleaning up the trash, cleaning up their lives, working their way to something better.

According to popular wisdom, I should never have found myself on welfare. White, educated, healthy, I grew up in a two-parent family in Roland Park, a middle-class neighborhood in Baltimore, and went to college. I was nothing like what most people picture when you say "welfare recipient". But then, in my years on welfare, with all the women and men that I met then and since, I never did meet anyone who fit that stereotype.

1
SECRETS

Even back when I was growing up in Baltimore in the fifties and sixties, Roland Park and Monroe Street were worlds apart. One Sunday, driving down Monroe to check on a patient at St. Agnes on the way out of town, my father sermonized about the problem of overpopulation, denouncing the way "worthless" people multiplied like rabbits.

"It won't be long before the world is overrun," he finished up.

My mother agreed. Looking out at the dilapidated rowhouses and the dirty steps, she said, "What we need is a good plague."

One of my brothers said, "But then we'd be killed."

My mother didn't turn her head as she replied, her voice tight and thin. "It wouldn't be my children who died."

I ignored them, as always. They were like the adults in the Peanuts comic strip: off-stage, making incomprehensible quacking noises. They had nothing to do with me. The second of six children, I learned early to stay off my parents' radar. I didn't know why I seemed singled out like the ugly duckling to be the one who didn't belong, but thought it might be because of my blond hair. Adults always commented on how I stood out in our flock of dark-haired children. *The iceman*, my mother would say, which made no sense to me. I was not cold.

My earliest memory is of lying stomach-down under the couch, my head sticking out, propped up on my elbows, so I could see the television. I was four, and Roy Rogers was one of my favorite shows. My brother—a year and a half older—sat on the couch and my sister—a year and a half younger—on the chair. We didn't talk to each other. The baby mumbled to himself in the playpen.

Over the television's whinnying horses came the clack of my mother's heels in the hallway. Quickly I scooted further back under the couch and put my hands over my head.

Her heels stopped at the door. There was a long pause, and then they started back down the hall again. I slid forward until I could see the television. My brother and sister hadn't moved.

As I got older, I found that as long as I got passing grades, showed up for dinner, and slept in my own bed, my parents never asked what else I did. It was not hard to stay out of their way; my father worked nearly all the time, and my mother was busy at home. She ruled the house with harsh words, backed up by the stinging threat of the yardstick or the wooden back of the hairbrush. I was amazed to learn later that it was normal for children to do things to attract parental attention. I wanted exactly the opposite.

I assumed other children were like the kids in books: happy souls with loving parents, lots of jolly friends and exciting adventures. My own siblings were like foreign countries to me. We didn't talk. I had closed my borders and withdrawn to my inner life. I was the invisible girl.

Escaping the house whenever possible, I roamed wild around the neighborhood, crawled into the head-high sewer pipes, and explored the woods behind the seminary. I found a refuge in the library's wooden alcoves where I liked to sit in the corner by the door reading about King Arthur. I dreamed of being, not a maiden meekly waiting in a turret, but one of the knights with their lonely quests and feasting camaraderie. I thought that was how people—adults—must really behave: living by some code of honor, loyal to their friends unto death.

Not that I had much chance to practice such loyalty. Trees were my best friends. They had personalities: the tulip magnolia with its child-friendly branches, the weeping cherry tree, the beech tree behind whose fans of leaves I hid, straddling a branch, reading. I wished I could fade into the trunk of a tree and disappear. Barefoot, I practiced walking as silently as an Indian on the cruel curled holly leaves.

We rarely saw any relatives. My mother's family came from a farm in

Delaware, but hard times and large families had reduced their holding to the small, plain farmhouse. The middle child, she claimed she was the disappointing second girl who could never measure up to her talented older sister or matter as much as her little brother. Chin lifted, her lips thinned with anger, she repeatedly described the same few incidents that proved her parents favored her siblings. She was uncomfortable with physical contact, so there were no caresses in our house, only rough combings of tangled hair or the hard grasp on my arm while she smacked my behind with the hairbrush.

My father grew up in a rowhouse in Waverly, then a blue-collar neighborhood in Baltimore. A brilliant boy, he was treated like a prince by his parents and sister. The Army paid his way through medical school, but he forever carried a chip on his shoulder because he'd gone to the University of Maryland instead of Johns Hopkins. Although as a doctor he was much in demand and much loved by colleagues and patients, he was caustic to the point of cruelty at home.

My mother said he was a genius and therefore not bound by ordinary rules of courtesy, but that didn't stop her complaining to us kids about the way he treated her and how miserable her life was. Her life was a soap opera, and she was the star. My brother took to calling her the Martyr Mother.

My parents almost never entertained; my father hated the idea. Neighborhood children didn't want to come over to play because there were always other siblings butting into one's games. Also, despite having six of her own, my mother had little tolerance for the noise and energy of children.

Although she wore her martyr's crown at home, in public my mother pretended that we were a Cleaver-perfect family. On the rare occasions that we went out as a family, she insisted on a silent crocodile of children, perfectly dressed and well-behaved.

With this social isolation, our house seemed like a place apart and the life we led there had nothing to do with the face we were supposed to present to the world. I knew better than to tell anyone about the arguments in the night or the bruises my mother covered with long-sleeved blouses.

While growing up in Roland Park in the fifties and sixties made for a seemingly sheltered childhood, there was always an undercurrent of fear. The hill behind our house fell away so steeply that my mother had nightmares about the house rolling down it, and hired men to dig railroad ties into the slope to prevent erosion. At school we spent long breathless minutes crouched under our desks with our fingers laced behind our necks, though how that would protect us from an atom bomb was never clear. The Cuban Missile Crisis had my mother poring over plans for building an air raid shelter in the side yard. My parents also worried that black people would move into the neighborhood despite the covenants prohibiting such a thing. There were stories of teenagers having rumbles up at the junior high and ripping up the bus seats with their switchblades. Rumors circulated about the White Car Man who drove around wearing only a trenchcoat and trying to get girls to come over to the car so he could expose himself.

Some nights I woke up to find my mother asleep on the rug next to my bed. I wasn't sure why my half of the room I shared with my sister counted as a refuge from my father's anger. What I didn't understand, I shrugged off.

Fearing his anger—he was enormous, almost six feet tall—I avoided him whenever possible. On the rare Sunday afternoon that my father was not working, he roared that he just wanted to watch the ball game in peace. Even when he was in a good mood and willing to wrestle with my brothers and sisters or tell stories about crazy medical students he had known, I kept my distance.

Eventually forced by a heart attack to stay home, he was shocked to discover that our lives went on without him, and hurt when, as darkness fell, my baby sister—his favorite child—solemnly told him that it was time for him to go home. She didn't even realize that he lived there.

He changed after that, taking more time off and trying to be home in the evenings. I began to hate dinnertime, a command performance, with my mother at one end of the table, yardstick at the ready, my father at the other. As the second oldest, I had to sit next to my father.

One night at the dinner table, after asking my brothers and sisters about their day at school, my mother rebuked one of my sisters for only getting 95 on a test. "Why didn't you get 100?"

I started to say something about the 100 I had gotten on my vocabulary quiz.

My father slammed his palm on the table between us. "Shut up! No one cares what you did." He turned away to looked at my youngest brother. "Did you have a game today?"

My eyes burned but I refused to cry. *I can be a rock,* I thought, grasping after the Paul Simon song. *I don't feel anything. He cannot hurt me.*

At the end of every meal, I had to carry my father's plate out to the kitchen, trying not to look at his cigarette butts stubbed out in the food, fighting back nausea. Both of my parents smoked incessantly.

When my sister saw pictures of a diseased lung in Biology class, she begged my mother to stop.

"Never," my mother replied. "My cigarettes are my only friends."

The stench permeated our clothes and our hair. We kids were always coughing and croupy once the windows closed for the winter.

There was a more immediate danger. In the car I always sat behind my father so he couldn't see me. Once, the cigarette butt he tossed out the window came back in through mine and fell onto the seat beside me. I didn't notice that it was there until my shorts flared up. He didn't want to stop the car to put out the fire, but my mother made him.

I didn't expect to understand my parents. After all, they were products of their time, a time before television, a time shrouded in history. My father did not talk about his childhood or his family, but my mother would sometimes say: *My father lost all his money in The Depression; boys I danced with one night were shipped off to The War the next day.*

When I was eleven, my mother began to throw secrets my way. Perhaps she sensed my lack of sympathy for the complaints she fingered over like rosary beads.

Cornering me in the bathroom one day, she told me that after my youngest sister was born, she had taken steps to ensure that she would not get pregnant again. She had to get the doctor to testify that she would not survive another pregnancy before they would let her get her tubes tied.

I wasn't sure who "they" were.

She went on. "We're at their mercy. The only thing of value you have is your virginity. If you lose that, no one will ever want you."

I must have looked skeptical.

"You think I don't know what I'm talking about? Believe me, it's not even enough to be good; you have to keep up the appearance of being good, or one day your husband will beat you for cheating on him."

"Why would he think that?" I asked.

"Why? Why? Just look at you," she said triumphantly, pointing a long finger at my face.

I glanced in the mirror and understood finally that my blond hair and freckles made me the cuckoo in my father's nest of dark-haired, olive-skinned children. *The iceman*, I thought.

As if being the stick he beat her with were not enough to make me a pariah in her eyes, she told me that finding out she was pregnant with me marked the lowest point in her life. Being pregnant again meant she could not leave the unhappy and abusive marriage.

"I thought I might be able to make it alone with one child but not with two," she said.

I wondered if I was supposed to feel guilty as well as sorry for her. *The Martyr Mother again*, I thought, rolling my eyes. I did feel sorry for her, but not sorry enough to wish I hadn't been born.

As news of the civil rights movement filtered into Roland Park, I began to pay attention. I had run across a book of newspaper accounts of lynchings in the South, which made me go cold with horror. Meanwhile, day after relentless day, the Eichmann trial brought images of concentration camp victims before my eyes. I became convinced that a lampshade in our house was made of human skin and refused to go near it.

My parents, though they condemned the camps, were convinced that Jews were behind a conspiracy to take control of the world. They also believed that the civil rights movement was clearly just a cover for a plot to murder all white people in their beds. Hippies and anyone who protested against nuclear bombs or the Vietnam War were Communists out to destroy the country. For that matter, Franklin Roosevelt's New Deal and Johnson's War on Poverty were obviously part of a plot to turn the U.S. into a Russian colony.

Watching them out of the corners of my eyes, I trusted the peculiar independence of mind that had come from my odd childhood where the only approval I had to look for was my own. I assumed that everyone else in Roland Park must have the same prejudices as my parents, but—walled off in my own world—I was free to make up my own mind about things. Equal rights for everyone seemed like common sense to me. After all, didn't I want the freedom to have a life I chose, rather than the one I inherited? Surely everyone else did too.

When Baltimore decided to integrate the public schools, my parents sent us to private schools rather than allow us to sit in a classroom with black children. I didn't want to go. I loved the public school where I played hopscotch with Sara at recess and Miss Hackman threatened to hang us out of the window by our ears.

I hated that private school. The first day, I looked at the groups of girls talking. They all seemed to know each other. I stood near one group, hoping they might include me. A girl with gleaming chestnut hair restrained by a black headband turned to look at me.

"I'm . . ."

"I know who you are," she said. "Go back to your public school. We don't want you here."

I went over and sat at my desk and waited for class to start.

Although I eventually made a couple of friends at that school, I mostly followed the same strategy I used at home of doing the minimum necessary to be left alone.

With the social unrest during the long hot summers of the sixties, I became even more disenchanted with Roland Park and its covenants prohibiting blacks and Jews from spending even one night on its green streets except as servants. They were prohibited too from being a part of my life, at least insofar as my parents could manage it. Catholics were suspect as well, Kennedy's election having proved that they were indeed plotting to take over the country and hand it over to the Vatican. My brother joked that our parents were equal opportunity bigots.

The girls at my school, with their easy assumption that the accident of their birth somehow made them better than other people, bewildered me. In the middle of the civil rights movement, they listened to Motown music while ordering around the black servants who picked their clothes up off the floor. My schoolmates, absorbed in planning their debutante balls, seemed to know nothing about the war in Vietnam, perhaps because only other people's brothers and boyfriends went off to fight.

I felt suffocated by the endless restrictions and covenants. I longed for a sword to cut through the tangled secrets, the sadness hidden behind bright smiles. When I left for college in 1968, after another summer of race riots, I swore I would never return to Roland Park.

My mother didn't believe in letting children make choices, so the first choice I was ever permitted to make was about applying to college. I was allowed to choose between two in-state colleges, Western Maryland and Washington. I offered to go to Towson State if money was a problem, but my parents didn't want me to live at home, so I chose Western Maryland.

I was grateful that I was able to go to college at all, knowing that it was only after a fierce battle between my parents: my mother wanted her daughters to have the college education she'd been denied, while my father maintained that girls were not worth educating. Like many people at the time, he believed that women's brains were simply inferior to men's, so the smartest woman in the world could never reach the level of the least intelligent man.

My mother sent me off to college with my father's old Army footlocker containing plaid wool skirts and mohair sweaters. But it was the sixties, so the skirts and sweaters stayed in the footlocker while I let my hair grow long and wore bell-bottom jeans.

Following my survival strategy of staying out of everyone's sight, I had not joined in any political activity while in high school, but once I got to college everything changed. Many of the students were vocal in their support of civil rights and their opposition to the Vietnam War. Finally feeling safe enough to venture out of my shell, I joined in and helped organize marches on campus and carpools to larger protests in Baltimore and Washington. I kept a journal that I stored in a drawer with my poems and short stories.

Through Christine, who had the room next to mine, I fell in with the small group of hippies on campus, delighted that they shared my politics and enthusiasms. We argued about books, marched in anti-war demonstrations, and indulged in a passion for music. In Baltimore, I had only listened to Motown and the Beatles, but now Christine and my other friends introduced me to Richie Havens, Cream, the Byrds, Donovan, the Grateful Dead, Janis Joplin, Joni Mitchell, Leonard Cohen, Tom Rush—we called him Tom Crush.

Sometimes we would escape from campus for a weekend, borrowing a car to go to D.C. or New York City. Occasionally we camped out in the woods near campus or borrowed an empty vacation home owned by one of our families.

One weekend in November of 1969, my second year at Western Maryland College, a group of us borrowed a one-room cabin in the woods out past Frederick. Musty and cold when we first unlocked the door, it soon warmed up once we got a fire going in the wood stove. There were about a dozen of us and, after unpacking our sleeping bags and food supplies, we spread out. Some people explored the woods while others curled up by the stove to read or talk. Later we fixed a big pot of spaghetti and a salad, put out some bread, and opened gallon jugs of red wine.

After dinner, we sprawled on the couch and chairs or sat on the floor in the soft light of the candles we'd brought. The wood stove roared as we reached for the wine. Jim and Charlie, brothers from New Bedford, Massachusetts, picked their guitars and sang Long Black Veil, drawing out the harmony at the end. Charlie strummed a final chord and bounced a little on his chair.

"That was great!" he said. He looked around at all of us, our faces lit by the flickering candlelight, lulled by the music, the wine and our friendship. Pushing back his unruly dark hair, his eyes bright, Charlie declared, "This is the perfect life."

It *was* perfect: the scent of woodsmoke, the sharp bite of the wine, the friends who were like family to me. I felt time slipping out from under me, nostalgic already for this moment.

Though most of us became friends for life, I lost touch with a few, like my first roommate. A gentle girl who whispered from behind her long curtain of hair, light reflecting off her round wire-rimmed glasses, she dropped out after only a few months of school and ran off with a musician to live the hippie life in New York. We visited her several times in her tiny, roach-filled apartment in Greenwich Village, the musician having long since abandoned her. Then she disappeared. We tried contacting her parents, but of course they had no idea where she was. It was common for families to sever ties with children who dropped out of school and vanished into hippie havens such as the Village or Haight-Ashbury. Sometimes it was the children who did the severing.

One night a friend dragged me down to the dorm's tv lounge to see a show that everyone was talking about. As Archie Bunker shouted and raved and threatened his wife, I shrank back into the couch. Why was everyone laughing? There was nothing funny about these people. They sounded like my parents.

By the end of my second year, I decided that it was time to make a change. I was too comfortable. It was as though the Green Knight had shown up and issued me a challenge. Unaccustomed as I was to making choices, this seemed like the right one.

I transferred to Clark University in Worcester, Massachusetts. The deal was that—unlike my brother and sister who were both permitted to go to out-of-state Ivy League colleges, all expenses paid—my parents would pay only my tuition; I would have to pay for my own room and board. I didn't waste time resenting the fact that my siblings were getting a free ride at top-notch schools. Accustomed as I was to my ugly duckling status, I didn't expect the same treatment. In fact, I was surprised and grateful to get the tuition. Many people I knew didn't have even that.

One of the reasons for moving to Massachusetts in 1970 was to escape the suffocating racism of Maryland. I didn't know much about New England, simply that it was the other direction from the South, where they turned fire hoses on black students and murdered young people who were trying to register black voters.

I felt at home immediately. When I crossed over the Tappan Zee Bridge and entered New England, I felt that I was waking up from the long stupor of my childhood, leaving behind my life in Maryland with its languid afternoons and heat-stunned evenings. I thought that I was experiencing morning for the first time, that clear, crisp, first-time-ever feeling.

My exhilaration vanished, however, once I reached Worcester. All I saw as I drove into town were auto body shops and funeral homes. *What have I done?* I thought.

Worcester was a New England mill town, most of whose mills had closed by the time I moved there in 1970. It was a struggling city that traded back and forth with Providence the distinction of being the second largest city in New England, Boston being the largest, of course.

The apartment I shared with a friend from Maryland was on a street of dreary triple-deckers, the local term for frame houses with three floors of apartments, often with porches stacked in front and in back. The surface of the narrow clogged street was broken up with frost heaves, and the air was permeated by an acrid smell I later learned came from barrels in backyards where everyone burned trash. Other barrels held bottles and cans that were collected, not by the city but by somebody our landlord hired, a grizzled man in a dirty Red Sox cap, flannel shirt, quilted vest and Dickie's work pants, who lifted the barrels as if they weighed nothing and tipped them clanking and clattering into the larger barrels on his truck. The streets were full of these trucks, rusted out but held together with wire and duct tape, rattling over the broken asphalt.

My friend and I were on the second floor, usually the best floor because you got some of the heat from downstairs and had the upstairs as insulation. The elderly couple upstairs sometimes locked their retarded daughter in a closet for hours, where she kicked the floor and screamed. The drug dealers downstairs were replaced after a few weeks by a veteran just back from Vietnam, who would turn up at our door claiming to have heard voices from our apartment calling him a murderer. I began to suspect that everyone in the city was crazy.

Certainly Worcester had pockets of wealthy people, an excellent art museum, and a large number of colleges that enriched the cultural life. But most people were working class, many of them immigrants who had come to work in the mills. In those days, the early seventies, you could take a map of the city and draw lines around the ethnic neighborhoods: the Armenians, the Irish, the Swedes, the Greeks. Late-coming Puerto Ricans blurred the lines somewhat as they moved into several different areas.

Because it was built on seven hills, my college friends often joked that Worcester must be, like Rome, the center of civilization. More often, though, people referred to it as the armpit of New England, dark and grim.

It was known primarily as the birthplace of diner cars—the original diners shaped like railway cars, slick with aluminum trim and Art Deco ornamentation. Worcester still boasted many diners where we would go to get coffee in thick white cups: the Miss Worcester, the Boulevard, the Top Hat. Nevertheless, whatever glory Worcester once had was gone before I arrived. The city seemed like a shell to me, like the grand Victorian train station on Washington Square that stood empty and ruined, open to the rain, covered with pigeon droppings and grimy streaks from the polluted air.

Although tempted to race back to Maryland, I stayed and learned to negotiate snowy streets without falling too often. As a student I had little money. My part-time job in the school library didn't pay much, so I mostly lived on Campbell's soup. Late one afternoon, finding it impossible to study with the family upstairs screaming at each other and a street hockey game going on in the driveway outside my window, I decided to go out and get something for dinner. I stumbled out into the grey gloom, wrapped up against the cold.

At the Cumberland Farms at the bottom of May Street, I counted out nickels and pennies on the counter for a can of Vegetarian Vegetable. Clutching my dinner, I trudged back up the hill, past rows of dilapidated houses with candy wrappers and plastic grocery bags caught on their steps. Overhead hung the dour October sky where a ragged V of geese called to each other.

I thought back to my long walks on Roland Park's serpentine streets, the aroma of brown beech leaves underfoot, white pine smoke curling from chimneys.

A car belching blue exhaust jolted over the broken asphalt and brought me back to myself. I caught a whiff of a rank odor that I already recognized as the residue of a burnt-out house.

I thought of a quote from last semester's Milton that had stuck in my mind. It was the thing Satan says, after he is cast out of heaven and thrown down to hell along with the other rebellious angels. He stands up and looks around and says, "'Here at least/we shall be free.'"

Worcester was my home now. I crossed my arms over my chest, hugging the can of soup close. I had no regrets.

2
CHOICES

I made friends at school and in town. My closest friend was Jill. At first, I didn't know quite what to make of her, small and fierce and totally honest, but I loved the way she seemed so at home in the world. She was a few years older than I, an artist whom I met when her four-year-old son marched up to me at a crowded demonstration against the Vietnam War and took hold of my hand. Looking up from under his rumpled blond hair, he smiled and refused to leave me. Serious, precise Richard and his impish younger brother, Michael, eventually came to seem like my own children. I loved hearing Jill's stories about them. One of my favorites had Richard hiding Oreos in his diaper, dismayed when he later found them to be wet and inedible.

Jill lived on Piedmont Street, which was only blocks from the university in distance but miles away in terms of status. No students considered living there. The triple-deckers were more run-down than those around the university and interspersed with commercial buildings. Piedmont Street's bleakness was compounded by an absence of trees, not to mention the empty lots where houses had burned down. Jill's apartment was on the second floor of a peeling grey house surrounded by an extended family on the first and third floors. Corrugated metal buildings of the plumbing company bordered one side of Jill's house, a vacant lot where a house had once stood the other.

Beyond the lot, a squat brick building housed a neighborhood activity center, a hangout for young people, which provided the soundtrack for the neighborhood. The loud music that poured from it all day and late into the night was a background to the mothers sitting on their front stoops calling out to any child within earshot who was misbehaving. I could hear them against the smooth, insistent R&B beat, calling.

"Leave that child alone."

"You stop that right now."

"Get out of the street – don't you see that car?"

Despite the ruckus around her, Jill carried a sense of normalcy with her always, an air of calm common sense. Whatever she did always seemed the most ordinary thing in the world to be doing, whether it was painting an old mailtruck purple and gold or creating life-sized portraits of her friends to glue onto a plastic tent. She was interested in everything I was. Our talks ranged from politics to poetry, from gardening to Buddhism.

An only child, she said, "We're so alike! Is this what it's like to have a sister?"

"No." Tormented by a younger sister who tried to copy whatever I did, I had worked out elaborate escape plans so that I could get out of the house without being followed. *Leave me alone* was my regular refrain. But with Jill it was different.

Although she was part Swedish and part French Canadian with a dash of Native American, Jill made me think of Joan of Arc: a slim, straight woman with dark hair, pale skin and a fierce honesty. I was surprised when I discovered that her income came from the Federal Aid to Families with Dependent Children (AFDC) program, the one most people meant when they said "welfare". I knew she worked hard, caring for her two sons, volunteering in neighborhood organizations, and creating playful artworks. But a welfare mom? Growing up in Baltimore, I thought that only black people were on welfare.

"Surprise!" Jill said. "White people can be poor too." She explained that in fact the vast majority of people on welfare were white and lived in rural areas, not inner cities. Jill had done a lot of research back when she had helped start the Worcester chapter of the Welfare Rights Organization. As Jill started introducing me to other welfare parents, I found they all were active in the community: taking care of elderly neighbors; providing child care so others could work; volunteering at schools, neighborhood centers, and the food co-op; not "sitting around on their cans", as my father used to say.

One evening when I stopped by, Richard opened the door. Immediately, he took my hand and drew me inside. His eyes were huge in his pinched face.

"What's wrong?" I asked.

"The puppy died." The previous day, Jill had told me that her puppy wasn't eating but that—with the vet so expensive—she was going to wait a day to see if it got better.

"Oh, honey," I said, putting an arm around him.

However, it wasn't the puppy that concerned Richard. "Ma's in her room," he said, gently steering me in that direction.

I paused in the doorway. No lights were on but I could make out Jill's form lying on the bed, her back to me. Sitting next to her, I touched her shoulder. "Jill?"

She kept her face turned away. Her voice thick with tears, she said, "We came home, and he was just lying there all stiff."

I lay down and put my arm around her. Her hand grasped mine. The streetlight glowed behind the curtains. I heard Michael mumble in his sleep in the other bedroom. Then Richard came in and lay down too. When Richard and Jill finally fell asleep, I slipped out and went home.

In addition to Jill and her sons, I also met Lewis, who lived in a flowered schoolbus, and his son Kevin who was the same age as Richard. Kevin's mother had left for California soon after his birth, giving Lewis sole custody.

I was twenty and in love for the first time. More than anything else, Lewis made me feel safe. Wiry and strong, he had long brown hair that he usually wore in braids and bright eyes the color of the big sky over Montana where he'd grown up. He had run away from home at fourteen to live in Haight-Ashbury. Afterwards, he tried several times to reconcile with his mother, but she always shut the door in his face. Later, he traveled with gypsies in England and ended up in Worcester when his motorcycle broke down there. He knew how to live in the world, something I wasn't at all sure about myself.

Sometimes he parked the bus on the empty lot on Castle Street, the next street over from Piedmont, where there was a row of dark-stained brick houses built in 1873. Once when he was away, the police—sure that a hippie schoolbus must have drugs in it—decided to break in but were scared off by Lewis's two German shepherds. Hearing that the police were planning to shoot the dogs, Lewis tried to watch out for them, but they drove up as he was giving the dogs water outside the bus. The dogs, terrified by the men and cars, ran up the hill to the playground. The policemen fired at the dogs and chased after them, continuing to shoot even as the dogs dodged between the children on the swings and seesaws.

The neighborhood was outraged at the callous disregard of the children's safety. "What were they thinking?" Jill cried.

We were all outraged, too, that the police arrested Lewis for assault with a deadly weapon: the dogs. Eventually he was able to get the charge dismissed.

I never knew for sure when I would see Lewis next. Sometimes he came to the apartment I shared with some other students, where I seemed to spend a lot of time sitting by the window writing in my journal and hoping to see him drive up in the schoolbus. He rarely stayed the whole night; he fought sleep as much as he could, resenting the time wasted.

Of course, my parents hated him. They met him only once, a few months after I graduated from college in 1972, when he drove a truck to Baltimore for our impromptu, do-it-yourself wedding in the living room, surrounded by my Maryland friends. It was Lewis's idea to get married. He didn't want me to be estranged from my family as he was from his, and thought they would accept me better if we were married.

I had tried to prepare her, but my mother took one look at Lewis's braids and put on her stiffest smile.

When she took me aside, I knew it would be bad.

"You have broken my heart," she started by saying.

"Okay." It wasn't the first time.

"Not that there's anything you can do about it now—you're damaged goods—so we simply have to get through this the best we can."

"Agreed."

We put together a buffet dinner of punch and sandwiches.

"There isn't time to make a cake," she said, glaring at me.

I apologized, not that it would make any difference.

To avoid contamination, she kept my younger brothers and sisters away from us, not only me and Lewis but my friends too. After it was over and we had seen my friends off into the cool night air, she turned to us and said, "Well, that's done."

Lewis thanked her and started to open the front door again.

"Where do you think you're going?" she said.

"I'm going to sleep in the truck tonight." He'd fixed up a bed in the box, part of a deal we'd made that he would put up with any amount of nastiness as long as he could retreat to his own space at night.

"Nonsense," my mother said. "I've prepared a guest room for you."

I wondered if she meant for both of us or if she intended for me to sleep in my sister's room as I had the night before. Tired of arguments and tension, I said, "Thanks, but we will sleep in the truck. We'll join you for breakfast in the morning if that's okay."

"Fine," she said. "Don't just stand there. You're letting all the heat out."

I turned and followed Lewis down the front path. She shut the door firmly behind us.

Later, back in Worcester, Jill presented me with a mug of chamomile tea and an appeal to tell her all about it. I tried to explain that the ceremony was never meant to insult my mother. "We didn't have to get married; we could have kept on living together."

Jill nodded. "You know, I can't even imagine dealing with six kids."

I hadn't thought of that. My sister had once asked my mother if she had meant to have six children. "Oh, yes," my mother had replied in that bright voice she used with teachers and my father's doctor friends. "As I walked down the aisle, I thought to myself: *I'm going to have six children, three boys and three girls.*"

Given the way she loved to run things, surely she would have preferred to keep working. At my brothers' school, they called her the General because of the way she jumped in and directed fund-raising activities. At the hospital's

Women's Auxiliary where she was President, they called her Mrs. Fullcharge. One household simply did not offer a wide enough scope for her drive, not even with six children.

Jill went on. "She must be really strong."

I thought of the girdle my mother wore every day and tried to get me to wear too. Those unused girdles were probably still sitting in my top drawer under the shepherd and shepherdess figurines she'd selected for my bureau.

When I went off in the schoolbus with Lewis, I knew what I was choosing. I dropped the idea of working my way through graduate school. As I expected, my family closed ranks behind me as if I had never been there, the same way Lewis's family had when he left for Haight-Ashbury and my college roommate's when she left for the Village. I was allowed to visit once or twice a year, but my mother was determined that I would not have an opportunity to infect my brothers and sisters with my wild hippie life.

I didn't care. Cooking rice over a hibachi improvised from a hubcap and oven rack, sitting out under the stars talking, listening to Lewis pick out a tune on an old guitar: my life didn't seem that wild to me.

I worked in an envelope factory and then as a secretary. Jobs were scarce in those days, even for college graduates. The glut of boomers with college degrees had flooded the job market, so an English degree was not worth much. A genius at fixing things, Lewis worked as a mechanic in another factory, keeping the lumbering old machines running. We lived in the schoolbus with a woodstove for heat, so it was a challenge to get to work without soot smears on my clothes.

We talked about getting some land and a farmhouse. The seventies "back to the land" movement was going strong, and we dreamed about raising our own food. I wanted a field full of orange pumpkins and a couple of goats.

Having lots of children was a part of my "country wife" vision, and I was lucky enough to get pregnant soon after we were married. Kevin too was excited about the new baby. Kevin was a bright, quirky elf of a boy whom I adored. We bonded so quickly that it made me impatient for the new baby to arrive so I could have two children to cuddle.

Pregnancy was a wonderful time for me, although sometimes people on the street remarked that I seemed too young to be having a baby. My cheeks still chubby with baby fat, I looked about 15, seven years younger than my actual age. I was never sick and felt hugely happy every day. I joked that it must be hormones, but being so in love with Lewis probably had something to do with it.

At night, the fire in the wood stove died out, and by morning the bus was freezing. If he was there, Lewis always got up first to light the fire, but he mostly worked nights. I was worried that the baby wouldn't survive a cold Massachusetts winter and insisted we get an apartment.

Lewis didn't want to be tied down by rent and heating bills. Finally he agreed, but the apartment never really became a home. We had no furniture other than a couple of beds and a table we found in the apartment. I had my grandmother's rocking chair that I had brought up to Massachusetts with me. All the cooking was done on a Coleman stove since we didn't have any appliances other than an old washing machine Lewis had patched together, and the windowsill was our refrigerator. Lewis insisted that we were only camping there and would soon move back to the bus. Although he had resisted the idea of an apartment, the rooms quickly filled up with engine parts and other projects of his.

Giving birth marked a turning point in my life. I was shocked when this wet, live, *separate* thing came out of me. Oh, I'd read the books, seen the films, listened to the heartbeat. But that intellectual knowledge was quite different from the miracle of this mewling little thing that had been me but now was definitely not me anymore. I was shocked too by my immediate and irrational devotion to this wrinkled red lump, a devotion that—as it turned out—never wavered during the sleepless nights that followed.

When I got home from the hospital, I called my mother to let her know she had a grandson named Jeremy. She congratulated me, told me I didn't know the first thing about taking care of a baby, and insisted that he be taught to call her *Grandmother*. No diminutives would be acceptable. Later, she sent a silver rattle and a teething ring with his name engraved on it.

What with Kevin, the baby and my job, I was exhausted all the time, partly from the birth and nursing, but also because Jeremy turned out to be a nocturnal child who, left to himself, would only sleep for a couple of hours in the afternoon and expected constant attention the rest of the time. Luckily Kevin adored his baby brother and helped entertain him. I had given up even trying to write in my journal.

Although the most competent man I had ever met—he could fix anything—Lewis couldn't hold onto money. He gave a lot of it away. Since we knew many people whose finances were so precarious that a car insurance payment or the bill for a tank of heating oil was a catastrophe, I couldn't blame him for wanting to help; in fact, his generosity was one of the things I loved about him. But I was furious when the rent check bounced because he had emptied the bank account to help out an elderly woman who was behind on her phone bill. Somehow, when the rent came due, I was always the one who had the money to pay it.

Lewis worked the third shift, 11 p.m. to 7 a.m., so we took turns caring for Jeremy and Kevin. Being at my secretarial job was in itself a respite from the demands of a newborn, but between staying up late to wash diapers in the old machine that walked across the kitchen floor as it spun, getting up to comfort a wakeful Jeremy, and rising early to pack a baby bag for Lewis to use during the day, I was worn out. It seemed as though 1-4 a.m. was the only time I could snatch any sleep, and that was when Jeremy was most ready to play. I spent endless nights rocking him and crying from pure tiredness. After a few months of this, I collapsed with a severe strep infection and recognized that I couldn't keep up that pace any longer.

Our problems started then: when, sick and exhausted with caring for a child who never slept, I told Lewis I had quit my job.

"But who will pay the bills?" he asked.

I stared at him. I knew that choosing a man with braids who lived in a schoolbus for a husband meant that we wouldn't have a traditional marriage, but I had certainly assumed that he would support me if I couldn't work for a while. "You won't?"

"Why should I? You're the one who wanted an apartment. I've tried to help out as much as I can, but it's your place."

I had thought it was ours. "You've been living here too."

"Well, of course I wanted to be with you." Puzzled, wary, he watched me.

"The doctor told me I needed to rest. He said I should quit my job."

"Doctors! What do they know? You're not in Roland Park anymore."

Tired, weak with illness and wakeful nights, I gave in to the anger that swept through me and lashed out at him, calling him names, accusing him of using me for a free place to live. We argued for over an hour until he finally left, saying he would come back when I was ready to be more reasonable.

The arguments continued for months, even though Lewis did agree to cover the bills for a while. We quarreled every day, made up in bed, and quarreled again the next day. Our fights brought out all kinds of unresolved personal issues that we had no idea how to work out without hurting each other. I knew that we were both in the wrong, but I didn't know how to make things right.

One night we were driving to Jill's to pick up Jeremy. Not wanting to take sides, she had offered to babysit so Lewis and I could have some time together, but we couldn't keep from rehashing our arguments. He started complaining about my not working.

I said, "I just don't see why do you think it's wrong to support us."

"I'm doing it, aren't I? But I shouldn't have to. Just because you're a woman doesn't mean you're helpless. You can take care of yourself."

Frustrated that he was turning my feminism against me, I wondered if he was right, if my independence so briefly asserted was worth so little that I not only expected but demanded to be cared for. "What about Jeremy?"

"How do I even know he's mine?"

I was too shocked to answer for a moment. My hands began to shake and my eyes burned. Helpless outrage consumed me. I said, "I'll get a lawyer and make you pay."

"No you won't. You can't afford one. But I can. Maybe I'll sue for custody and then you'll have to pay *me* child support."

I felt light-headed with shock. "You don't want custody."

Lewis laughed. "I'm the one with a job. The judge might very well decide I'm the better parent."

I hated it. I hated myself and the way we were treating each other. "Stop," I said. "Stop the truck. I want to get out. I want to walk."

"Don't be stupid."

Desperate to get away from the argument, I opened the door and tried to climb out. Asphalt flashed by under me and then Lewis grabbed my arm and dragged me back inside.

"Are you crazy?" he screamed. "Shut that door."

I wasn't crazy. But I couldn't bear all the anger. And I was baffled that he didn't want to support us, miserable and afraid that he didn't love me after all. I wanted to do what I had always done: run away and hide.

He was equally baffled by the way—as he said—he went from being someone who could do no wrong to someone who couldn't do anything right. Acknowledging that both attitudes were wrong, I still hoped we could work things out.

When I discovered that he had acquired a girlfriend, I was devastated. I wanted to shut the door, curl up under the blankets and cry. He took Kevin and went to live with his new girlfriend, coming by occasionally to visit me and Jeremy. Sometimes he stopped by at dawn on his way home from work, crawling into bed next to me, and I welcomed the familiar strength of him, remembering how happy we had once been.

As a last-ditch effort I tried to get Lewis to go to marriage counseling with me.

"You must be crazy," he said. "That will never happen."

There was nothing more I could do.

Later I thought that maybe if I had remembered the way his mother had treated him and Kevin's mother had run out on him, I would not have been so surprised that he was quick to see a door closing and move on. But at the time all I could think of was that he didn't care about me and probably never had. To him, I was only an easily replaceable stopgap for that empty place Kevin's mother had left behind when she took off for California.

Lewis told me that he would not be able to give me any alimony or child support. He didn't make very much money and was afraid—not without reason—that if he got behind on regularly scheduled payments, the Department of Social

Services would have an excuse to take Kevin away. It was unusual enough for a man to have custody of a child. As a long-haired hippie, Lewis was already suspect, and he wanted to stay out of the system.

Most of the poor people I knew shared that fear of having their kids taken away for some real or imagined infraction. "It's how they keep us in line," Jill said.

Jeremy was almost a year old. Sturdy and imaginative, he held long conversations with his oatmeal-colored teddy bear. I read him the Christopher Robin stories and Milne's other books. Jeremy especially liked the poem about James James Morrison Morrison Weatherby George DuPree, thinking he must be a cousin or something.

I searched for some kind of work where I could keep him with me during the day. Jill helped me look for a communal living situation but we had no luck finding a place that would open its door to someone who could not contribute financially. For the next few years, at least, the cost of child care would outweigh any salary I could make.

In June I found a live-in job in Worcester with a family who treated me and Jeremy like members of the family. They gave me room and board in return for cleaning the house, fixing dinner, and keeping their ten-year-old daughter company. They all adored Jeremy. He was a loving child, learning early to laugh and generous with his hugs. The biggest problem was keeping him from eating the dog's kibble, which made the little dachshund retreat to the kitchen doorway, barking helplessly.

I liked all of them too and found the work easy. There was plenty of time during the day to take Jeremy and the daughter to the park, where the sight of young couples kissing under the trees made me shake with what I thought was rage. At night, once the children were in bed and the house quiet, I cried into my pillow, but in the morning I set my bitterness and grief aside to face the demands of the day.

With this family, I felt that Jeremy and I had found a precarious safety, as though—like Road Runner or Daffy Duck—I had run off the edge of a cliff and in falling had caught hold of one frail sapling and dangled there in mid-air, holding onto my son with the other hand.

As in the cartoons, the sapling's roots did not hold. Jeremy and I could not stay long at that house. I was pregnant again, the result of one of my last nights with Lewis. We thought we had been careful, so the pregnancy was a surprise to both of us. Lewis said he doubted the baby was even his, no matter what I said. He renewed his threats to try and get custody of Jeremy, saying that then no one could go after him for get child support.

I swallowed my fury. There wasn't time for anger and tears. Another baby on the way meant that I had to make other arrangements. My employers were generous, but not prepared to have two babies in the house or to cover my medical expenses.

There weren't very many options open to me. I couldn't earn enough to support the three of us. Jill couldn't help me; she was on welfare herself. My other friends were recently out of college and struggling to start careers and pay off college loans.

Out of possibilities, I called my mother to confess that my marriage had failed. I barely got past my first statement.

"How dare you let your husband leave? Who do you think you are?"

When she yelled, it made my head ache. I said, "There's more. I'm pregnant."

"Whose child is it?"

"Lewis's. Of course! What did you think?"

"When are you getting an abortion?"

"I'm not."

"No man will ever want you."

"Good." I was ashamed of my failure, the failure of my marriage, but wasn't going to admit it to her.

"Well don't even think about coming back here. You've made your bed."

"What do you mean?"

"I don't want you ruining your sisters and brothers with your bad example. And besides, what would people say, you here with two babies and no father, not that he was anything to write home about."

"Okay." The habit of obedience was too strong for me to even consider arguing with her.

"You should beg him on bended knee to take you back," she went on.

"This will be better for all of us," I said.

"Better? You don't deserve better. What makes you think you have the right to be happy? Do you think I'm happy? You don't see me leaving your father."

I had no answer for that.

Her response was not unexpected. My mother and I had never been close, even when I was a child, but by 1974 we were on opposite sides of the chasm that divided the country. It was the year of the Watergate trials, coming after all the years of civil rights demonstrations and anti-war protests. In my parents' eyes, I had gone over to the enemy long ago.

Nearly everyone I knew advised me to get an abortion. I was not opposed to abortion, but knew that I would keep this child no matter what. It often seemed to me that if those opposed to abortion really meant what they said, they would push for better funding for welfare in order to make it easier for women to keep their children. Some people even suggested that I ought to give Jeremy up for adoption so that I would be free to pursue a career.

Yet I knew that my decision had to be based on what was best for the children. They didn't have a choice. They depended on me.

Jill offered no advice, saying, "Whatever you choose to do is okay with me."

"How did you decide to go on welfare?" I asked her.

"When I got pregnant, I went to the Children's Friends Society for help and they were not too positive about the possibility of welfare. To them, that was like being a ragpicker, like something out of Dickens. Then I ran into David, a friend from high school, who said 'Why don't you just go on welfare? My mother raised me on welfare.' And that made it real. Doable."

"I'm afraid I'll be on welfare forever."

But Jill told me that was not likely, since the average time to be on welfare was less than two years.

It was October by then, by the time I realized I had to leave, and the darkness closed in early. The house was empty and silent, the family having gone out for the evening. There were no curtains in the window of our sitting room on the third floor. I stood close to the window and looked at the small bright stars in the black sky, so far away. With Jeremy absorbed in stacking and sorting blocks, I went over and sat at the table to count up my assets. I was 24 years old. I had an English degree, no money, a fifteen-month-old son and another child on the way.

There were three piles of paper next to my journal on the table. One pile consisted of the Help Wanted ads torn out of the paper and lists of other possible jobs. I had checked them out, but I had next to nothing to offer in the way of skills or experience, and even the factories didn't want to hire someone visibly pregnant. A second pile contained the brochures from day care centers. Childcare for children under three was almost non-existent and very expensive. Some individuals provided day care for infants and kids under three in their homes, but they were not licensed or inspected, and they charged the earth. The third pile, the most disorderly, slipping this way and that were the old envelopes, napkins from Friendly's, and other stray pieces of paper on which I'd been scribbling budgets for weeks.

Jeremy came over and crawled into my lap. I held him with my left hand and with my right moved the budget papers back away from his questing hands and spread them out. I'd kept trying to make the numbers work, but looking at them now, it seemed clear that the salary I would have to make simply to pay for room and board and childcare was well out of my reach. With no alimony or child support, I would have to work two or three jobs just to survive, but who would watch the kids? I wanted to raise them myself, not dump them in some group home for sixteen hours a day, even assuming I could find such a place.

As I looked at the pile of much-erased and rewritten budgets, I realized that with no job, no money, no child support, and looming medical bills for pre-natal care and the new baby's birth, I had no choice but to go on welfare, a "choiceless choice" as Jill called it. I had fought against going on welfare for so long, trying to find a communal living situation or a stay-at-home job. The idea of taking handouts, asking for charity made me cringe, but I didn't see any other way to provide for my children in the coming months. Welfare seemed to be the only door left open to me.

Getting welfare, I reasoned, was like getting unemployment; I had paid taxes for years and would again someday soon. It would be, as it was meant to be, a temporary safety net during a difficult time, as if we'd survived some natural disaster. Indeed, I felt like the victim of a hurricane. My life had been picked up and shaken around and dumped to the ground, leaving me without resources of my own to care for my children.

Welfare was not an attractive option, even in 1974, even in Massachusetts where the allotment was one of the best in the country. I had seen what it was like for Jill: in return for food stamps and barely enough cash to pay rent on the cheapest apartment with minimal utilities, she was subject to surprise inspections from social workers who were entitled to criticize every aspect of her life. When she handed over food stamps at Stop & Shop, the other shoppers inspected the contents of her cart, ready to condemn anything frivolous. She often had to fight to keep her meager allotment from being cut at some administrator's whim, dependent on an office where social workers were told to act as if the money were coming out of their own pockets.

As Jill sometimes cried in frustration, "How bad do your choices have to be before welfare seems like your best choice?"

I felt so old, as if I'd lived a hundred years already. I'd taken to sleeping with a pillow, hugging it against me all night. Extra warmth, cushioning for my swollen breasts, yes, but it was more than that. I ached for Lewis. Me, who'd never been lonely before. He'd been my whole life, my chance to be a part of life and not be alone. His letters were stuck in my journal, all higgledy-piggledy, angry letters, sad ones, loving and threatening. They seemed like telegrams from another world. I was embarrassed that I loved him so much and still wanted him, even when he'd made such a fool of me.

I had only one bit of philosophy left, one motto to hold my life together: *The kids come first.* Every decision had to be based on what was right for the kids, Jeremy and this new baby. I was all they had.

I raised my head. Darkness filled the corners of the room, beyond the feeble circle of light from the table lamp. I shivered and held Jeremy closer, crossing my arms over his tummy and pressing him back against me. He craned his head back to look at me with wide surprised eyes.

"It's alright, sweetheart," I said and kissed his neck, inhaling his baby smell. "Everything's going to be okay."

"O-gay," Jeremy repeated as he patted and stroked my cheek with his small square hand.

We were like the Babes in the Wood, but I couldn't allow us to lie down and die. I had to be an adult, though I barely knew how, having relied on Lewis's knowledge of the world since leaving school. The lives of two children depended on my making the right choices. The October wind rattled the window, threatening our precarious refuge. Hazards of all kinds pressed in around us. In deciding to go on welfare, I had the sense that a door had slammed shut behind me and I was stepping out into the cold, setting off on a journey with no maps, without even knowing what my destination would look like. All I knew for sure was that I would never give up my babies.

3

FOUND

At that time, you could not apply for AFDC unless you were a head of household and able to prove that you had a place of your own. Staying with friends or family disqualified you. I had struggled to put together cash for a security deposit, a first month's rent and utility deposits, about $300 total. The requirement to get an apartment before applying for welfare struck me as absurd. If could lay my hands on that kind of money, why would I need public assistance?

I scoured the Classifieds and went to look at any possible apartment, no matter how unlikely. I pushed Jeremy's stroller up one street and down another looking for "For Rent" signs, trying to find a house that could be a home. I dreamed of a farmhouse with a quilt-covered bed high under the rafters in a whitewashed garret, a wooden table in a large kitchen with a stone fireplace, but in truth, I would have settled for anyplace that didn't have rats or roaches.

In the end, Jill found the apartment. She had been looking too since the house where she lived on Piedmont Street was to be torn down, and she finally found a place where all three apartments were empty. We both moved into the red house on Newbury Street, a few blocks away from Piedmont.

It wasn't the famous Newbury Street in Boston, the one most people know about, in the heart of town among shops, banks, and the Public Garden with its swan boats. Worcester's Newbury Street was very different. Only two blocks long, it was lined with clapboard triple-deckers, most of them in need of repainting or new siding, and featured a tot lot containing a swingset, a damaged seesaw, and ground strewn with broken glass and litter.

Frost heaves and potholes broke the surface of the road, and leaves clogged the gutters. A few trees along the street held empty branches up to the November sky. Our house had a small maple tree out front. Some of the houses in better neighborhoods were decorated with gingerbread or colored glass, but not ours. Plain as a farmhouse and painted barn-red, it had no porch, only a front stoop made out of wood. A driveway led through the tiny side yard to a cinderblock garage that listed dangerously to one side, which the landlord had warned us to avoid.

Jill took the second floor, and I the first. Sharing a place would have been cheaper of course, but would have disqualified us both from getting welfare. We each had two bedrooms, a living room, kitchen, tiny bathroom and even tinier pantry. It was more space than I had ever before had to myself. I scrubbed everything down and painted the walls white.

That first night in the new place, I tried to put Jeremy down in his crib in the small second bedroom but he refused to settle. The way the house groaned in the night wind and the muffled but steady bark of a neighbor's dog were still new enough to keep us both awake. Over and over, I padded across the empty echoing living room to comfort him and pat his back till he quieted down.

I let him cry for a while hoping he'd wear himself out, but then I was worried that he'd wake Jill, Richard and Michael in the apartment above us. Finally, I brought him in with me into my sleeping bag on the floor of the front room. I didn't have any furniture beyond Jeremy's crib, my grandmother's rocking chair, and the wooden table from our old apartment.

Shifting my hipbones on the hard floor, I whispered to Jeremy, "Guess I'm not a princess. If I had one mattress, they could put hundreds of peas under it and I'd never feel them."

He didn't answer, but wriggled around trying to get comfortable.

We lay awake, dozing a little, listening to the rumble of the occasional car going by outside.

The neighborhood where I'd grown up had been quiet. Lying there in the darkness, for the first time I felt naked, unprotected by my parents' world, a protection I hadn't even been aware of before. Now I faced this new territory alone.

Then the creak of Jill's bed overhead reminded me that I was not really alone. I thought about her steady support: *Whatever you choose to do is okay with me.* Shutting out thoughts of Newbury Street and its shadowed houses, I concentrated on my own apartment.

Lying there, I had the sensation of expanding, not my body, but somehow my presence swelling to fill the four white rooms of my apartment. This, for the first time, was a place of my own. I felt a dark responsibility not only to fill it but to defend it against all the forces that seemed to threaten us. I hushed Jeremy as he curled against my tummy where the new baby was growing. I didn't feel strong or frightened. I felt tired. In the long stretch of the night, protecting my family, my beloved babies, seemed like just one more thing that I had to do.

Wait here," I said to Jeremy. "I have to get a diaper."

Leaving him standing in the middle of the bedroom, still wrapped in a towel, I stepped into the living room where early sunlight slanted across the floor and the basket of diapers I'd brought in from the clothesline the night before. Late November in Massachusetts meant leaving them out for several days, frozen, swinging stiffly in the wind before they finally dried. I stood in the sun for a moment, one hand on my belly. Five months gone, but at least I'd never had a problem with morning sickness.

"Wear this." Jeremy appeared in the doorway, towel gone, holding up a pair of blue shorts.

"Those are for summer," I said, grabbing him and nuzzling the damp curls on his neck.

He wriggled to get down and, after some protest, allowed me to dress him in the layers necessary to withstand Worcester's winter.

I quickly packed a diaper bag with books, toys, bottles and diapers. Then I collected a squealing Jeremy from where he was hiding under his crib, outfitted him with shoes, snowsuit, hat, scarf and mittens pinned to his sleeves with diaper pins, all hand-me-downs from Jill and other friends. Then I stowed him in the stroller with a blanket tucked around him. Grabbing the diaper bag and my purse, I backed the stroller out the front door and reversed to lift the wheels carefully down the steps.

"Whoopsie!" Jeremy cried with each step. Craving motion and attention, Jeremy only seemed to quiet down when he was riding in the car, being pushed in the stroller, or listening to someone read to him.

It had been several days since the last storm, and the snow on the sidewalks had packed down into an uneven and slippery coating. I struggled with the light metal stroller, finally giving up and walking in the street.

Jeremy twisted around in the stroller, his face rounded by the hat and the hood of his snowsuit, his cheeks apple-red already. "Let's sing!"

"Okay," I said and started on *Puff, the Magic Dragon*, knowing that once we started Jeremy would want to sing the same song over and over.

After we turned the corner onto Pleasant Street, the traffic sent me back to the sidewalk. The front wheels of the stroller went this way and that, following the ruts in the packed snow. As the stroller lurched, Jeremy held onto both sides to keep his balance. Out of breath from climbing the hill, I had to stop singing, but Jeremy went on in his thin voice, singing some approximation of the words.

When we finally got downtown, the wide sidewalks were clear. I turned onto Walnut Street and stopped at the plain soot-stained building. Inside that door was the welfare office.

Inside, I gazed with dismay at the steep stairs. Before starting up, I unzipped Jeremy's snowsuit and took off his hat and scarf so he wouldn't be too hot, and did the same for myself. I struggled with getting the stroller backwards up the stairs.

In the room at the top, a woman with elaborately coifed dark hair sat at a desk filing her nails. Behind me, on a metal chair sat a girl with colorless skin and undernourished eyes, two children playing on the floor at her feet. My resolution faltered for a moment. This was a big step I was about to take.

Then, facing forward again, I approached the dark-haired woman. As she looked up I said loudly, "I'm here to apply for welfare."

A few days after our trip to the welfare office, I sat on the front stoop, buried in my coat, while Jeremy ran back and forth in the scrap of yard yelling "Putt! Putt!" He loved the stories about Toad of Toad Hall, that demon motorist. At sixteen months, Jeremy radiated energy. He had fine blond hair that curled a little at his neck and a determined chin.

"Stay in the yard," I said. I myself had felt like Mole, shut in by the whitewashed walls and desperate to get outside. Once out there, though, I couldn't think of anything to do but sit on the stoop, arms folded over my five-month belly. The baby-weight pulled my whole body down into a lump, even the bones of my shoulders sinking lower and lower.

There was no snow on the frozen ground, although a grey November sky hovered overhead. Whatever colors the surrounding houses may have been originally, they had all worn down to shades of grey. The blank windows revealed nothing, making the houses appear cold and withdrawn, hunkered down, barely separated by a driveway or bit of yard. I remembered from four years ago my first sight of Worcester, the funeral homes, auto body shops, and burnt-out houses.

A truck with a rusted fender drove past, clanking as it hit a pothole. It was one of those scrappy little trucks that cruised Worcester's streets with a snow plow in winter and an array of rakes in summer, their homemade wooden bodies advertising moving and hauling services. I was always surprised by the way people seemed to scrape a living somehow.

In the pale light, the only colors came from Jeremy's faded red snowsuit and the green of my VW bug parked in the driveway. I'd bought the car right after Jeremy was born, for just $100. It looked like it had been parked in a pond for a couple of years: the bottom was all rusted out, so that whenever I drove through a puddle, water would splash up over me. Almost immediately, of necessity, I started learning how to fix it. I asked Lewis to teach me, but instead he gave me a book and a socket set so I could teach myself.

The main thing he taught me was to use whatever was at hand. One Sunday night when the two of us were driving in a thunderous rainstorm, the driver's side windshield wiper had stopped working. Lewis pulled off to the side of the road, Route 20. We were surrounded by woods; there were no houses nearby.

Worried about getting rear-ended in the rain, I turned to Lewis, but he spoke first. "Let's take a look," he said, ducking out of the car. When he pulled on the wiper, it came off in his hand and he hopped back in to look at it under the light. He turned on the wipers again and we could see the empty spindle turning. He turned them off and held out the wiper.

"See how this screw is supposed to hold it onto the spindle? The spindle must have worn away so the screw doesn't grip it anymore," he explained.

"Where are we going to get another wiper?" I asked. "I guess we'll have to spend the night in the car,"

"No need," he said, getting out of the car again to rummage in the trunk.

By the time he got back in, he was soaked, water dripping off the ends of his braids. He held tin snips and a soda can. Cutting a strip off the can, he grabbed a flashlight and screwdriver and jumped out into the rain again. Holding the flashlight in his mouth to free up his hands, he wound the aluminum strip around the spindle, making it thick enough so that he could screw the wiper down onto it firmly.

"That should do it," he said, grinning, as he got back in the car. And it did.

Excited at finally owning a car, I named it Celia, initially because my friend from college, Christine, had named her VW bug Roz for the letters on her license plate. *As You Like It*, with those great friends Rosalind and Celia, was one of our favorite plays. But as I spent more and more time poking with greasy fingers in Celia's engine, lying on the ground under the chassis threading a clutch cable, and kneeling by her side probing at the brake adjustments, I realized that her name had a second meaning. I started singing slightly modified lines from a Paul Simon song as I drove, usually under my breath but sometimes, late at night, at the top of my lungs, begging Cecilia to get home.

One morning when Celia wouldn't start, I found that the battery, normally located under the back seat, had fallen through the rusty floor and was lying on the ground under the car. I lifted it back up, wedged a piece of plywood under it, and refastened the battery cables. The battery worked fine after that.

As I gazed at it there in the driveway, that old rustbucket looked beautiful to me because I knew every inch of it. I had buried my arms in her engine to change spark plugs. I had adjusted points and replaced gaskets. I had edged underneath her to grease the clutch cable to keep it from corroding. I had rewired lights and mended gaping holes in the body. I knew what that car was capable of and what she wasn't.

Behind me, Jill's sons burst through the front door. At four and seven, Michael and Richard seemed to have endless energy. "Hi," Michael yelled as he barreled past me.

Jeremy threw his arms up in delight and soon the three boys were running about, criss-crossing the small strip of yard and driveway, circling my car.

"Stay away from the garage," I called. I was terrified that it might collapse as the landlord had predicted. Richard waved to show he'd heard.

We were lucky to have found apartments we could afford, even if it was a stretch. Otherwise we would have ended up in one of the low-income highrises. I'd never been to one, but imagined them covered with graffiti and smelling of urine.

The door opened again and Jill came out and sat next to me on the stoop. "Brrr. Couldn't keep them inside once they heard Jeremy out here."

"Sorry."

"No, it's good. Maybe they'll tire themselves out."

I watched the boys chase each other.

"Your furniture get here okay?" Jill asked.

"Yeah, but it's awful, made out of cardboard and masking tape."

Having almost no furniture, I had applied for Emergency Assistance, one of the concessions that the Welfare Rights Organization had won. The fixed list included appliances, bed, curtains, dinette set, living room suite, and kitchenware. The only problem was that the furniture was the cheapest stuff possible, flimsy, made out of particle board and a little foam rubber. The way it worked was that for each item, like a bed, for example, the welfare office found the store with the lowest price for a bed and gave you a voucher for that amount made out to that particular store with a notation that it could only be used to purchase that bed and that it could not be used in combination with cash to get something different.

Jill shook her head. "Vouchers! What? Give us actual money so that we could buy a good second-hand sofa instead of a cheap living room suite that'll fall apart in no time? Oh, no. We're little children who can't be trusted with cash."

But I felt more relief than anger. "If it hadn't been for you and Melinda, I'd still be sleeping on the floor and sitting on a milk crate."

"We did some good things. Mostly we were just trying to make them follow their own rules. The way they acted didn't make any sense."

"I never expected to be on welfare," I said.

"Me neither. It never even occurred to me to have children," Jill said. "Seeing my mother, it seemed like kids were an all-consuming activity, as if they'll drop dead if you stop watching them for a minute. And anyway, I was busy with art school and politics."

Jill had gotten involved in the civil rights movement in the early sixties— "It seemed a natural thing to do"—when she volunteered with the Worcester Integrated Summer Project to help integrate the Clayton and Laurel Street areas. Through the program, she met Ruby Jarrett, a married woman who owned her own property and was active politically, and other activists like Jan Selby, Betty Price, and Abbie Hoffman, whose sister was teaching in the project.

Ruby took Jill and others to New Jersey for the 1964 Democratic National Convention, where Jill heard Martin Luther King, Jr. speak. She participated in sit-ins to support the Mississippi Freedom Democratic Party, a political party formed that same year as an alternative to the Mississippi State Democratic Party. The new party came to the convention to win seats for their slate of delegates, elected by disenfranchised black Mississippians and white sympathizers, on the grounds that the all-white slate of delegates from the State Party did not represent the people of Mississippi. They argued that it was almost impossible for black Mississippians to register to vote, and the small minority of blacks who succeeded in registering could not participate in the segregated State Party conventions that selected the Mississippi delegates to the Democratic National Convention.

Jill's life took a different turn when, as a college senior, she got pregnant in late 1966. Her elderly parents felt terrible for her. Even though they didn't say anything, Jill was aware that her mother wanted her to keep the child while her father wanted it put up for adoption. She talked with several agencies and also thought about abortion, which was illegal then.

Jill said, "Finally I decided to just do the next thing. I thought, *I can have this baby, at least do that.*"

The three boys stopped running around, dropped to their knees and started digging in the hard ground with a stick.

"And here you are," I said, looking around. "On this ugly street."

"How can you say that? Look at that window." She pointed to the house next door. "That little one with the small panes. That's lovely. And look at the gable on that house over there. And the shape of the maple tree."

I realized Jill was right. Newbury Street wasn't as bad as I would have expected for a poor neighborhood, with its mixture of welfare parents and blue-collar workers. Both sides of the street were lined with trees—bare now, but still—and every house had a bit of yard front and back, some with shrubs or blue and white shrines, some with a little of last year's dried-up grass. Back in Baltimore, there were neighborhoods where the flat-fronted brick rowhouses came right up to the sidewalk and you could go for blocks without seeing a single tree or even a bit of earth in which to plant one.

Jeremy pulled something small out of the ground. "No, Jeremy. Dirty," I called. "Put it down."

Richard looked up at me. "It's okay. I'll make sure he doesn't put it in his mouth."

Jill laughed. "The kids are always coming home with their pockets full of stuff they pick up: rocks, old spark plugs, broken bits of china. I should start doing found art."

"What's that?"

"You haven't heard of found art? Duchamp started it but you've seen Rauschenberg's stuff, haven't you?"

I shook my head. "Collages?"

"Yes but more that that. He stuck found objects onto his canvases. The thing is, you see something ordinary like a quilt or a broken toilet seat differently when it's taken out of its normal context. It makes you pay attention."

"I guess even a toilet seat can be beautiful if you really look at it," I said. "I never thought about it before."

"Come upstairs," Jill said, standing up. "I think I have some of Rauschenberg's work in one of my books."

Richard and Michael beat us upstairs, abandoning their coats on the floor. Jill's apartment always looked like a great wind had swirled through, leaving the floor littered and Jill's quirky, mismatched furniture awash with clothes, books, papers and toys.

The worn Oriental rug, a gift from her parents, was barely visible under the clutter, but I knew it was clean. An old upright vacuum cleaner stood in the middle of the floor—"How else would I remember to use it?" Jill had said.

There was pile of clean clothes on the electric blue cushions of the couch, vying for space with shoes, a stuffed animal, and a cereal bowl full of carefully collected stones. I made a space for myself and started folding clothes while Jill went to find the book she wanted to show me.

Against one wall was an old-fashioned wooden bureau with three drawers, the middle one sitting half-open. The top of the bureau held a jar of paintbrushes, a tipped-over pile of books—one on Zen Buddhism lay on top of a copy of *Green Eggs and Ham*—and some papers covered with Jill's large, looping handwriting. Jill had been writing down her dreams on stray scraps of paper, curious as to whether she could see any patterns emerge.

Living in that kind of chaos made my teeth ache, but Jill didn't mind it. Each thing was there for a reason.

"There are never enough hours in the day," Jill had said to me once. "I can spend my time cleaning or spend it painting." The walls were covered with her artworks: paintings, collages, an assemblage of nails and strings.

"I like that one," I said, pointing to a painting of a heavyset woman with an apple-shaped face. "That from one of your photographs?" Jill had been painting color-drenched versions of old photographs, the black and white changed to rainbow splashes of color, light brought into the darkness.

"Yes. It used to be about half again as big, but the canvas got torn. I cut it down and restretched it."

"How did you think to do that with the photos?"

"Oh, I just started playing around with them. I wasn't sure what I was going to do. Then I thought, well, these women. They didn't live black and white lives."

I thought Jill was like a prism, finding colors where they weren't obvious.

She brought an open book over to me and held it out. "Here, look at this. This one's Rauschenberg."

I always enjoyed looking through Jill's art books. She introduced me to artists I'd never studied back in high school, people like Judy Chicago, Red Grooms, Käthe Kollwitz. The all-girls school where my parents had sent me after the public schools were integrated didn't offer much math or science, but did have required courses in music appreciation and art appreciation so we could be ornaments to our husbands.

It was almost lunchtime when Jeremy and I headed downstairs. I had to drag Jeremy away from one of Red Grooms' paintings of New York City, the one with the alligators in the sewer.

We used the front stairs. Jill and I always left our front doors unlocked so the kids could go back and forth, relying on the locked front door of the house for security. I held Jeremy's hand as he negotiated each step, lowering first one foot and then the other. Inside the apartment, he ran over and threw himself at the square couch which was upholstered with olive green burlap.

Maybe I could cover the couch with that old Indian paisley bedspread left over from my hippie days. I went into my bedroom to look for the spread and saw on the bureau my collection of little white stones and shell fragments. They seemed like magic tokens to me, not only because they reminded me of summer days at the beach, but also because they had been broken from some larger stone or shell and polished by the sea, purified really, scrubbed clean. I touched them with one finger, rearranging them slightly.

Next to them was a book Jill had lent me: *Be Here Now.* The way she had talked about using what you have, perhaps that was related to her practice, the Buddhism she studied, being mindful of the world around you.

The white walls of my room reminded me of my childhood fantasy of living on the ceiling. Lying on my back, looking up at the ceiling, I had wished I could be in that blank, white place, away from the oppressive clutter of furniture, immoveable knickknacks and emotions. I had yearned for that clean, empty space. And now I had it. I had never thought about creating a home before, and certainly never expected my home to be beautiful. Peaceful, maybe. Austere. Beauty was just a word. Truth, though, that was something else. Clarity.

What I liked best about Jill was her transparency. She was clear straight through, not clouded by ambition or deceit. No need to wonder about a hidden agenda. I thought about how Mole left his hole and found himself in the strange world of the river with only his new friend Ratty to show him the ropes. But then later Mole came back to his white walls and found not a prison but a place that felt like home.

Jeremy ran in and plopped down on the rug. He had a Matchbox car in each hand and began running them back and forth, making engine noises.

I sat on the bed and, picking up my journal, wrote some ideas for how I could decorate my apartment, what kinds of free things I could look for that would make it more homelike. Artist friends from Maryland had given me some pictures, a silk screen of a barn, a painting of a girl on a swing. Maybe, after all, I could make something of this place where I found myself. I wrote: *I can be the artist of my own life.*

4

SENSE

When I went off to college, I was confident about fitting in, sure that I'd find the school a place where I could be my real self. I thought I knew everything because I knew myself. However, one of my teachers showed me how much I had yet to learn.

Esther Smith, sister of Lillian Smith who wrote *Strange Fruit* and other novels and memoirs, taught in the theatre department. We all revered Miss Smith, entranced by her generous integrity, fiery gentleness, and tough fragility. An elderly woman, she moved through the classroom with expressive grace.

The course was Oral Interpretation, a course about working up a part, grasping the core of a character simply from the play's dialogue. She nurtured in us the empathy needed to enter into a character's struggles and concerns, an empathy that carried over into our dealings with each other.

I presented some of Emily Dickinson's poetry for my final project. During our prep session, Miss Smith questioned me closely about my vision of the author.

"Well, she was a poet," I said. "And a recluse. She must have been dreamy and ethereal."

"Must she?" Miss Smith asked. "What do her poems tell you?"

And I looked again at the poems I had selected, setting aside what I thought I knew about the Amherst poet. What I found was a sturdy girl with bright snapping eyes and a quirky smile, far from the fainting maiden I had been picturing.

Of the many lessons Miss Smith taught me that have helped to shape my life, the most important was one that she didn't so much say out loud as exhibit in her every encounter with another person. Whether they were students, parents or teachers, she listened, really listened to what they said, watched what they did, and responded to their concerns. I wrote in my journal: *Each person has value. I have to look past what's ugly or strange to find what's important. Look past stereotypes and clichés to see what is really there.* It was not an easy lesson to sustain.

Jeremy had a restless night, getting me up several times to quiet him. Each time, I slipped back into bed, hoping it would warm up quickly so I could fall back asleep. Each time, I lay there, hugging my pillow, watching the streetlight cast shadows through the flimsy polyester curtains.

I didn't cry at night as I had when Lewis first left, nor did I lie awake fretting over everything that had gone wrong. Hormones again. Being pregnant was like wearing a thick down coat: I didn't feel the cold winds howling around me; if I bumped up against something hard I barely felt it. Still, some part of me knew we were in a jam.

When the sluggish December dawn finally greyed the room and outlines of furniture began to creep out of the shadows, I took a deep breath. *Things always seem better in the daylight.*

Jeremy was calling out to me, so I threw back the covers and went to him, turning up the space heater as I went. Once he was changed, Jeremy ran to the kitchen and crawled up into his high chair.

I sat at the table drinking coffee while Jeremy mangled a banana. Outside the window the round clothesline frame hung off the back porch, its worn grey ropes sagging. Beyond the driveway loomed a grey wooden triple-decker with no signs of life behind its blank windows. Above that house, a spot of sullen sky heavy with clouds was visible. Eyes gritty from lack of sleep, I bent over the mug, letting the steam rise into my face and the strong smell of the coffee drown my senses.

I picked up an old envelope and started jotting down expenses for the next two weeks. I knew exactly how much money was in my purse: $11.53. It looked as though I would need three times that much to get through the rest of the month, and that was without doing anything special for Christmas. The pile of money that had seemed like a fortune a couple of weeks ago had melted away faster than a freak snow in May: a pacifier here, a tube of Desitin there, a surprise fee from my bank because the checking account I needed in order to cash my check had fallen below the bank's minimum balance.

There was a knock. I reached behind me and opened the back door. "Jill! Come in. Coffee?"

Jeremy windmilled his arms happily at Jill. Bundled in a thick sweater, he was as round as a snowman.

"Hello, you beautiful baby," Jill said, sitting on Jeremy's other side. "Are you coming with me today?"

Jill and I traded kids one day a week, so that she could have an art day and me a writing day. Too often, though, I ended up washing the kitchen floor or taking a nap on my day off. Jill was more focused than I, completing a number of life-sized flat plaster portraits of friends and more of the rainbow paintings based on old photographs.

Jeremy bounced in his high chair and held out his arms to Jill, talking excitedly.

"Wait; let me wipe him off," I said.

Jill picked up the old envelope I'd been writing on. "Running short?"

"It's different only getting paid once a month."

"I can lend you some."

"I should be okay. I didn't expect that electric bill so soon."

"No. If they were really smart they'd have all the bills be due right after the first." Jill laughed.

"I feel so stupid. I've always been good at budgeting."

"Well, it's not like we actually get enough money to cover expenses. I just get so angry. They have this idea that we're poor because we can't manage money. We're so incapable of functioning that we need a social worker to tell us what to do."

"I don't feel very capable," I said.

"You know your math. You finished school. Some poor people do need a social worker to help them. But it would wonderful if we could free up the social workers who aren't needed so they can help other people. Their caseloads now are too big for them to be effective."

"I guess you're right." I remembered when I was a student having to count out nickels and pennies on the counter at Cumberland Farms to see if I could afford a can of soup.

Jill pushed her coffee aside and sat up straight. She looked more than ever like Joan of Arc. Her voice was calm but I could hear the outrage behind it. "It's insulting and degrading to look someone in the eye and tell them they have to learn to manage their money, when they pay nearly their entire income in absolute expenses, like rent, heat, lights. To say we can't manage our money correctly when we have no money to manage is insane. When you sit down and add up the figures, and find that your disposable income is in the negative numbers, then of course it isn't a problem of not knowing how; it's a problem of not having the resources."

I sighed. "Twenty dollars more a month would sure make a difference."

Jill's outrage was what led her to start the Worcester chapter of the Welfare Rights Organization. After she left with Jeremy, I recalled the bits and pieces she had told me about those heady days.

When she went to apply for welfare, even with her college degree, Jill was bewildered by the complicated and contradictory regulations. First they told her she had to have the baby before she could apply. "They made it impossible to plan ahead," Jill had told me. "It's as if they want people to be irresponsible."

Then after she had the baby, they told her she had to live with her parents in order to apply, which was not true. At that time her father had recently been diagnosed with cancer and her mother couldn't deal with both a dying spouse and a baby.

Benefits given out by the welfare office were intentionally inconsistent. Two women in equal circumstances could go in and one be given food stamps, Medicaid, housing assistance, and emergency assistance for furniture and winter clothing, while the other was not even allowed to apply. It was up to the whim of the social worker and how strongly management enforced the dictum to keep back whatever they could get away with. It was up to the applicant to know what to ask for and be willing to make a fuss to get it.

Jill's friend Ruby, the one who had taken her to the 1964 Democratic convention to support the Mississippi Freedom Democratic Party, gave her a book, *Mothers for*

Adequate Welfare, put out by a woman from Boston on welfare who had researched the statutes to find out what you could and couldn't get. At that time, in the sixties, there were no state-wide regulations; each city had its own. When Jill returned armed with the booklet, they did allow her to apply, even though she still wasn't living with her parents.

Some of the social workers didn't know the rules themselves, while others had been instructed to withhold whatever benefits they could, either by not volunteering information about them or by actively putting up roadblocks. As a strategy to keep the welfare rolls low, social workers routinely denied requests for aid and waited to see if the person appealed the decision. Since most applicants didn't know they had the right to appeal, this strategy often worked.

Although the inequality made Jill furious, what really got to her was the behavior of some of the social workers toward the women who came in for help. If the women weren't treated like little children, then they were regarded as somehow immoral or corrupt.

"There's this stigma," Jill said. "There's something wrong with you, you're lazy. We had one of the supervisors come and give a lecture at the health center and she portrayed welfare mothers as just sitting around drinking coffee all day. You know that this is simply bizarre. The fact that you have to go in there with your child—because of course you have no money for a baby sitter—and you have to fill out voluminous forms telling them what you do not have, like boats and vacation homes. And then they make you wait and there's no place to wait, just some hard chairs. And you also clearly are taking care of children. There's some work involved. Not just drinking coffee. Especially if you're a very poor woman."

One day Jill herself had gone into the welfare office because of an issue with her check. Grey rain ran down the grimy window behind the receptionist's desk. Past the railing stretched a large room cluttered with metal desks where social workers talked with clients, the hum of their conversations overlapping and drowning out the sound of the rain against the windows.

Waiting on the hard metal chairs, Jill noticed a woman she knew from high school and greeted her. The woman waved back listlessly.

As she sat there, trying to keep Richard from tumbling down the open staircase, Jill couldn't help overhearing a social worker with another client, a middle-aged woman who sat in the chair before him like a prisoner in the dock, her feet tucked under her.

"Please," the woman said. "I just need a little extra for a pair of shoes. These are no good anymore."

"Didn't you get your check this month? What's wrong with you? You should have saved out some money if you needed shoes." The thin, balding man frowned, his hands folded on the desk in front of him.

The woman seemed to sink deeper in the chair. "Yes. I know. But there wasn't anything left after I paid the heat bill." Her wisps of faded hair started to shake. "Please. The soles are gone and the stitching on the side. I put in some cardboard but the rain ruined it."

"You have to wait for next month's check."

Jill turned to her high school friend and said, "How can they do that? It's not their money." But the friend shook her head and tried to melt into the wall. The last thing she wanted was trouble with the welfare office.

The older woman's voice wavered. "Please. I'm afraid I'll catch pneumonia walking around with wet feet."

"Let me see, then. Take your shoes off."

The woman shrank in on herself with embarrassment. "Here? In front of everyone?"

Jill couldn't take anymore. She stood up and said loudly, "Just give her the money. It's only a pair of shoes."

"Wait your turn!" the man said without looking at Jill.

"No," Jill said, advancing on him. The room fell silent.

"Sit down."

"How dare you make her beg like that? For a pair of shoes! What's the matter with you?"

As the woman started to cry, the man slammed his hands flat on the desktop and turned on Jill, his face reddening. "Shut up! This is none of your business."

A buzz started up. Everyone was looking at them.

Jill stood her ground. "Just give her the shoes."

The man looked around the room, then shook his head. "Alright," he said. He pulled out a form, filled it out quickly, and thrust it at the woman. "Go on. Get out of here."

The woman scurried out without looking at Jill.

Jill returned to her seat, resolved that she was going to do something about this situation.

Having quickly found out that it was illegal to organize a group to change legislation, Jill started having little kaffee klatsches with poor women. She went from door to door in her neighborhood introducing herself and explaining that she was on welfare and wanted to change things because they didn't seem fair.

Her main goal was simply to have the system be consistent.

"It doesn't make sense," she told her neighbors, "that they would tell me I wasn't eligible when I clearly was. It doesn't make sense that I had to have a child in my arms before I could apply."

Most of the women agreed with her and wanted to hear more.

Jill pointed out that, since you didn't get things if you didn't ask for them, you were penalized for your ignorance. The people newly on welfare were the least likely to know what they are entitled to, so in effect you were punished for not being a long-term welfare recipient.

Also, you were penalized if you wanted to do more with your life. If you earned over a certain amount of money, all of your benefits changed and you had to keep providing the welfare office with pay stubs and other documentation. And then your case would be reopened for any little change. Even something as predictable as a five-week month meant that all of your benefits would change, and you had to go back to the welfare office and renegotiate everything.

Jill's first meeting was at the house of a welfare recipient named Mary Lou. About thirty people showed up. Jill brought the book Ruby had given her, which turned out to be one of her most valuable resources. It was very difficult to find out what the regulations were because even the social workers themselves didn't have access to the official manuals. After discussing the information in Jill's book, the people at that first meeting decided to go to the welfare office and ask for something they should have been given.

They found that everybody got different results: "Wait, you got a bureau?" "School clothes? You're kidding."

Initially Jill's group worked not so much to make big changes in legislation but just to have the office adhere to the law. Their primary weapon was the appeals process, which at the time was rarely used and very intimidating. If you could work up your nerve to speak out—unlike Jill's high school friend who had wanted to melt into the wall—you had go into the office for a fair hearing before a referee, where everything you said was recorded by an official sitting at the table. "Oddly enough," Jill told me, "when you brought your own tape recorder and put it there opposite his, he would get very nervous and very upset, so they clearly knew this was a method of intimidation."

The welfare office didn't take them seriously at first, these poor women. Jill said that they tried to blame outside agitators. Anything rather than believe that these mothers could actually be intelligent enough to organize.

Through the meetings, Jill got to know a number of other women on welfare. "What struck me," she told me, "was their strength, their beauty, their intelligence, their willingness to work their butts off for their children, for what they believed in, and even in horrifying dead-end jobs. What always amazed me was that most people really tried to work, in spite of the hassles from the welfare office, in spite of having their rent go up, in spite of losing health care benefits, in spite of all the extra expenses involved in working, in spite of inadequate day care, and in spite of all the extra work to get your babies off to day care."

Jill mentioned one woman who had three children of her own and ended up with five more when her second husband left her with his children too. "She would go out and get these jobs, and she would get sick because she couldn't work nights and take care of eight children during the day, live in a cold-water flat and do everything. Surprise, surprise. And, you know, she was one of those 'lazy' welfare mothers. It was just amazing."

Sitting at my kitchen table remembering these conversations with Jill, I knew I had these women to thank for everything around me. Their efforts to standardize benefits and educate social workers and recipients alike were the reason I was able to give my children this home.

I got up to put some beans on to cook. I loved my stove with its built-in space heater, but of all the furniture and appliances I'd gotten through emergency assistance, the thing that gave me the most joy was the washing machine. Laundry was a constant, since Jeremy wore cloth diapers. The new disposable diapers were too expensive, and I couldn't get them with food stamps anyway. With a washing machine in the kitchen, no longer would I have to balance a garbage bag of dirty clothes and stinky diapers on top of the stroller and spend half the day at the laundromat. Little wonder that I was in love with my washing machine.

When I went upstairs to get Jeremy that afternoon, Melinda was there, a friend of Jill's since those early days of the Welfare Rights Organization. I got a cup of coffee and joined them at the kitchen table, sitting between them, our mugs crowding the table. A heavy-set woman with lank brown hair, Melinda's face seemed closed and expressionless. She reminded me of Gertrude Stein in that painting by Picasso, like an unapproachable monolith. I couldn't imagine what she thought of me, who was such a novice in her world.

She looked past me to address Jill. "So what do you think about Great Brook Valley? I can't believe they're building it so far out of town."

"I can," Jill said. "That's the whole point."

Melinda eyes tightened slightly at that. "You're right. Keep them out of sight."

"People are so generous," Jill said to me. "If they see someone in trouble, they try to help. That's why the politicians put public housing projects like Great Brook Valley way out of town and don't run city buses out there very often. They want poor people to be invisible. Never mind that it makes it that much harder for the people to get to jobs or city services."

"Wall them up somewhere out of sight. It's not like they're human beings or anything," Melinda said in her peculiar monotone. She looked at me, not moving, just shifting her eyes. "When you go on welfare, the system tries to demean you, debase you, discourage you. If they could kill you, they might."

Melinda lived on Piedmont Street, across from Jill's old place. She never tended the scrubby yard but it grew lush with lilacs, ailanthus and chicory anyway, as though the mere force of her expectation somehow made the yard flourish. Always supportive of Jill, she would show up on rainy days to give her a ride or, later, loan Jill her car to learn to drive on. And Melinda was politically savvy. She had been instrumental in having the Model Cities funds taken away from the Community Action Council, which represented business interests and given to the kind of community groups for which they were intended.

When Melinda and her husband split up, leaving her with twin toddlers and another baby on the way, she too had gone on welfare.

At first, the group of women had gone round and round about what their next step should be. Finally, Melinda had stood up and said "I'm sick of meetings. I'm sick of talk. On Monday morning I'm going down to the welfare office, and I'm not leaving until I get what we need."

The others decided to join Melinda, and so the first sit-in at the welfare office was organized.

They lived in the office for two weeks the first time. Taking shifts, some people would come during the day, and others lived there day and night. And of course, they all had their children with them.

Each woman decided what she was going to contribute. One woman wrote a newsletter. Another ran a free store, where everyone could bring clothing and trade. Every day when the children came home from school, the women and children put on fashion shows.

Others heard about the sit-in. The Women's International League of Peace and Freedom came down to the welfare office and brought food. Various church groups, mainly African-American churches, offered support. Reverend Hargrove, the minister at Second Baptist Church, actually came down and sat with the protesters.

Meanwhile, the welfare office couldn't shut down, so had to work around them. At night, police officers were assigned to guard the offices and the jumble of women and children camped out there. Night after night, Melinda talked with them about why she was on welfare, the amount of money that people got.

One policeman said, "But no one can live on that."

Yup.

The policemen were also amazed at what people had to do to get the money. Although stand-offish at first, many of them became sympathetic to the cause.

Eventually the women won what they wanted, which was simply to have minimum standard guidelines. The win was a huge boost for the nascent group, showing them that the process worked.

Jill was named the first president of the Worcester Welfare Rights Organization. They tried to raise public consciousness about the plight of welfare recipients, challenging a church group to live for a month on the amount of money they would get if they were on welfare, or putting on a dinner for local politicians made solely from the recipes on the cans of surplus food.

Melinda and Jill went on local public television and radio in an attempt to de-stigmatize welfare recipients. To combat the stereotype of a lazy welfare mother, Jill described her experience and degree, and said that she would take any job, no matter how hard, if they would include day care. She didn't get a single offer.

They also networked with others, such as the Mothers for Adequate Welfare organization in Boston and a group from Clark University that wanted to help. The Teamsters Union gave them money and support, because the union recognized that welfare mothers, too, were a union.

Jill went to Washington and arranged an affiliation with the National Welfare Rights Organization (NWRO) started by George Wiley in 1967, an outgrowth of his work in poverty and civil rights. He had been involved in CORE (Congress of Racial Equality) as early as 1961 and later started the Poverty/Rights Action Center. Wiley had been shocked when he started to look into the federal Aid to Dependent Children program (later named AFDC) and found a pattern of disregard for the law by the state and local governments that administered the program. After Wiley pushed the federal government to investigate, the Department of Health, Education and Welfare found that thirty-nine out of fifty states were not in compliance with federal regulations.

In 1967, the NWRO sent an organizer to Massachusetts who worked with the Worcester group among others. Bill Pastreich came from Syracuse where he had been trained in organizing methods used by Saul Alinsky, a successful community organizer. Pastreich had also worked for Cesar Chavez's United Farm Workers movement and later went on to organize Justice for Janitors.

Melinda said, "Bill was trained as a labor organizer; that's where his strengths were. He would line up lawyers to bail us out in case we got arrested. He did a lot of advance planning because he didn't want anybody to get hurt. He made connections with politicians and did a lot of fund-raising for us. He was a smart guy."

However, she added, "We strictly ran our thing. We didn't want to be nationalized. Same with Boston. Worcester always wanted to be on our own. We had some good people, some intelligent women."

It was never about power. It was about the children.

Their main philosophy was that everyone deserved to live at least at poverty level. But the WRO looked at other factors that exacerbated poverty. They were the first organization in Worcester to provide translation services for Spanish-speaking people. They also arranged for free clinics to provide immunizations for children.

In addition, remembering the difficulty that newcomers to the welfare system encountered, volunteers from the group agreed to witness when people needed to meet with their social worker, the way Jill had offered to go with me when I applied. Not only would the person not have to go in alone, she would know she had support. Jill said that it made all the difference in how they were treated, adding, "It made me very sensitive to how little mistakes and little power trips can really impact other people."

However, Jill was always careful to note that the social workers themselves were like anyone else: some were wonderful, some terrible, and some just doing the minimum to get by. Some were so helpful that Jill was amazed that they could function inside a system that pushed them to be the opposite.

As the women in the WRO became friends, they developed into a support network for each other. When Mary Lou got burned out of her house, she came to live with Jill for a while. When Jill—who didn't drive—needed to go somewhere, someone would always volunteer to take her. They all helped clean Melinda's house. She in turn would drive people around, since she was one of the few who owned a car, albeit a ramshackle Ford Fairlane that had once been a police car.

In 1968 the Poor People's Campaign was going on, and the group in Worcester was able to join the March on Washington, thanks to a local Catholic Church, which provided a bus. Energized by the march and the speeches, Jill and three other women decided to have a poor people's march in Worcester. They weren't sure what would happen, but went ahead and organized it by lining up speakers, putting up posters, giving out flyers, and writing speeches.

Hundreds of people showed up for the march in Worcester. They marched down Main Street and congregated on the Common in front of City Hall. Melinda, Mary Lou and others gave speeches to the assembled crowd.

Jill said, "It was funny. All the politicians were rushing in to try and grab a piece of the stage. They clearly didn't know what was happening."

To Jill, organizing the march was like making a piece of art. "You start with a concept, build on the concept, see what's going to happen," she said. "And you try to maintain as open an attitude as possible and be as thorough as possible."

Then they organized a second sit-in.

"The issue at hand," Jill had once told me, "was clothing allowance for children to go back to school. Some people had gotten extra money for that, since there certainly wasn't money in the budget to get things like coats and jackets and school clothes for children, and that was a big crunch, especially for people like Melinda who had three babies. Even though Melinda's kids weren't going to school yet, she was looking out for the future. And for other people too. She was very much involved in the community."

The second sit-in didn't go quite so well as the first one. The women were arrested and taken along with their children to jail on charges of trespassing in the welfare office.

Jill said that it made her realize that what she was involved in could be scary. "Not jail—we were nice white moms with kids, so nothing much happened to us—

however, we were taken to court on the charges. They even wanted to charge us with sedition in addition to trespassing."

Melinda and Mary Lou were found guilty of trespassing. Jill and the others who came later had their charges dropped because the welfare representatives didn't want to present the whole case again.

"But the idea that they could say that our sit-in amounted to sedition," Jill said, "when we were just sitting there in what was supposed to be a public building, a waiting room for welfare recipients. When we were just saying we need school clothes for the kids."

I asked Jill and Melinda why the group had died out.

Jill said that as it grew, it became divisive. "Our philosophy at the beginning was that we didn't care who you were or what you did besides the fact that you were on welfare." Later on, however, some members of the group became judgmental: "People were saying, if you don't have my lifestyle, if you're turning tricks on the side, we're not going to accept you."

She noted too that there were some chilling things that happened, many accidents. For example, the NWRO founder, George Wiley, drowned in a boating accident.

"At times it was scary," Jill said. "You'd get phone calls saying they were going to kill your kids. Anonymous calls. But also wonderful calls, people saying thank you for doing this. My mother raised me on welfare and so on."

Melinda added, "Part of it was that as time went on, the tactics we used were no longer effective. Part of it was that we had been successful. But it died when Kennedy died." June of 1968 was when Robert Kennedy was shot, a few months after Martin Luther King, Jr.

Perhaps the biggest reason why the group died out was that key leaders like Melinda got jobs and didn't have time anymore. Jill added, "They didn't stay on welfare. Some got married, some got jobs, things changed—thank God—for all of us."

Besides Melinda, who was working now, the woman who had run the newsletter during the sit-in went on to head up the Main South neighborhood center. Mary Lou ended up teaching courses in welfare law at Quinsigamond Community College.

Melinda said, "It was an exciting and meaningful time. Something was happening. There was also the sense of power and control. I truly believed in the effectiveness of change."

Later I wrote in my journal: *When I left home, I thought I knew everything because I knew myself. It took Miss Smith to open my eyes so I could see what was in front of me. Jill and Melinda aren't that much older than I am, both of them around thirty. Yet they are veterans of a war fought and won while I was still in high school. They stood up, not only for themselves but for that woman who needed shoes and the kids who needed school clothes.*

They look so ordinary. No wonder the people at the welfare office didn't believe Jill and Melinda would have the power to change anything. Jill seems too slight to take on the powerful and Melinda too immobile. But if you push past the way they look, you find that level-headedness, that need simply to have things make sense. You find a way of being mindful of each person around them. And you find courage. Lots of courage.

5
FAMILIES

Since deciding to go on welfare, I hadn't seen Lewis. He hadn't wanted me to do it, afraid they'd come after him for child support, although in fact they did not.

I wasn't angry with him anymore. However, I felt that if he wasn't going to give us any child support, if he wasn't going to commit to being a regular part of Jeremy's life, then he shouldn't come around at all. Only twenty-four, I didn't know much about being a parent, but I did know a child wasn't a toy you could set aside when you were tired of it.

Despite being exhausted and wondering if I would ever again be able to sit down and read a book without being pulled away to change a diaper or kiss a boo-boo, I was completely in love with Jeremy, the soft curls of his hair, his big snaggle-toothed grin. I was surprised that Lewis was apparently immune to baby love. Not wanting to be around me made sense after the way I'd been such a harridan, but how could he stay away from Jeremy?

Some people are simply no good at relationships, I wrote in my journal. I had failed as a wife, and was still trying to puzzle out how to be a parent. The one thing I seemed to be okay with was being a friend, not only with Jill but with my Maryland friends who stayed in touch even as I moved further and further from the life we had shared.

We were more than friends. We had called ourselves a family and helped each other out at school in all kinds of ways: studying together, pooling money for late-night treats, lending cars and clothes, providing comforting arms when needed. We were always ready for games: duck-duck-goose in the quad, O.K. Corral shootouts outside George's Diner, sneaking around like outlaws in the cornfield. It was like a drug, those moments of connection, looking around at my friends' faces as we lounged on the steps of Baker Chapel, listening to Jim and Charlie play their guitars. Despite being scattered all over the country, we called, wrote letters, and even got together now and then.

Listening to the Bob Dylan songs that Jim and Charlie used to sing made me blue. I was overwhelmed by a kind of desolation, fearing that my new life was too far removed from theirs. So I was thrilled when Christine came to visit me on Newbury Street soon after I moved in. Christine had been my closest friend at Western Maryland, sharing my enthusiasms. Electricity seemed to fly off of her. Tall and energetic, she had overflowed with ideas for adventures back in college, such as pretending to be Nancy Drew or creating a huge collage out of an old refrigerator box.

Always on the lookout for ways to ease our transition to college life, Christine would prepare a feast of toast with strawberry preserves during exam week, suggest we break curfew with an illicit campout in the nearby woods, or spend an entire afternoon napping to old Beatles records. Every now and then we would have a food orgy, skipping lunch in the cafeteria and spending all our pocket money on junk food from the corner store. We sat on the Oriental rug in her dorm room and ate ourselves silly while listening to Rimsky-Korsakov's Scheherazade. Even though my own taste ran more to farmhouses and simple Shaker furniture, I loved the splendor of those food orgies Christine put together.

When Christine transferred to a college in New York after freshman year at her parents' behest, I visited as often as I could. She was given Roz, the VW bug who became Christine's magic carpet, taking us everywhere. We zipped up and down the Garden State Parkway, shadowed a pickup truck decorated with ball fringe, and stopped at every diner in Morris County to sample their apple pie.

The summer after our sophomore year—right before I moved to Worcester— she and I shared an apartment in Bay Head on the New Jersey shore working as waitresses. We both loved the ocean. Just sitting and listening to the cleansing rhythm of the waves or walking along the sand picking up shells was a sure and certain comfort.

By the time I was living on Newbury Street, she and her husband had relocated to Washington State, driving a red and yellow schoolbus across the country in 1972. Luckily she came back East pretty regularly and usually managed to fit in a visit with me.

With our maritime history, it was inevitable that on this visit we should decide to go to the ocean, which was only a little over an hour's drive away. Christine insisted that we visit Rockport, a town that had acquired mythic status for us because of Tom Rush's tune "Rockport Sunday". Even with the addition of Jeremy bundled up in his red snowsuit, I felt as though Christine and I were setting off on one of our old adventures. I couldn't resist the lure of the past. Here I was, barely over the threshold of my new life as a welfare mother, already needing the reassurance that I wasn't losing everything that had come before.

It was one of those colorless days you get sometimes in December, when it seems as though the cold has leached all the life out of the earth and the sky. Celia forged bravely down the highway. With Jeremy absorbed in the passing scenery, Christine and I were able to catch up a little. After telling me about their house in Washington and the cats' latest adventures, Christine asked how I was adjusting to single life.

"In some ways it's easier. I only have the two of us to worry about."

"Has your mother forgiven you yet?"

"Oh, we always work things out," I said.

As we zipped into the seaside town, Celia hugging the road, all three of us sang "Old MacDonald" and Donovan's "Sunshine Superman" to keep our spirits up, even though neither Christine nor I could sing very well.

I was afraid that Christine, with no children of her own, would have trouble fitting into my baby-centered life, but so far she and Jeremy were getting along fine. They were both Leos, their birthdays only three days apart, so maybe that explained it. They both were so full of energy.

"The ocean," Christine exclaimed as I slid the bug into a parking space. "Smell that air!"

We walked around the half-deserted waterfront, rimmed by white frame buildings that had withdrawn into themselves now that the summer tourist season had faded. The wood of the pier was worn and silvered by the salt air. In his stroller, giggling as the wheels rumbled over the seams of the wood, Jeremy glowed bright as a robin, his wind-whipped cheeks matching his red snowsuit.

We found a bench near the end of the pier, and listened to the roll and hiss of the waves on the pebbly beach. Seagulls perched on the pilings and flew off screaming. The grey sky blurred into the sea, the horizon obscured by mist. Jeremy, good-humored as always when he was out and about, kept up a conversation with his stuffed bear and the seagulls.

Listening to the waves, I began to understand why the hypnotic chiming guitar in Tom Rush's tune had made me dream of the ocean as I lay napping in my dorm room.

"This is so peaceful," Christine said. It was unusual, though, for her to sit still for long, and it was only a few minutes before she said, "Brrr. Look at the red cheeks on that boy. Let's go look at the shops."

There were a few good craft places, pottery and leather, and one with those shore paintings that all look nearly alike with waves cresting behind a grass-topped dune. The other storefronts were the usual seaside tourist trinket shops. While Christine looked for something with blue whales on it, I tried to maneuver Jeremy's stroller away from an enticing display of toy boats.

After that, we headed to a seafood restaurant, more formal than I would have chosen if I'd been alone, but Christine insisted that the day was her treat, and I was happy to go along.

It was midafternoon by then, and the place nearly empty, so we could sit by ourselves where Jeremy wouldn't disturb other diners. We peeled off our layers in the welcome warmth, and sat by the big windows overlooking the water.

"This feels so right," I said, looking across the table at Christine, but I meant *familiar*. I had barely taken the first step into a new life by moving into the red house on Newbury Street. I didn't know what it was going to mean to be a single parent, a poor person, a welfare mom. With only Roland Park as a frame of reference, I had no idea what the future held. Looking at Christine, though, I knew that I hadn't lost the best part of my past, and that was good enough for now.

She raised her water glass. "To many more adventures," she said.

"More oceans," I added.

"More food orgies!" She laughed, and we drank.

When the bill came, Christine pulled out her wallet, one of those super-efficient ones with lots of compartments and a built-in change purse. I made Christine show me all the different pockets and compartments while the waitress went off with Christine's credit card. In my age group, at least, Christine was the only person I knew who had a credit card.

"Thanks," I said.

"No problem. I'm the one working, after all."

Watching Christine play with Jeremy, making him laugh with her funny faces, I said, "You know, I was a little afraid that having him would change everything."

Christine understood. "I told you I didn't ever want to have kids."

"Right. All those years babysitting your neighbor's kids used up your maternal drive."

"I love those kids!" she cried. "You would not believe how big the twins are now. But it took everything I had, and there were other things I wanted to do."

"Back when I decided to have Jeremy, I didn't realize how much of a full-time job it was," I said. Of course it didn't help that I hovered as though Jeremy would drop dead if I stopped watching him for a minute. When he was out of my sight, my vivid imagination came up with one nightmare scenario after another.

"You see."

"But we can still be friends."

Christine leaned forward. "When we're eighty, we'll be sitting next to each other in rocking chairs on some porch looking out over the water."

"Cackling over our youthful adventures," I added.

I had never thought about whether or not to have kids; they were merely part of the vision I had of what my adult life would be like. But old age? That was going to be me and Christine.

Being an adult, to me, meant making my own choices, but my sense of responsibility freighted every choice with consequences and costs. For instance, with an active toddler to watch, I could no longer give in to my longing to bury myself in a book; struggling to make ends meet meant that pride and saving face were no longer so important; I couldn't afford the luxury of flouncing away from my family.

After my mother told me I wasn't welcome at home, my first inclination was to stick my nose in the air and say: *Okay, I'll do this on my own then*. However, having seen how hurt Lewis had been by the estrangement from his mother and how much Kevin missed having a grandmother in his life, I made up my mind to keep the lines open with my family. I didn't want to deprive my children of the possibility of a relationship with their grandparents, no matter how difficult it was for me to deal with my mother.

And then, I didn't completely believe she meant it when she disowned me and barred me from the house. She loved melodramatic scenes—ever the Martyr Mother—especially those that reflected the romances she devoured. It might take a while, but I thought she would eventually accept some kind of relationship, even if it was simply talking on the phone occasionally. My father, with his animosity toward me, would be a harder sell. I didn't expect that they would ever offer to help me financially, given their strong prejudice against "welfare bums".

At the same time, I mulled over my childhood, trying to understand how to be a parent without repeating my mother's mistakes. Part of raising children is working out how much of your parents' methods to use. I wanted to give my children the autonomy I had enjoyed and to ensure that they had the chance to be alone. At the same time, I wanted them to have the caresses and the conviction of being loved that I had lacked. I wanted them to be able to be islands if they wanted, but not to feel that they had to be in order to hang onto themselves.

"I'm just trying to keep it all together," Jill said when I asked for parenting advice. She found every day a struggle to balance taking care of the kids with creating her art and trying to get off of welfare. She claimed that she never knew what she doing and looked to me for level-headed strength. I thought it was the other way around.

We were both caught up in the women's movement. It was 1974, and issues of work versus home were hotly debated. Even though we didn't work outside the home, we both struggled to carve out time, Jill for her art and me for writing. More than that, we were trying to create our lives from scratch. We were like pioneers settling a new country, learning how to be women in a world where the old rules were gone and new ones not yet written. Living without precedents forced me to act and react honestly, to examine my motives and choices. We read biographies of women artists and writers voraciously, looking for role models. I admired the way Jill was quick to throw out social norms—like cleaning her house regularly—if they didn't fit the life she was putting together.

I questioned Jill about her childhood, looking for alternative ways of parenting and hoping to understand what had influenced Jill. The only child of elderly parents, Jill's experience was different from mine but didn't offer many clues.

She told me a lot about her mother, whom we all called Nana. Like me, Nana was the oldest girl in her family and had spent much of her childhood off by herself, reading fairy tales and roaming the nearby woods marveling over each violet and Jack-in-the-Pulpit.

A generation older than my parents, Nana grew up in a world that seemed like ancient history to me. She remembered the lamplighter coming around every evening to light the streetlamps, and the big day when the entire neighborhood gathered outside, sitting on the front porches that looked across to Holy Cross College hill, waiting for the electricity to be turned on for the first time. When the lights came on, everyone shouted and cheered. Her mother said, "It's like stars coming out all over!"

The women in Jill's family were hard workers. Leaving school at fourteen in the midst of World War I, Nana got a job in a cartridge belt factory to help out. A year later her father died of influenza, and her mother went to work as a saleslady at Denholm's, a local department store. When the war ended, Nana got a job at the Bachrach Photo Studio, and by the time she was sixteen earned enough for her mother to stay home and care for the house and younger children. Even while supporting her family, though, Nana had managed to take free art classes at the high school and later at the Worcester Art Museum.

I knew less about Jill's father who had died before I met her. He grew up on a farm in Maine that had no electricity or indoor plumbing. After his mother died when he was two, his fourteen-year-old sister Ethel took care of the youngsters, the house, chickens, and garden. One day, after he had grown and gone, Ethel just sat down in the rocking chair and died. Of exhaustion, they said.

Jill invited me to come with her to visit her mother. Jeremy joined Richard and Michael in the backseat of Jill's car, and we headed across town.

Nana's house was a small grey bungalow, located on a short, dead-end street tucked in behind Norton Company, the factory where Jill's father had worked. Protected from the street by a low white picket fence, the house nestled among leafless azalea and forsythia bushes that rattled in the December wind. Above the bushes, the windows glowed bravely against the bleak day.

When Jill opened the front door, the warmth of the room poured out. I followed Jill and the boys into the brightly lit room, which stretched the width of the house and had white walls that bounced with light.

Next to the front door hung a marvelous hand-stitched quilt depicting a street scene, including houses and trees, cars and garages.

"My mother did that," said Jill. "It's the whole neighborhood. See, there's her house, and Mrs. Fortier's dog, and that bratty boy from down the street. She even included the trash cans."

"It's wonderful," I said.

I turned away from the quilt and looked through the far doorway where I could see kitchen cabinets and the corner of a table. Then Nana appeared in the doorway, a stout woman with white hair that stuck out this way and that. Jill had warned me that her mother regularly hacked her hair off with an old pair of scissors, never bothering to look in the mirror. With Jill's parents being nearly fifty when she was born, they behaved more like grandparents: indulgent, never yelling at her. When Jill had a tantrum, they simply ignored her till she stopped.

Richard and Michael ran to hug Nana. She smiled at me over their heads as Jill introduced me.

"And this must be Jeremy. Why he's a regular Gerber baby, isn't he?"

"They don't come any cuter," Jill said.

"Except for these two." Nana looked down at Richard and Michael. "Oh, you're so big. I hardly recognized you. And what cold hands! How about some cocoa?"

The boys dropped their coats on the floor as they followed Nana into the kitchen. I picked the coats up, tilting Jeremy as I bent and making him giggle. Then I held out my arm for Jill's coat.

"Thanks," she said as she set the milk she'd brought on the counter and slipped off her coat. She pointed to a bedroom off the kitchen. "You can put them in there. That used to be my room."

"The one you painted dark blue?" I asked.

"With silver stars and never thinking how dark it would be in the daytime." Jill shook her head as she reached for a saucepan from the drain.

"Oh, let me hold him," Nana said, as I came back into the kitchen with Jeremy. She sat on one of the dinette chairs and held out her arms for him. "Aren't you the sweetest thing?" she said as he smiled up at her complacently, used to being adored.

While Jill fixed the cocoa, Richard and Michael clambered onto chairs at the table. Michael chattered to Nana about a car he'd seen that he wanted when he grew up. Jeremy stretched out his arms to Richard, and Nana handed him over.

I looked around the warm, bright kitchen. All the cabinet lights were on as well as the overhead, and they reflected off the cheerful wallpaper decorated with red and yellow teapots.

Jill put tea mugs on the kitchen table and poured water into them.

"So, what was Jill like as a child?" I asked Nana, having a hard time imagining Jill as a little girl. I thought that her strength and self-assurance must be the result of maturity and hard times survived.

"Jill was always so creative," Nana said.

As she tilted her mug and looked into it, Jill said, "I don't know about creative. I just did things backwards, like picking up things with my toes so I never used my hands till I was ridiculously old."

"And she made her own clothes," Nana went on.

Jill looked at me ruefully. "Like the dress I made out of a shower curtain, never thinking how sweaty it would be."

"You were the most wanted child." Nana looked fondly at Jill. "I walked on air the whole time I was pregnant. I made ridiculous promises to God if he would let me keep this baby, and you were born beautiful and perfect. The nurses put a huge pink bow on your crib and when I asked why, one of them said it was because you were the most wanted baby in the nursery."

I tried to imagine what that would be like, to be the only child, the most wanted child. The silence stretched as Jill fiddled with her spoon, moving it to the right, turning it upside down.

Finally I said, "But you didn't wrap her up in cotton wool." Jill had told me stories of being put out in the yard to play, with the dog, an Irish setter, to watch her. He did a good job, too, blocking her way when she tried to toddle off, making her infant escape. Jill beat on the dog's side with her tiny fists, but the dog only turned to lick her face indulgently.

Nana stirred her tea again. "The whole household revolved around her. It was ridiculous. My mother was the worst of all. Jill was a small angel to her, and as she grew to be two or three years old, my mother thought I should keep her away from all the kids in the neighborhood."

Jill snorted.

Nana went on, "She said they would spoil her, and I would lose my angel. This was one of the few times I went flatly against my mother and encouraged every kid around to come into the house to play or lunch with Jill."

I knew that Jill had been a sickly child, with one illness after another. How much braver of her mother, then, to resist being overprotective.

We heard the boys' voices raised in an argument over a book, and Jill called out to them to behave and then got up to collect our tea mugs. As Nana went into the front room to see to the boys, Jill turned to me and shook her head. "I love those boys to distraction, but I must be doing something wrong, the way they fight all the time."

I tried to reassure her. "It's normal. My sister and I were much worse than they are."

"I don't know how siblings behave toward each other. I was always treated like just another person in the family."

"Not just any person—an angel!" I teased her.

"Yeah, right."

Jill's art school friends had loved Nana, eccentric as she was, and often visited with her even after Jill moved out. That seemed to be one indication of a good parent, so I was pleased that neighborhood children came to my apartment to play with Richard and Michael, who spent a lot of time with us. A few even came back to play with Jeremy sometimes, handing him the toys he threw out of his playpen. Since he was such a gregarious child, he was thrilled by their company. And I was thrilled to be able to hang clothes out on the line or do the breakfast dishes without Jeremy's constant demands for attention.

One young person I met through Jill was Dorian. She needed someone to babysit for her in the mornings between the time her mother left for work and the time school started. Jill asked if I'd be willing to do it.

I said that it was okay with me, but I didn't actually meet Dorian till the day when there came a knock at the front door. Surprised, since most people used the back, I crossed the living room and opened the door.

There in the front hall that smelled of mildew and old wallpaper, stood a half-grown child, about nine, in a puffy black jacket and forest green knit cap. As she pulled off the cap with one hand and extended the other, I realized that this was a formal occasion.

"I'm Dorian," she said. "You're Barbara."

I nodded. She had a very firm handshake. I stepped back quickly and said, "Yes, Jill told me you would come by. Please, come in. Let me take your coat."

She marched past me into the living room and then faced me with her hands on her hips. She looked like some tough Disney tomboy, with her short blond hair still tousled from the cap and freckles across her nose.

"I've just come from Jill's. I can't stay," she said. "I want to make sure that everything is clear." She looked around the room and saw the playpen with Jeremy holding onto the rail and beaming at her.

"This is Jeremy," I said.

"Hi, kiddo," she said, crouching down and handing him a plastic ring from the floor.

"Can I get you something to drink or some cookies?" I offered.

"No, thanks," she said, standing up. "Here's the thing. I can watch out for myself, of course, but we don't want Social Services on our case."

"Jill told me. You're going to come here when your mom leaves for work, have breakfast, and hang out till it's time to go to school."

Dorian nodded.

I went on. "We usually have oatmeal, sometimes eggs. Is that okay or do you want some kind of cold cereal?"

"I'll bring over some Cheerios for days when I don't want oatmeal," she said. Apparently our business was finished since, after another handshake, she pulled her cap on and left.

After that, Dorian always came to the back door. I was happy to have her come over and share our breakfast, thankful to have someone willing to play with the ever-gregarious Jeremy. I didn't know much about her home and had never met her mother. All my dealings were with Dorian.

She was tough. And as practical as my friend Christine. She didn't like her name, so decided she wanted to be called by her middle name. We talked about the story of Dorian Gray which she thought hilarious. She went around telling people she was really thirty years old, which I might have believed, seeing her sturdy independence.

One morning, she dropped her backpack by the back door and dragged off her green cap. Without taking off her coat, she sat at the kitchen table, collapsing like a day-old balloon and curling her thin legs in scruffy blue jeans under the chair. She hadn't brushed her hair, and it stood up in a tangle in back.

"You look really tired," I said, setting a bowl of oatmeal in front of her. This was clearly not going to be one of the mornings we talked over breakfast.

"Mmm," she said, not looking up. She pushed the bowl away and put her head down on her arms.

"Is anything wrong?" I asked.

"No," she mumbled. "Just tired."

"Don't you want to go lie down?"

"No," she muttered.

"At least take off your coat. You should go to bed earlier," I started. "School is important and . . ."

She let out a loud, prolonged groan. "And Jill said you were cool," she said with disgust as she turned her head away.

I let her alone. Jill had said, *I was always treated like just another person in the family.* I realized that was all I had wanted from my parents, to be recognized as a person in my own right, rather than only a tool in their war with each other.

A few weeks later, Jeremy got bronchitis and was up most of the night crying and coughing. I finally was able to fall asleep a little before dawn and only woke up groggily when Dorian called my name from the bedroom doorway. I could tell by the light on the wall that it was late.

"I have to go to school, so you need to get up," Dorian said, glancing behind her.

"How did you get in?" I asked.

"Through Jill's house," she said, turning to go.

She must have come through the front hall. I rolled out of bed and followed her into the kitchen where Jeremy was already ensconced in his high chair with a banana and a bottle of juice.

Dorian handed me a cup of coffee. "He's changed. His pajamas weren't wet so I left them on."

"Dorian, I don't know what to say." I looked down at her, such a thin child, no taller than my shoulder, freckles smudging her pallid skin.

"Drink your coffee. I have to go." She paused, drawing her eyebrows together in a frown, looking up at me sternly. "You know, you should go to bed earlier," she said. She held the look for a moment, but then let out a yelp of laughter, her whole face opening up.

The next morning when I let her in, I handed her a key. "I should have given you this at the start," I said.

She narrowed her eyes and examined me for a moment. Then she said, "Right."

6
RULES

Dorian helped me realize that if I set aside my pre-conceived notions about children, they would teach me how to treat them. If I applied what I'd learned from Miss Smith, maybe I would do okay as a parent. At the same time I wasn't at all sure I was—or wanted to be—an adult. I missed Christine and the games we'd played together. I missed the food orgies and camping trips with our group of friends, but most of all I missed that feeling of having them all around me, like a family, the way a family ought to be. Little by little, though, I was starting to build a group of friends in Worcester. I felt like the girl in the fairy tale who'd lost her brothers and set to work weaving shirts out of stinging nettles to bring them back.

One of my new friends was Sherry, whom I had met at Elm Park the summer that I worked as a live-in maid-housekeeper, after Lewis and I had split up. When I first saw her, Sherry was crouched down in the sand with the kids, arms and legs angling out in all directions. She seemed little more than a child herself, with her big grin and wide cheekbones. She looked up at me, her face open and alight, with an air of eagerness, like a puppy ready to play.

Her eyes startled me: one was blue and the other brown with a wedge of blue in it. It was hard not to look from one to the other, willing them to change and be the same.

Her daughter Rora—short for Aurora—was about the same age as Jeremy and they hit it off together right away. While the kids played with my brother's rusty old yellow Tonka trucks in the sandpit, Sherry and I sat on the bench and talked. She told me she thought her eyes were ugly.

She talked with everybody she met and was interested in everything: yoga, macrobiotics, theories of child rearing. Her words tumbled over each other in her haste to get them out.

"I want Rora to have everything I didn't," she said, waving her long, strong arms. "Education, a career." She paused then, slanting a look at me.

"She has you," I said.

"Yes!" Sherry leaned forward. "Exactly. I don't want her to ever be sad."

I asked Sherry about her family. She wouldn't talk about them, but everything else poured out: the man she'd gotten involved with, and the way he had tried to be decent when she got pregnant.

"He really tried to help me." When she looked at me with those trusting, mismatched eyes, she made me feel like a big sister who ought to be watching out for her. A part of me wished I could be more like her and think the best of everyone.

Whether he actually helped her or not, now here she was: alone with Rora and without resources, so she had turned to welfare to keep the two of them going until she could get a job.

Lacking a car, Sherry rode everywhere on a bike with Rora strapped into a yellow plastic childseat on the back. At the end of a long day at the park, she still lifted Rora with ease and settled her into the childseat. She would turn her head and grin as she swung onto the bike and started off, her long legs spinning the pedals.

It was a relief for me to be with someone who didn't know Lewis. Sometimes when I met people who knew him I could see the distance come over their faces when they realized who I was, and I would think: *Shoot. Another one. What has he told them about me?* Sherry hadn't needed to choose between us or wrestle with staying friends with both of us, as Jill did. Sherry didn't even know Jill or any of my other friends.

I invited Sherry over to see our new home on Newbury Street. I hadn't been to her apartment. "It's awful," she had said. "I'm looking for a new place." I had the impression she didn't have much in the way of furniture: a mattress for the two of them, plastic milk crates for toys and clothes.

Even though it was December, Sherry was still riding her bike. She moved so gracefully, as she wheeled the bike onto the back porch and lifted Rora down, that it was hard to believe she thought of herself as ugly and clumsy. Watching her with Rora, it was clear that she had the most gentle hands.

In the kitchen Sherry exclaimed over the appliances I'd gotten under Emergency Assistance, stroking their clean white surfaces. "They're so new."

"They don't let you get used ones with vouchers," I said.

We went into the living room where I had arranged the furniture under the windows and covered the couch with the Indian paisley bedspread. Further along the wall was my old footlocker and against the far wall was the second space heater, normally the only type of heat in Worcester apartments.

"It's so empty!" Sherry said, and then, in a rush, "I mean, there's so much light."

"No, you're right," I said. "This is the first time I've really been able to do what I want with a place." Trying to build a home instead of merely a place to stay was still new to me.

In front of the space heater was the playpen with Jeremy standing in it, holding up both arms and demanding his freedom. I lifted him out while Sherry unwrapped Rora from her snowsuit. Rora was a square, compact child with light flyaway hair and firm ideas about the world and her place in it.

I put out the Matchbox cars for her and Jeremy to play with. The two children lay on their stomachs running the cars over imaginary roads while Sherry sat at the kitchen table. I gave her some tea and went back to chopping parsnips and turnips for the beans soaking on the stove.

Sherry stirred some honey into her tea and then looked up at me. "This place, I don't know if it's the furniture or what, but it feels like a grownup's house, not an apartment."

"Maybe it's the vibe of the house. From the start it just felt right. Jill found it, you know." I didn't know how Jill had known about the house, through what arcane connections—an art school friend or Welfare Rights contact—she'd heard about it.

"She's upstairs?"

I nodded. "And her friend Erica is on the third floor. I only met Erica a few days ago. She and her friend Andrew are into yard sales, and their apartment is absolutely crammed with stuff. It's fun, all kinds of silly things, but I couldn't live there." I could hear Erica's voice in my head: *Look at that lamp with the belly dancer! Isn't that a scream?* Erica liked to tease me and Jill. *You welfare mothers,* she'd say, *cunning as foxes, manipulating the system to get as much as you can.* Jill would just laugh and agree.

"How does she know Jill?" Sherry asked.

"I'm not sure. I think they were in high school together."

"Jill must know everybody," Sherry mused. "Are you two still doing your babysitting exchange?"

"Yup. It's even easier now that we're in the same building. Would you be interested? Maybe you and I could swap Rora and Jeremy another day of the week," I said, dumping the vegetables in the pot and turning on the burner.

"Oh, yes. Let's do that. Or a few hours anyway, since I'm still nursing Rora. I can't afford babysitters, so that would be a great help. I can use the time to look for a job."

At that moment we heard Rora yell, "Mine!" and then a howl from Jeremy as she slugged him on the arm.

"No, Rora darling," Sherry said as she ran to pull her daughter onto her lap and hug her. "I love you, but you mustn't hit other children."

I comforted Jeremy who seemed more offended than hurt.

Once the children were happily playing again, we went back to the kitchen and talked about some of the issues coming up at the food co-op to which we both belonged, a power struggle between two factions, one led by a newcomer and the other by his one-time mentor.

The food co-op was only one of my community efforts, determined as I was to make this new life a good one. I also worked with some friends to start a land trust as a means of preserving open land and family farms, and Jill encouraged me to join her women's group. I made lists of things to do and tried to work out a structure to organize my days. Despite being mother to a lively toddler and pregnant with a second child, I sometimes felt like I was a kid myself, setting off to school in September with a new pencil case.

This time it was Jeremy who grabbed a car out of Rora's hand, and Rora who started to wail. I took the car away and tried not to laugh at Jeremy's mutinous scowl.

"You know better than that," I said to him firmly. "Tell Rora you're sorry or you can go have a timeout in your room."

Jeremy gave me a dark look and then mumbled, "Sorry."

Rora was squirming in Sherry's arms, struggling to get down. Finally Sherry set her back down by Jeremy.

As we watched them start playing together, the incident forgotten already, Sherry said tentatively, "You know, children who misbehave just want more attention. I think timeouts just make them more unhappy."

I laughed. "Yes, my friend Fay thinks I'm too strict with Jeremy too. But then my mother, on the rare occasions that we talk, says I'm criminally permissive, so I must be doing okay."

After Sherry and Rora left, I called my mother to give her my new phone number. I had been putting it off; talking with my mother was worse than picking stinging nettles.

Since the conversation when I had told her my marriage had failed and she had said I could not come home, I had called her a couple of times, not to ask again for help but simply to chat. Some of my friends called her "The Rock" for the Rock of Ages. Certainly she held strong opinions. She had made it very clear to me that she thought I was ruined, first when I ran off in a schoolbus with Lewis, then when I married him, when I got pregnant, and again when Lewis and I separated. Each time she excoriated my choice and prophesized disaster.

However, I always managed to work out at least an awkward peace with her. After all, I was far away, and not her problem anymore. I hoped it was clear even to her that I accepted the consequences of my decisions and tried to make the best of them. And, too, I was grateful for my odd, solitary childhood. It had taught me to be alone, all those days roaming the streets of Roland Park and sneaking into overgrown gardens.

My mother's voice came through the static on the line. Before I could say anything, she started talking about what she had made for lunch and some shoes she had just bought. Then she told me about what my siblings were doing, those people whom I felt as though I only knew now through her anecdotes. She didn't ask about me, what I'd had for lunch, not even about Jeremy. Ever since I had slipped the leash and deviated from the path she had laid out for me, she had lost what little interest she'd once had in me.

I listened to my mother's stories and then told her about Jeremy's latest antics, whether she wanted to hear them or not. Finally, I explained about my new apartment and gave her the phone number.

She said, "Is that child still waking up at night?"

"Jeremy? Yes. I don't think he'll ever sleep through the night."

"Not if you keep picking him up. You have to let him cry. Be hard with him. Don't go to him. Let him cry. After a while he'll realize it's not working anymore."

I looked over at Jeremy, seated now in the high chair eating a banana. He didn't seem to have that level of cunning. "I think he's just a night person like his father."

"That man! No wonder the child acts the way he does."

I knew where this conversation was headed. "I have to go now."

"You need to get married again," my mother said. "Isn't there anyplace you can go to meet a nice young man, someone with a job?"

"I'm not actually dating right now." I looked down sheepishly at my swollen stomach.

My mother knew about my pregnancy, but she was very good at ignoring things she did not like. "Next you'll be burning your bras. I hope you're wearing one, or you'll be sagging to your waist by the time you're thirty."

Of course, my conservative mother hated the women's movement, but I was excited by it. The nascent women's movement was opening up new doors, encouraging women to consider careers formerly closed to them, even plumbing or car repair. I wasn't in a position yet to be thinking about a career, but equal pay for equal work just seemed like common sense to me.

But big questions—like politics, equal rights—didn't interest me the way they had back in the days when I had marched for civil rights and to end the Vietnam War. Now I focused on what was right in front of me: diapers, bottles, being pregnant. Finding a meaning for my life was no longer an issue: I just had to raise my kids the best way I could.

Usually when Sherry came to pick up Rora, she'd stay for a while. As we'd gotten to be friends, Sherry had opened up a little more about her family. There was a certain panicky look in her brown/blue eyes sometimes that led me to believe that she had been abused. She finally admitted that she had left home at fifteen, lived for a year with an older sister, and then been on her own until she had hooked up with Rora's father. Sixteen seemed way too young to have to fend for yourself.

My questions brought out more of the sad story: her father had indeed been abusive toward her mother and all of the children, three girls and one boy. Sherry was the youngest, her siblings being five, eight and twelve years older. I thought perhaps her mother had abused the children too, but Sherry said no, she mostly neglected them, locked in her room crying. Her mother even tried to drown herself in the creek out back.

"But my brother and sisters sometimes picked on me. One time, my brother tried to kill me by packing snow down my throat. I told my mother, and—you won't believe this—she made me kneel in front of a picture of Jesus and beg forgiveness. Me! When he was the one trying to hurt me."

"No! That's horrible." I rubbed her shoulder in sympathy, and thought about the little girl in the fairy tale weaving shirts for her brothers. They had been turned into swans, but if she threw the shirts over their heads at the right time they would turn back into themselves, and she would have a family again. There were always hard things you were being asked to do, whether it was setting out on your own or letting a child cry at night.

One day Sherry and I were in the kitchen folding diapers and other clean clothes when I heard Michael from the living room telling Rora to stop what she was doing.

I was on my feet quickly. "What is it, Mike?"

He pointed to the small bedroom. Going in, I saw Jeremy sitting on the floor with a toy car in his hand, and Rora standing by the window looking up at us defiantly, her lower lip stuck out.

"What happened?" Sherry had followed me. "Are you hurt, sweetheart?"

"She was chewing on the windowsill," Michael said.

"Oh, no!" Sherry ran to grab her up. "Sweetie, Momma's told you about that."

Rora twisted in her mother's arms and started pulling at her shirt. "Nurse. Nurse."

"I should never have let you out of my sight." Sherry plumped down cross-legged on the floor to nurse Rora. Looking up at me, Sherry said, "She knows better. I've told her about lead paint."

I thanked Michael for his vigilance. He was only four, but no matter what pranks he himself got up to, he was always careful with the little kids and watched out for them.

Once the children were playing quietly again, we settled back at the kitchen table with the piles of laundry. Rora seemed old to be still nursing, but Sherry was determined to let her nurse "until she falls off". I had had to stop nursing when I got sick a few months after Jeremy was born, but I remembered that sweet sensuality, the sense of connection when he looked up at me. I thought with the new baby I might follow Sherry's example if I could.

There was a tap at the back door and Jill came in.

"Hi," I said. "Come in. We should stop and have some tea. Richard okay?"

Jill filled the kettle and put it on. "Yes. He's upstairs building Lego things. Hi, Sherry." I had been pleased to be able to introduce someone new to Jill.

Rora ran through the kitchen, and Sherry grabbed her as she went past. "We have to leave soon."

"No," Rora said, sticking out her lower lip. My mother used to say: *Be careful or your face will freeze that way.*

Jill said, "You have that lip stuck out so far a crow is going to come along and sit on it."

Rora studied Jill for a moment, letting her mouth hang open in a soft "o". Then, making up her mind, she said, "No way," and clamped her mouth shut again.

Sherry said, "Okay, a little while longer then."

Jill and I did not look at each other.

"Do you want some tea?" Jill asked Sherry as the kettle started to whistle.

"No, thanks," Sherry said.

Transferring the piles of folded laundry back to the basket, I said, "I was just telling Sherry—Rora was chewing on the windowsill—that lead paint tastes sweet. That's why kids lick it."

"True," Jill said. "At least the paint's not chipping off in this house."

"Oh, no!" Sherry jumped up. "Do you think that this house has lead paint? Was that really what Rora was chewing on?" She looked at Jill appealingly.

"If it is, she probably didn't get very much," Jill said. "The top coat of paint is fresh."

Sherry ran into the living room and grabbed up Rora in a hug. The child wriggled and squirmed to get down, but Sherry only held her tighter. Finally, Rora bit her mother's arm. Sherry reacted, instinctively pushing Rora away, holding her out in mid-air, hands under Rora's armpits.

Startled, Rora wailed loudly.

Immediately Sherry relented and hugged her close. "Oh, I'm sorry, darling. Momma loves you. Shh. Shh. I would never hurt you. Shh."

Sherry continued holding and stroking the child till Rora calmed down and began lifting Sherry's shirt, saying, "Nurse. Nurse."

"But you just . . . Okay."

Later, after they left, Jeremy crawled into my lap and Michael into Jill's. Richard was still upstairs.

"She's going to have trouble with that child," Jill said.

"She doesn't want Rora to ever be unhappy. She doesn't want her to ever cry."

"Who was doing the most crying today, then? Oh well." Jill stroked Michael's blond hair and he slumped back against her with his eyes closed, long black lashes lying on his cheeks, cheeks that were streaked with dirt even though he'd been playing inside all day.

"Mm," I said. "Rora is different when Sherry's not around."

"I guess all kids are, one way or another."

Compared to Sherry, I felt ancient, practically middle-aged. I wanted to pass on to her some of what Jill had given to me, but didn't feel qualified to give out advice, especially about discipline.

Jill took Jeremy once a week to give me a day to write, but it was hard to make myself do it. Given the chance, I seemed to spend hours simply trying to remember who I was. When Jeremy was over at Sherry's I tried to write too, in between whatever other chores or errands had to be done, but rarely managed to get much down on paper. I was sure if I could just be more organized or more self-disciplined I could manage it. Those to-do lists I made every day never got finished.

Jill comforted me. "Look at all you have to do: a baby to run after, the welfare office to deal with, and being pregnant's no joke."

It just seemed like I should be doing more.

I wrote in my journal: *Why am I so bad at disciplining myself? I can discipline Jeremy okay. I think I've found a pretty good balance with him. Even though I'm not as controlling as my mother, I don't have a problem getting him to follow my rules, though he does ask 'why' over and over until he takes me back to my first principles.*

Sherry is so fearful of hurting Rora that she avoids disciplining her at all. I love that gentleness in Sherry. She makes me believe in the stories of monks brushing ants off the path so they won't step on them, or wearing masks to avoid breathing in gnats. But it doesn't seem like a very effective way to raise a child.

I was excited about our first Christmas at Newbury Street. Christmas brought out the kid in me. One very cold day in mid-December, Richard and Michael came with me and Jeremy to buy a Christmas tree. It was my day to have Jill's boys, and I needed their help. Our venture started out badly when I returned to the house to get the boys, who had been putting on snowsuits and mittens, and accidentally locked the keys in the car. The four of us stood there helplessly on the sidewalk while Celia, nicely warmed up by then, putted gently at the curb.

A bare-headed boy I didn't know came swinging down the sidewalk. A lot of people used Newbury Street to cut across to Chandler Street, so I didn't think much of it till he stopped beside us. He looked about eleven and wore jeans and a puffy nylon parka.

"What's up? Locked the keys in the car?" he asked.

We nodded glumly.

"Want me to let you in?"

What else could I say? "Yes, please."

He turned his back on us, pulling something from inside his jacket. I couldn't see what he did, just a quick movement of his shoulders and he was standing aside, holding the door open.

"There you go," he grinned.

"Wow. Thanks," I said.

The boy refused the money I offered him. "Merry Christmas!" he called as he swung off down the street.

Richard looked up at me with a serious expression. "Well, Barb, if you're going to lock your keys in the car, at least you picked the right neighborhood to live in."

Michael's eyes were dancing. As he opened his mouth, I cut in. "Don't start on me, Michael, please. I admit I'm an idiot. Help me get Jem into his carseat."

"Okay," Michael said, and slid into the back seat to give me a hand.

We went on and got the tree, laughing and struggling to tie it on top of the car with tangled nylon ropes and bungee cords. Celia held up well under the abuse and we got the tree home safely and set it up in my living room using my mother's old trick of sticking it in a bucket and adding rocks to prop it up. The tree was a good shape, a Scotch pine about four feet tall and very full. I put the bucket on top of the footlocker to make the tree seem taller and also to keep it away from Jeremy's eager hands. Richard, who was seven but tall for his age, helped me tie fishing line from the top of the tree to some nails in the window frame for extra stability.

The next day I went to the Little Brown Toyshop near Elm Park and looked longingly at the wonderful but expensive toys: trucks made of natural wood, Caran D'Ache crayons, little musical instruments. I ended up getting Jeremy a used Fisher-Price farm set from Goodwill. It was in pretty good shape and had most of the pieces. I wrapped it in old Sunday comics pages, wrapping each person and animal separately so it would look like more, and put the packages under the tree.

My mother hadn't sent any presents for Jeremy. We seemed to be on speaking terms, given our phone conversations. Maybe she thought he was too young for Christmas presents. Or maybe they merely hadn't come yet.

A couple of days later, I invited Sherry and Rora over to help decorate the tree. Richard and Michael came down too and brought one of their friends from the neighborhood. I loved having Chance over. Though small for his age, he was smart, very quick to pick up on things. No matter how rowdy he could be when roughhousing with the older boys, he was always gentle with Jeremy and generously entertained him for long stretches of time.

It turned into a party. I popped a big bowl of popcorn for stringing and eating and got out the home-made Christmas cookies. We had cider too, in plastic cups for the children. With Christmas records on my old stereo, it was quite festive.

Only Richard had the patience and dexterity to string the popcorn without breaking it, so Michael cut out strips of red and green construction paper while Chance and Sherry helped the toddlers paste the strips into chains. Coming back into the living room with more cookies, I felt the place was bursting with life, the air fragrant with pine and cider, rich with the children's chatter and their bright clothes. The older boys wore sweaters in primary colors over their jeans, while Jeremy and Rora had on corduroy overalls, Jeremy in royal blue and Rora in red. The two of them were roly-poly with diapers that made them stagger about bow-legged like tiny cowboys.

The satisfaction only lasted a moment. Tiring of the chains, Jeremy pasted a strip of green paper on Michael's back and, letting out a deep belly laugh, overbalanced and plopped down on his bum. After a little bit of mayhem, as Michael retaliated by pasting a red strip on Jeremy's forehead, much to the child's delight, I organized the children into a game of pin the strip on the kid. Mike volunteered to be the target and I used scotch tape to attach the strips wherever the blindfolded children placed them, Chance and Sherry supporting the toddlers' uncertain steps when it was their turn. Only Richard refused to be lured away from his task and continued to sit in a corner of the couch calmly stringing popcorn.

I asked Sherry if she had been in touch with her family, if she didn't miss them now that it was nearly Christmas.

"This is my family," she said, waving her arm, taking in the children, the happy mess.

That night after everyone had left and an exhausted Jeremy had for once gone right off to sleep, I looked around the living room and had to laugh. Strips of colored paper hung off the walls and furniture as if there had been an explosion. Only the tree was free of them. It held the old colored Christmas lights my mother had given me to decorate my dorm room with when she switched to white ones, and Richard's popcorn strings.

Jill came down to admire the mess and stayed to chat over hot cider with cinnamon. While I finished up the abandoned chains, she took some sheets of white paper and cut large intricate snowflakes to hang on the tree.

After Jill went back upstairs, I turned out all the lights except for those on the tree and sat in the rocking chair admiring it. I thought it was the most beautiful tree that I had ever seen. It had been hard, saving the money to buy the tree, but it was worth it. Making the transition to welfare, creating a home for my children, carving out a life for myself—nothing had been as hard as I'd expected it would have to be for this kind of reward, seeing ugly ducklings turn into swans and swans into family to celebrate Christmas with me.

After all that, I gave away the tree on Christmas Eve. Dorian's family didn't have a tree and no money to get one. I reckoned that with Jeremy still so little, Jill's snowflakes on the little potted Norfolk pine and a string of colored lights tacked up to the ceiling molding would be magical enough. So I gave the tree to Dorian, missing the sticky pine smell, but loving the grin on her freckled face.

On Christmas morning I woke up to silent snow. I'd been in New England long enough to recognize that unmistakable hush that lets you know snow has fallen during the night, even before you open your eyes. Still an hour before dawn, the windows were lit with that pale glow of ambient light reflecting off falling snow. I lay in bed for a moment savoring the quiet, and then got up and pulled back the curtains to see a street transformed by the still-falling snow into a magical landscape. There was no wind, no movement but the fine snow that carelessly, ineluctably filled in the cracks in the world, that light, dry kind of snow that seems like it will go on forever.

I went into the living room, barely seeing the outlines of the couch and chair in the grey light, and turned up the space heater. Plugging in the lights, I admired the wash of colors down the pale walls even as I heard Jeremy stirring. I changed him, zipped him back into his thermal footed pajamas and pulled a baby blanket around him for extra warmth. Then I brought him out to see the lights and after that over to the window to see the snow, white as the swans at Elm Park. Jeremy, silent for once, seemed overwhelmed. He watched the snow for a minute, and then looked around at the lights. Still without a sound, he buried his face in my neck, so I took him over to the rocking chair.

I settled him on my lap and kissed the top of his head, inhaling his lovely baby smell. His feathery curls tickled my chin. The creak of the wooden rocking chair was the only sound in the early morning stillness as Jeremy nestled on my lap. Outside the snow fell steadily, shutting out the world and sealing us in our rainbow-washed cocoon. I tightened my arms around Jeremy and the bulge in my tummy, thinking: *I chose you. This isn't where I thought I'd be and certainly not the life I thought I'd be leading. But I have you.*

7

BARTER

After the excitement of Christmas, I felt a little bleak, writing in my journal: *Must be the dreary rain, days and days of it. Beginning to doubt a little the felicity of the life I've chosen. A strange fear, too, of losing this baby when there's no reason to think so. It just feels like I've lost so much lately. But there's no place I'd have chosen differently, I think; very little I regret.*

Eventually I decided that instead of sitting around, I should do something to make my world a little better. I thought about the way people on Piedmont Street helped each other out. I also thought about the informal way my college friends helped each other out, and compared that to the more formal systems such as the food co-op and land trust, as well as the communes Jill and I had visited. It seemed to me that I could come up with some kind of synthesis, maybe expand on that neighborly impulse to help each other out by creating an informal system of bartering services that would help us help ourselves. It might even be enough simply to put people with different skills in touch with each other, so they could barter work rather than having to pay for it.

Sherry and I started exchanging child care. Once, Rora came to stay for an entire week while Sherry was painting the new apartment she had found. I was happy to have Rora, figuring it was good for Jeremy to get a taste of not being an only child before the baby arrived. However, the tantrums multiplied as the week went on, the two of them taking turns to dissolve in fury and frustration. With an extra child, the diaper bucket filled up so fast that I could barely wash them fast enough. Diapers became my zen thing, like archery or motorcycle maintenance.

I also took care of Richard and Michael for a few days while Jill was struggling to finish artwork for a show at a co-op gallery.

"It would be great sell to a few pieces," she said one night when I expressed concern. Her color was never good, but that night her face looked parched and drained.

She did get everything done in time and the show was a great success. At least, a lot of people came and praised Jill's work. But she didn't sell anything.

I went ahead with my plan to set up an informal work exchange, mining Jill's contacts, putting people in touch with each other, talking to people at the library and the food co-op. I kept a list by the phone of people's names and what they could do. It grew to several pages and I had to put them on a clipboard, an old one from high school, still with my class schedule written on it. My own contribution was usually babysitting or minor car repairs.

I found ways to cut costs. Jill and I and some other friends had gotten together to buy bulk food from Erewhon, a natural foods distributor, splitting up the fifty-pound bags of beans and rice. I had an old hand grinder from when I lived with Lewis so I could grind wheat berries into flour, whole oats into oatmeal. Anything to save a few pennies.

Fresh fruit and vegetables were a challenge, being so expensive. On the kitchen table was a wide flat soup bowl with some water and the tops from the carrots and turnips that had gone into last week's stew. The tops had already sprouted new greens. Another bowl held an upended canning jar, its mouth covered with cheesecloth, a handful of alfalfa seeds sprouting inside.

On the stove, a pot of milk sat on top of one pilot light slowly turning into yogurt. On the other, a bowl of bread dough was rising. A healthy life, idyllic even, and close to my vision of what life would be like in the farmhouse I wanted to buy someday. However, making everything from scratch took a lot of time.

Hanging diapers out on the round clothesline came to be one of my favorite parts of the day, a brief moment to step outside alone, Jeremy napping or confined to his playpen. The diapers would freeze solid as boards and sway back and forth on the line, but eventually they would dry and I could bring them in and fold them.

Another favorite part of the day was storytime, with Jeremy on my lap, his head tucked under my chin, perhaps Rora or Jill's boys cuddled up next to me. I would read book after book, using different voices for the characters. Some years after this, my sister told me that she had no memory of ever sitting on our mother's lap. I said that by the time each of us was old enough for memories, there were one or two more babies to monopolize whatever lap-time was available. Anyway, I hadn't been interested in laps since I was always reading or wandering off by myself. It was only in my twenties, with this baby boy cuddling close to me that I felt I was experiencing a real childhood, even if it was at second hand.

Sometimes, if things got too much for me and I started having that old trapped feeling, that pacing-the-cage feeling, I would bundle Jeremy into his carseat and we would drive around Worcester or out Route 9 toward Amherst, singing songs like *Morning Has Broken* at the top of our lungs. I loved seeing the barren trees that crowded up against the road give way to the wide stubbly fields.

One day in February, I took Jeremy, Rora, and Michael to the park. We liked to go there even in winter, when it seemed to take forever to bundle the children into snowsuits, scarves, mittens and boots. The park felt quiet without the ducks and geese, the pond frozen and the rhododendrons bowed down with snow. The snow creaked underfoot as we walked over to the playground.

I brushed snow off the swings and went from one to another, pushing the children in turn. Then, hopping off the swings, they ran around shouting in the clear cold air. They dropped to the ground to make snow angels and got up laughing, with cheeks flashing bright red, ice crystals clinging to the scarves in front of their mouths, and archipelagos of snow on the mittens pinned to their snowsuits.

Finally we trudged home, only to find a strange van parked out front and a group of men huddled in their coats on the stoop. A tall man with shaggy blond hair stepped forward and I recognized Walt, one of my Maryland family of friends.

When he stooped to wrap me in a bear hug, his face against mine was freezing. "Come in," I said and broke loose to unlock the door. "Is this your band? Come in where it's warm."

Walt helped me get Jeremy and Rora inside. Jeremy recognized him and demanded music instantly. Walt laughed and said, "In a little while, buddy."

"Give him a chance to warm up, Jeremy. Could you go be with Rora?" Alarmed by the strangers, she had taken refuge in Jeremy's room.

Walt looked at me ruefully. "I meant to call. We've been on the road forever."

"That's okay," I said. "You all need a place to stay? There's only the floor."

He grinned, relief showing in his eyes. "That would be great. We have a concert here in town tomorrow."

Michael was trying to help the others bring in their instruments from the van, but they were reluctant to entrust them to a four-year-old, however cute. Walt went back out to tell them to bring in their duffle bags too. Gradually the chaos subsided, and the members of the band introduced themselves, apologizing for bursting in on me like this.

"Don't be silly," I said.

I looked over at Walt joking with Michael. When Jill and I had gone to upstate New York looking at communal situations, he had put us and the children up for a weekend, no small gift from a man with no children and a house full of valuable instruments.

In truth I was thrilled to have them all in my home. It was a new experience, having a home of my own and welcoming guests into it. Walt, with his light heart and ready grin, always cheered me up. And then there was the music. Instrument cases were stacked in a corner of the living room or spread around the floor while the guys picked out tunes.

Soon my little apartment was bursting with music. Jeremy was beside himself, trotting from one set of knees to another, reaching for guitar strings. Michael was able to coax Rora out of hiding before Jill called for him to come upstairs, and Rora followed Jeremy in his rounds, one finger in her mouth.

When Sherry came to pick her up, I introduced her to Walt and the others.

"You play the guitar, don't you?" I asked her.

"Just a little."

Walt immediately handed her his guitar and took up a banjo. After only one tune, though, Rora started pulling on Sherry until she agreed it was time to go home.

As she left, Sherry leaned close to me and said, "You're so lucky."

I was. Friends made all the difference. I closed the door behind her, stepped back into the warm living room, and pulled the tatters of my old life around me. I lumbered about, feeling hugely pregnant, yet at the same time feeling like my old self, the girl who had gone racing through the cornfields back in Maryland and camped out in the woods, showing up for breakfast at Baugher's Restaurant with twigs in my hair and a flannel shirt that smelled of wood smoke.

Of course, Jeremy wanted to show the guys the farm set which had been a big hit at Christmas, and soon had them all down on the floor making animal noises for him. Then, while I talked with one about art, another actually let Jeremy pluck at his mandolin, the only instrument small enough for the child to hold.

Sometime later, Walt and I were in the kitchen exchanging news about our mutual friends. Talking about them reminded me that there was a world outside of Worcester. I thought about my farmhouse dreams, the restlessness of curtains blowing, gauzy white curtains billowing over that bed under the rafters, a crazy quilt, a rag rug.

Then Walt said, "So, is it horrible? Being on welfare?"

"Not really. I mean, there's never enough money, but it's okay."

"I pictured you down and out in some drug-infested tenement." He looked around the kitchen with the walls I'd painted white and the new stove and washer. "You seem to be managing all right!"

I laughed. "Yes. And can you tell how proud I am of that?"

He tilted his head as if considering. "People don't treat you badly?"

I shrugged. "It's only been a couple of months, but I think it'll work out." I didn't want to think about the ugliness when I was having such a good time.

"You seem pretty happy."

"I am." It was hard not to smile around Walt. "Or it could just be pregnancy talking."

Pregnancy agreed with me. Not only did I never have morning sickness, but I was happy every day. It had been the same when I was carrying Jeremy. In fact, it was how I had known I was pregnant again: I woke up one morning so full of joy that I jumped up out of bed singing a hymn—Holy, Holy, Holy—at the top of my lungs.

I thought, *I haven't been this happy since . . .* And then, *Uh-oh.*

A pregnancy test had confirmed it and now the baby was due in about six weeks. I had crashed back to earth after Jeremy was born and expected it would be the same with this baby.

Walt's concert was the next night, at Holy Cross, a college in Worcester. Jill and I and the children went up with Walt and the rest of the band. There was still snow, of course, but the streets were clear.

Nights out were pretty rare for me and Jill. At the door to the coffeehouse, excitement washed over me, as though I were Cinderella headed for the ball. As I walked into the dim room, however, the feeling faded into a sense of déjà vu. When I was a student, I used to go to coffeehouses and concerts in Worcester all the time. Partially subsidized by the colleges—there were eleven colleges in the Worcester area—the prices were low and the quality of the music high. The folk revival was still going strong, and the concerts drew all kinds of people, lowering the barrier between townies and college students.

Jill and I sat at a round table near the front, off to the side a little, while Walt and the rest of the band set up. People filtered in, students and older people from town. They gradually filled up the other tables, keeping the bar busy. Looking around, I was surprised by how young the students seemed to be, like children not much older than Richard, a peculiar sensation since I was only a couple of years out of school myself.

I listened to them flirt with each other, talk about exams, and gossip about professors. My mood deflated even more, like a leftover party balloon, and I turned to Jill hoping to catch some of the excitement in her bright eyes.

"This is so much fun," she said. "I'd forgotten how great it is to go out." On the other side of her, Michael was bouncing up and down in his seat, eager for the music to start. Richard sat next to me holding Jeremy. Jeremy adored him, and I knew I could trust him to be responsible. Richard seemed much older than his eight years, maybe because he was tall for his age and serious.

Then the music started. No matter how many times I heard Walt play, his music always seemed fresh to me. All around me feet were tapping to the lively bluegrass tunes. When Walt got out his hammer dulcimer, he set a scorching pace, driving the rest of the band to play even faster, their fingers flying over guitar and mandolin strings.

Jeremy scrambled down from Richard's lap and crawled up close to the stage where he fell asleep in front of the speakers. I worried about him damaging his ears, but he seemed to love the vibrations, the feeling of being enveloped by the music.

The band played favorites I'd heard before and some that were new to me. The applause grew louder after each song, and some folks started to clap in time to the music. When the band swung into a slow ballad, people around us sang along softly. The diverse crowd seemed to pull together under the spell of the music, sharing a story, a mood, an evening.

By the end of the concert, all three children were asleep. The guys helped us carry them to the cars and later into the house.

The next day, bundled against the cold, I stood on the stoop with Jeremy on my hip, waving good-bye as the van pulled away. It was hard to go back inside, even after the street had settled back into itself and some of the neighborhood boys came out to play street hockey.

The bustle of having Walt and his friends at my house was fun, but then they were gone and I was back to diapers and economizing. The welfare check only came once a month, and after the first disastrous month when I had nearly run out of money after two weeks, I had come up with a budgeting system that seemed to work for me, using some small green envelopes I'd been given back when I had worked at the envelope factory. As soon as I cashed my monthly welfare check, I divided the money between the respective envelopes for rent, heat, light, phone, milk, car, non-food groceries like laundry detergent, and emergency. There was rarely anything left in the emergency envelope by the second week, but at least my method kept me from the financial crises I saw among some of my friends as the cash ran out toward the end of the month.

When the February cold seeped up from the basement, I tried to keep the heat turned down to save money—Jeremy and I could always put on more sweaters—but as the month wore on, I began to think that Cinderella had the right idea crouching by the fireplace. When we first got up, Jeremy and I had to huddle around the space heater until the kitchen warmed up a little.

Despite my efforts, though, every month was a struggle. After rent and utilities, I only had about $20 a month left over. It had to cover everything that food stamps didn't: gas and oil for the car, laundry detergent, toilet paper, even baby supplies like Orajel and Desitin. There was no margin for error. If I had to buy a new distributor cap for the car, the cash had to come from somewhere, but what could we do without? Soap? Trash bags?

Then there were the arguments with the welfare office. The good part was that Medicaid paid for pre-natal visits for me and well-baby check-ups for Jeremy. I had found a pediatrician with an office near Elm Park who accepted Medicaid. Getting medical assistance had been the weight that had finally tipped me over into welfare, and I could not do without it. I could never have afforded medical care on my own.

But it was not uncommon for me to spend the whole day at the welfare office, torn between trying to keep Jeremy quiet and fighting over a check gone astray or an accounting error that suddenly gave me half the expected amount of food stamps.

It was a crapshoot. No particular social worker was assigned to my case and we were not allowed to make appointments, so in effect it worked like a clinic where we saw whoever happened to be in the office. I never knew if I would get one of the social workers who practiced the director's policy of pretending every penny came out of his or her own pocket, or one of the good ones, who was as frustrated as I was by the vagaries of the system which so often seemed designed to keep us down.

One day I got home in such a fury that Jill came down to see why I was slamming doors.

"It wasn't even the social worker!" I said. "He was fine."

"What happened?" Jill said, kneeling down to take the snowsuit off an unusually silent Jeremy.

"We were walking home, up Austin Street, you know."

Jill nodded. It wasn't the best neighborhood, to be sure, with some derelict houses, a few burnt-out shells, and trash scattered across the dirty snow. But using it to walk downtown and back avoided the heavy traffic noise on Chandler or Pleasant.

"And this man in a car slowed down next to me—me! pregnant out to here and a baby in a stroller!—and starts in with his *Hey, baby, want a ride? Come over here. Those are some big knockers. How much for a blow job?*"

"They are such fools," Jill said, finishing with Jeremy and standing up. "They think because you're walking in this neighborhood, you must be a prostitute."

It was true that prostitutes in Worcester commonly looked for customers by pretending to hitch-hike, but it still made me furious.

"I'm pregnant!" I said. "With a stroller. There was no way he could have thought I was a prostitute. They just do it because they can."

"Crimes against us don't matter," Jill said.

I still believed in barter. I kept my lists up next to the phone. I managed to get a man with plumbing experience to fix an elderly woman's burst pipes in return for an ancient wood-burning stove she plan to junk anyway. Maybe my work exchange idea could still succeed.

Also, Sherry, Jill and I continued our babysitting exchanges. One day Jill stopped by as Sherry was dropping off Jeremy. We stood in the living room talking about the problems at the food co-op while the two kids moved off toward the bedroom.

"Let's sit down," I said motioning toward the couch and chair.

"For a minute," Jill said. "I have to start dinner, but I need to talk about lead paint."

"Jeremy, keep an eye on Rora," I called. "Let me know if she licks the paint again."

Sherry leaned forward, hands clasped between her knees. "All these landlords should have to strip it off right away. How can they live with themselves knowing that their houses are poisoning children?"

Jill let out a cynical laugh. "It's not that simple. For one thing, it's almost more dangerous when they start taking it off, especially if they don't do it right. If they start chipping or sanding it off, you've got poisonous dust and paint chips everywhere."

"I hadn't thought about that."

I looked at Jill. "And for another thing, . . . ?"

"It's expensive," Jill said. "It's hugely expensive, so no landlord's going to do it till he's forced to. And then it becomes something he holds over you."

"Like your landlord on Piedmont Street?" I asked.

Jill had been the last to move out of Piedmont Street, and terrified by the time she finally left. She explained that the landlord threatened to evict all of them if they got their kids tested for lead poisoning, but Vicky's kids from the third floor were in Head Start, and lead testing was required. When the kids tested positive for lead, the landlord evicted everyone: Vicky, her mother Ruth on the first floor, and Jill. He wanted them to get out before the court order to remove the lead paint took effect.

"But Head Start!" Sherry protested, straightening up. "I mean, it's so good for children."

"Of course. That's the point," Jill said.

Jill, Vicky, and Ruth got together to sue him for evicting them, but they lost. Their Legal Aid lawyer disappeared in the middle of the whole process, just up and decided to move to the west coast to start a new life. Even though they lost the case against him, the landlord still had to remove the lead paint. He told the workmen to make life miserable for the tenants. Luckily the workmen hated the landlord, so they disobeyed his orders and treated Jill, Ruth, Vicky and the children kindly.

"But are you sure it was him?" Sherry said. "Maybe he only wanted you to find someplace better."

"I could hardly mistake the phone calls all the time, during the day, in the middle of the night, threatening to burn the house down."

Sherry leaned forward. "But . . ."

"Then after Vicky and Ruth found somewhere else to live," Jill continued, "the calls escalated. They said they would kill Richard and Michael if I didn't move out. Kill my children. I could hardly mistake that."

Sherry looked out the window. I leaned over and touched her arm. She turned to me, smiled, and sat up straighter, untangling her long legs, Jill's cynicism rolling off of her.

Jill went on. "Of course, as soon as I moved here, the landlord called off the workmen and had the house pulled down."

"Well, at least you're safe here now," I said.

"We're not home free here, either," Jill said, looking at me. "That's what I wanted to tell you. I found out there's a suit pending against our landlord brought by someone who lived here before. Apparently there really is lead paint here."

"What if he loses? Do you think he'll evict us and pull the house down? Or torch it?" I was terrified of fire. Too many houses in Worcester conveniently burned down.

"Maybe," Jill said grimly. "We'd better start looking again."

I hung up the phone and sat down at the kitchen table. It was the beginning of March, and the baby was due in a few weeks.

I looked out at the empty driveway and rubbed my forehead. One of my attempts at barter had just backfired on me. It started when the clutch cable on my ten-year-old VW bug fell off again. I had stopped Celia in front of the house, turned her off, and let up on the clutch cable, as I'd done a hundred times before. Only this time the pedal kept coming. The car was so old that the floor had rusted out under the restraining tab on the clutch pedal, allowing the pedal to fall completely forward on its face and the cable to slip off its hook.

It had happened twice before. The last time, after fixing the cable, I had wedged a crushed soda tin under the clutch pedal to compensate for the disintegrating floor. That had lasted for a few months before the tin slid out. I knew how to fix the problem, but was so big around from my pregnancy that I couldn't get down between the steering wheel and the front seat, even with the seat pushed all the way back.

So, consulting my contacts list, I arranged for a young man named Alan to fix it for me in return for the loan of the car for the weekend to go see his girlfriend in Amherst. I hated to let him take Celia. Not only did I feel helpless without a car for the weekend—what if the baby came early?—but also I hated to have anyone else to drive her. She was so rickety. I wasn't sure anyone else would be gentle enough and nurse her along the way I did.

I didn't have much of a choice, though. Garages were too expensive, and I didn't know anyone else who could fix the clutch cable. I might have been able to talk Jill through the repair, but she was always nervous about cars and was afraid to work on mine. So I agreed to Alan's terms, and kept a close eye on him as he worked, pleased that he did such a good job. Then I waved good-bye, Jeremy pulling at my leg, as Alan drove off in my car.

He must have had a good time. The phone call was from a humble and repentant Alan telling me that he fell asleep on the way back from Amherst and rolled the car. He wasn't hurt but the car was totaled.

Celia was gone. And along with her not only my independence but something of my connection with Christine. Roz and Celia (those Shakespearian cousins), our Rockport Sunday. Gone too were the fun times with the children, driving around Worcester with Jeremy singing *Puff the Magic Dragon* or *Morning Has Broken*, getting the Christmas tree with the boys. I felt as if all my magic charms were gone, the little things that I used to ward off sadness. It was all well and good to try and make a game out of being poor, but this was not a game.

I sat at the kitchen table wondering what I was going to do. Even when I didn't have money for gas and the car just sat in the driveway, I still needed it to be there. Celia seemed like my escape hatch, my way out. I could not afford to buy another car. Even if I could come up with the cash, I could no longer call on Lewis's expertise to ensure that a cheap, much-used car still had some life left in it.

My carriage had turned back into a pumpkin. Being nine months pregnant meant that walking downtown to the library or the welfare office had become nearly impossible. Cabs were too expensive. I would be stuck with buying groceries at the expensive corner spa except when Jill drove me to Iandoli's or Stop & Shop. I didn't want to rely on Jill to drive me everywhere, even though I knew she would if I asked—too many favors could damage a friendship, and my friendship with Jill was about all I had left in the magic charm department.

I could have said no to Alan, insisted on repaying him some other way. Or simply left the car, done without it for a month until I was able to fix it myself. Young, impatient, trusting, I still somehow believed that the world would not hurt me, that people were basically good, that they wanted to do the right thing. When I lost Celia, I lost not just my mobility, but some piece of me that had held out against the casual treachery of landlords and social workers, the life I was living, the person I had become.

8

INVISIBLE

"I know it's my week, but I can't get the milk," I said. "Do you think you could go and I'll make it up to you later?"

Now that Alan had wrecked my car, Jill regularly offered to lend me hers. I mostly refused, wanting to save the favor for when I really needed it. Asking for help didn't come easily to me. And then too, with the baby due in a couple of weeks, I had a little trouble fitting behind the wheel of Jill's tiny car.

Then Jill brightened. "Actually, why don't we all go? It'll be fun to get out."

Normally Jill and I took turns driving up to the dairy in Rutland. It was an outing that the kids looked forward to every week, a chance to get out of the city.

We piled into Jill's VW bug, me struggling to buckle the seatbelt, the three boys in the backseat. As usual, we took the back way and stopped at Holden Reservoir.

Early March meant that it was still cold, but there wasn't any snow on the ground and the sky was a deep clear blue. Jill and I walked through the ranks of dark pine trees, fanatically straight rows planted as part of the WPA effort during the Depression. They seemed like zombie trees to me but they smelled like Christmas.

The boys ran ahead toward the water. Calling to each other, they scattered to run up and down the beach.

I sat down heavily on a log.

"You're not going to have that baby on me, are you?"

"Not today."

"You welfare mothers are all alike: having more babies so you can get a bigger check." Jill sat down next to me. "It's not like you actually love them or anything."

"Yeah, right," I said. "I'm rich, I am. Can't you tell?"

Newspaper articles referred to us as the "greedy needy". I asked Jill why they didn't simply give us money for child care. That plus health insurance would mean we could survive on a low-end job. Maybe if we were working, we wouldn't be so demonized.

"Wouldn't that make sense?" she said. Then she went on to tell me about a Government study that found child care assistance for poor women would actually cost more than the AFDC program. "It's cheaper for them if we take care of our own children."

At that moment the boys ran up to us, their pockets knobby and heavy with stones they'd found.

"Cows," Jeremy said. "Let's go."

We set out again, and eventually left the highway and drove up a side road lined with aspen and maple trees, still bare in early March, to the dairy. Jill parked between the farmhouse and the barn, and the boys were out of the car immediately.

"Look, Jem. Cows!" Richard said, pointing to the stately Guernsey cows.

Jeremy held up his arms, and was scooped up by Richard. The three boys went over to the fence. Michael, always the bravest, reached out to stroke one cow's caramel-colored shoulders. As the head swung slowly around, he opened his palm to the cow's wet black nose and soft lips.

The cow let out a loud "Moo" right in their faces, startling the three boys, so that they jumped back, and Jem started to cry.

I went over and took him from Richard. "There, there, Munchkin," I said, patting his back as he hid his face in my shoulder.

He looked back at the cow and scowled. "Bad cow!" But I knew that in a few minutes he would be demanding the cows again. He always liked best those things that he was afraid of.

Since it was my week to pay for the milk, I set Jeremy down and sorted through my bag. I always got three half gallons. Never anything extra, like cottage cheese.

Every food stamp, every penny was already allocated. There was no such thing as an impulse buy in my world. I had learned to walk through Filene's and Jordan Marsh with the sure and certain knowledge that I wasn't going to buy a single thing, no matter how many free lotion samples I rubbed into my hands.

After Jill and I got back from the dairy, we sat in her kitchen, drinking coffee and leaning in toward each other to talk over the din of the boys in the other room.

"Here," Jill said, giving me the latest jumbled mass of papers covered with her big, loopy handwriting. "You can look at this, if you want, while I see what the kids are up to."

Both Jill and I had started writing down our dreams, me in the journal I kept in an old notebook from Clark University, Jill on flyers and other scraps of paper. Neither of us had the cash to actually buy a pad of paper.

Jill's dreams were always full of unexpected images, some of which she used in her artwork. This dream was about a car stuck in the sand.

Jill came back into the kitchen. "You know, amazing things happen. One day—this was back when we lived on Piedmont Street—I decided to take Richard and Michael to the beach."

"That beach near Rhode Island where we went that time?" I asked, laying down the papers.

"Right. Well, halfway there the car broke down. There I was, hitchhiking with two little kids, and this cop stopped. I told him I was so disgusted with the car that he could have it. He asked didn't I have anyone to call, and I said no. So the cop—he didn't know us at all—he pushed the car all the way to a repair place. And the people at the repair place fixed it for five dollars even though it took them three hours."

"Five dollars? That's nothing." I would have been wondering what the catch was.

"You got it. While they worked on the car, I looked after their kids. You know, here were these kids playing around the shop, and I was afraid they'd fall into the pit, so I took them for a walk."

"Sounds like the kind of thing you'd do."

"Well, I wanted to do something for them since they were helping us out. And then, it was so late when we got to the beach, I decided that instead of trying to get home we would just sleep in the car there in the parking lot. But we met this woman while we were walking on the beach, and she invited us to stay over at her house."

Taking children into a stranger's house seemed awfully risky to me. She could have been an axe murderer or something.

The phone rang, and Jill got up to answer it.

Her story reminded me of back when I first got Celia, before my marriage fell apart, and I had been afraid she would break down, leaving me stuck by the roadside with baby Jeremy. Celia had been such an old car and not in very good shape. That was why I had bugged Lewis to teach me how to fix whatever broke. I didn't have Jill's faith in the kindness of strangers.

Car repair: that was a skill. Sitting there in Jill's kitchen, I daydreamed about getting a job once the baby was born, working in a garage. If I could only figure out how to manage child care, I could be off of welfare in a few months.

When Jill got off the phone, she asked me when the baby was due.

"Soon. A couple of weeks."

"You look like you're ready to pop now."

With all the furniture and appliances I'd gotten through Emergency Assistance, there was one voucher I hadn't used yet. It was for a crib, a second crib for this new baby. The voucher was made out to The Mart, a discount store on Main Street where they supposedly sold a crib for the price on the voucher.

The welfare office policy was to find the lowest price in town for the item and issue the voucher in that amount, with a caveat that the recipient could not add funds to purchase a more expensive item, an attempt to keep stores from cheating welfare recipients with a bait-and-switch sales tactic.

Running out of time to get the crib, I went to The Mart, awkwardly holding the glass door open to push Jeremy's stroller through, and walked past the tables where old ladies in zippered housedresses fingered messy stacks of nylon panties. I presented the voucher to a salesman. He was middle-aged, balding, with very pink cheeks and a tie holding the unbuttoned collar of his short-sleeved dress shirt together.

"No," he said. "We don't have a crib for that price."

"But you have to," I said.

"We don't." He started to walk away.

"Hey," I said. He turned back. "This voucher, the welfare office has you down as selling a crib at this price."

He looked down his nose at me, the florescent lights gleaming on his forehead, one side of his upper lip curling. "We don't. We used to, but it costs more now." He turned away.

I stood there gripping the metal handle of Jeremy's stroller, not sure what to do. The social worker had been very clear. She was not allowed to change the value of the voucher, no matter what the circumstances, even if the store raised its price. It was this voucher or nothing. And I couldn't make up the difference, per the caveat on the voucher.

All my childhood training back in Roland Park, all those *Good little girls don't make a fuss* admonitions told me to back down and leave without an argument. I looked around, embarrassed and hoping none of the other women had overheard our conversation.

I thought briefly. The baby could sleep in a cardboard box or a bureau drawer. Maybe we could get by until Jeremy no longer needed a crib.

Then I heard Melinda's voice in my ear: *I don't know about the rest of you, but I'm going to go to the welfare office and not leave till they give me what's right.*

I stood up a little straighter. Jeremy twisted around to see what I was doing. And then I—the child who'd always hidden in the shadows, slipping into neighbors' yards and hoping no one was looking out of the windows—raised my voice.

"So," I said, loud enough that the little old ladies with their tight curls and pastel housedresses looked up. "So, you won't sell me a crib at the price you promised."

The old ladies started to murmur.

"So," I said, raising my voice a little more, and laying a hand on my ninth-month stomach. "You want my baby to have to sleep in a cardboard box."

"Imagine that," the ladies muttered, dropping the nylon bits they'd been looking through and starting to move closer.

Jeremy looked up at the salesman with a scowl. "You're a bad man," he said loudly.

The man stepped back. He looked to his right and to his left. The store was silent as everyone listened to what he had to say.

"No," he stumbled. "No, of course not. You can have the crib. Of course we'll honor the voucher."

I kept my hard look on him as the ladies sighed and turned back to their shopping. "Thank you," I said. "Now please show me which one it is."

He even threw in delivery free of charge. I set up the crib in the small bedroom, the two cribs end-to-end across the far wall. Jeremy's battered hand-me-down crib was a blond wood with stencils of Bo Peep and her sheep on the headboard, while the new crib was dark brown with a stencil of Jack and Jill carrying a pail.

The next weekend, my friend Jim came to visit. Lewis had hated that I kept up with my Maryland friends. Of all Lewis's betrayals, the one that cut the deepest was that he had read my journal. He claimed it was to find out if I was telling the truth about the extent of these so-called friendships. He was most suspicious of Jim, who visited us sometimes. Jim had sung at my wedding to Lewis, the Tim Hardin song "If I Were a Carpenter." I had read a poem at his wedding, "Havens" by May Sarton. Although I explained that it was Jim's brother Charlie who had been my boyfriend and that Jim was like a brother to me, Lewis had never believed me.

I'd spent uncounted hours listening to Jim and Charlie play music. They'd sit facing each other, feet tapping the floor, slender backs curved, shaggy brown heads bent over their guitars as they harmonized on Child ballads and Dylan songs. Sometimes other friends played or sang along, but I could only listen. I wished I could play an instrument, or even just sing in the right key.

After I moved to Worcester, Charlie went off to Europe, so I hadn't seen him for a while. Jim, however, moved to New Bedford, which was not that far away, and came to visit regularly. A gentle soul, he adored Jeremy and would sit cross-legged on the floor, hands on his knees, elbows sticking out high to the sides, to commune with the child. Even after Jim's marriage fell apart, we stayed close. I could tell him anything; I trusted him, right to the core. If my friends were my family, then Jim was the best of my brothers.

"Hey," he said, appearing at my door on a Saturday afternoon, lanky as a plant that had bolted and grown too tall to support itself.

"Hey, yourself. Get in here," I said.

"Wait." And he went back to his car and opened the back door. He pulled out something large and, turning, set it on the sidewalk for me to see.

"Oh, Jim." It was the most beautiful cradle I had ever seen: long and sturdy, made out of pine.

"It's a Shaker design," Jim said.

We had spent a lot of time talking about the Shaker aesthetic, about New England's clean lines versus Maryland's Victorian excesses. I thought about the kind of person I'd had to be in The Mart to get the crib and felt my eyes start to burn.

"Aw, come on," Jim said, setting down the cradle and folding me into a hug. "Cut that out."

Jeremy pulled on the hem of Jim's jacket. "Hi," he said.

Jim let me go and knelt down. "What's going on?"

Jeremy held out a hand. "Come on," he demanded and led Jim off to examine his collection of Matchbox cars, culled from my brothers' toychests and the shelves at Goodwill.

Later, over tea, I tried to thank Jim for making the crib.

"You can't stand to have anyone do anything for you," he said.

"I don't know how to repay you."

"Don't worry about it," he said. "I just wanted to see if I could do it. Pass it on to someone else when you're through with it."

I used to quote Faulkner's words about the past not even being past in order to mock Roland Park and the way it seemed to be stuck in a fifties time-warp. However, Jim's embarrassed face and the way he fumbled with his mug of tea opened up another more positive meaning to Faulkner's words. My past, my Maryland friends were not going to abandon me. They may not understand the path I had taken or even agree with it, but they would help me when they could.

It was an odd feeling. My solitary childhood had taught me that I had only myself to depend on.

When I was in first grade, my older brother was supposed to walk me home from the public school a few blocks away. Usually he was conscientious about making sure I was following him, but one day he ran off with a friend. I ran after them, but quickly lost my way. Finally, out of breath, I gave up trying to catch them and looked around. The street had no landmarks I recognized, the houses alien and forbidding.

I was scared, of course, but decided I'd keep walking till something looked familiar. I turned down what I thought was the right street and looked at the house numbers. When I got to 107, though, I saw that it was not my home, but a strange brown-shingled house. Terrified, I wondered if a house really could stand up on chicken legs and stalk away like Baba Yaga's, letting some other house come in and settle down in its place.

It never occurred to me to knock on a door and ask for help. I hated the feeling that people in the houses might be looking out at me and wished I had a magic cloak that would make me invisible.

I stood there for a bit, gripping my copybook and pencil case. Then I turned back the way I'd come, determined to keep trying every street till I found the one where my house had gone. Luckily the next street I tried turned out to be the right one.

Newbury Street was my home now and—with all its shabbiness—precious to me. It was the home that I had created by myself. I looked around and thought: *no, not by myself.* Jim's crib, Walt's records, the silkscreen of a barn by Christine's husband Will: my family, the one I had created, was all around me.

That was the moment, with the baby due any day, that the landlord decided it was time to remove the lead paint in my apartment.

The first I knew of his decision was a knock at the front door, the door we rarely used.

"What's that?" Jeremy asked.

I opened the door to a couple of workmen armed with propane torches.

"But I haven't prepared. I didn't know you were coming," I protested.

The men shrugged and came inside.

I sent Jem upstairs to Jill and frantically started packing clothing, dishes and toys away so they wouldn't be contaminated.

After looking around, the men walked into my bedroom.

I dropped an armful of toys and followed them. "At least let me take down the curtains," I said, dragging the bed away from the wall and yanking down my Chelsea-Morning gold curtains.

They lit the hissing torches and started burning the paint off the window frames. A terrible stink filled the air.

Suddenly part of the window molding burst into flames. The man jumped back yelling, "Hey!"

I ran to the kitchen and filled a pot with water. Then I ran back to the bedroom and threw the water on the flames, dousing them and creating an even worse stink.

The two men looked at each other. "Okay," one said. "We have to talk about this. We'll be back." With that, they collected their stuff and left.

I went upstairs.

"What's that smell?" Jill asked.

I told her.

"What a bunch of incompetents," she raged. "You'd better stay up here for a while. No telling what they'll do next."

I felt cheated of this special time, this last nest-building time alone with Jeremy, but agreed.

That night I woke up at about three-thirty. Shifting uncomfortably on Jill's couch, I decided I must need to pee. Once I got to the bathroom, though, I stayed, feeling nauseous.

After a while, Jill came in. I don't know what woke her. Narrowing her eyes, she asked, "Are you having that baby?"

I wasn't sure, but knew she was right to be concerned. I hadn't been in labor long with Jeremy, only four hours. I decided to go to the hospital.

Jill called a cab for me. She needed to stay home to care for Jeremy and her two boys, so I had to go to the hospital alone. I went out to the stoop to wait for the cab. The cold March wind seeped into the coat that wouldn't close over my swollen midsection and rattled the bare branches of the maple tree. I peered down the dark street and waited. After a long time, I began to despair and almost went back inside to ask Jill to call again, but then I saw headlights coming slowly down the street.

When the driver got there, he got out of the cab and met me on the sidewalk. He wasn't much taller than I, dark-skinned with a misshapen nose and lower lip, as though he might have been a boxer when he was younger. He took one look at my body and said, "No way."

"What do you mean?" I asked through teeth clenched against the cold.

"No way you're getting in my cab."

"But I need to get to the hospital."

He crossed his arms and said, "I don't want you messing up my cab, and I sure don't want to be stuck with delivering no baby."

I stood there shivering and looked at him. I didn't know how long it would be before this baby popped out. What would I do if he didn't take me? I started to cry.

Finally, he shook his head, saying: "Aw, okay, but don't be having that baby in my cab." He went way over the speed limit, covering the handful of miles to Hahnemann Hospital in minutes, but even so we barely made it.

Once inside, I was gowned, gurneyed, and left alone. I lay in a little room by myself, no one to coach me this time or rub my back or give me ice chips. I tried to remember the breathing patterns, but eventually gave up and counted the dots in the ceiling tiles when the pains came.

I knew that this child wouldn't get a silver rattle like the one my parents gave Jeremy; they had not wanted me to have this child. Even the nurses were unsympathetic; to them I was just another welfare mother having another baby. But he was my baby, and I wasn't going to give him up. I remembered Jeremy's birth and how I'd known Lewis would make sure nothing bad happened to me, how he had run to get the nurse when I needed something, how he had slipped me a magazine in the recovery room when I was bored, not having had anesthesia.

This time I was alone. But I wasn't afraid. I knew I could do this. In any case, I hadn't been lying on the gurney very long before I felt the baby's head. I yelled for the nurse, pushed the call button, yelled again.

To my relief, she stuck her head in the door. "What?" she demanded.

"The baby's coming."

"That's impossible. You just got here." The door swung shut again.

"Wait," I yelled. "Come back!"

I kept on yelling till she returned.

"Would you please look?" I begged.

She did and immediately started calling for the doctor. Scolding me for waiting so long to say anything, she hustled me into the delivery room. The doctor arrived just in time to catch my son as he entered the world. I hadn't been there even an hour.

I was put in a room with three other women who talked incessantly about their husbands, children, homes. I tried to be friendly but felt like I was from another planet. They each had lots of visitors and vases of flowers. I didn't expect either. None of my friends had money for flowers, and it was hard to arrange for babysitters in order to come visit.

I didn't mind. I felt independent in a way I rarely ever had. Alone I decided to have this baby; alone I carried it through to the end and went through those painful pre-dawn hours.

When I'd had Jeremy I couldn't wait to get home and have him all to myself. This time, though, I begged the hospital to keep me longer than the customary three days. I didn't have an apartment to go back to, what with the de-leading, and I was so tired. The hospital refused, saying that they could only keep me longer if there was some medical complication.

None of it mattered, though, when I held my tiny baby boy. Ten fingers, ten toes. He was perfect. I wrote in my journal: *These fierce passions, these startling devotions that surprise and shake me. How I adore these babies!*

Jill surprised me by coming to visit the day after the baby was born, my second day in the hospital. She pulled one of the orange plastic chairs over to my bed.

"I stopped by the nursery. He's beautiful, Barbara."

I had to laugh at that. "Come on, he just looks like a baby."

"He's special, and you know it."

"So what's going on at home?"

"Jem's fine."

"What about the lead paint?"

Jill shifted in the chair. "You aren't going to like this. The workmen came back yesterday, while you were here, and went into your apartment and started sanding—the idiots—sanding the paint off the woodwork."

"But then . . ."

"Right. Lead paint dust everywhere."

I groaned, picturing the poison dust sifting into drawers full of baby clothes and wool sweaters, between the dishes in the cupboard, lying thickly on the toy shelves and on the crib, in among the interstices of the crocheted baby blanket. I didn't know what to do. I felt helpless, weak and still exhausted from the birth. It was too much.

Jill looked at me with concern. "Don't worry. It's okay. Erica, Sherry, Fay and I went in last night and cleaned it all up. We took all the dishes out of the cupboards and washed them. The shelves, too. We cleaned all the toys, and scrubbed all the surfaces."

"What . . ." I started.

"We ran everything we could through the washing machine and even—oh, you would have laughed to see us—remember the rain last night? We carted your furniture outside and let the rain clean it for us." Jill sat back with a big smile and waved her hand like a magic wand. "All done. Everything's ready for you."

I was stunned by what Jill and the others had done for me. Even as a small child, I had put on and ripped off my own Band-Aids. When I got lost, I had to rescue myself. Nothing like this had ever happened to me before.

9
PATIENCE

The few trees that lined Newbury Street delayed putting out new leaves, as though reluctant to start the whole thing again. Even as the first frail litter of leaf pods began to fall, clumps of last year's leaves still clogged the gutters. The weary triple-deckers looked more dilapidated than ever, paint peeling in new places, a piece of aluminum siding partially torn off and twisted by a winter storm.

It was the spring of 1975, and the city no longer allowed people to burn paper. The air had lost its rancid, yesterday's fire stink, but it still smelled dirty, like exhaust from a coal-fired factory.

People began to emerge from inside to sit on their front stoops in the pale sun. The houses were too far apart for the people to converse, even if their New England reserve had allowed such a thing. So they listened to the occasional car navigating the street's new frost heaves and potholes. They watched the maple seedpods twirl down to the asphalt sidewalks. The kids called the seeds "nosies" and "helicopters" after the games they played with them.

When I called to tell her about the new baby, my mother surprised me by insisting I come visit. After she'd forbidden me to come home when I told her I was pregnant and alone, I'd assumed I would never be invited back to Roland Park.

"Nonsense. What kind of mother would I be if I didn't help a daughter out with a new baby? You'll have to manage the children yourself, though. I don't have time to wait on you."

Trying to navigate her changing moods and rules was difficult. She had never offered to help me out in any way, financial or otherwise, so this invitation seemed to come out of nowhere. But in typical fashion, my mother had it all planned out. One of my mother's neighbors who happened to be in New England would drive me and the children down.

When I walked in the door, my mother immediately took the baby away from me, saying that I didn't know how to hold him correctly. Then she noticed Jeremy dancing around her trying to say hello.

"For goodness sakes, child. Yes, I see you." She handed the baby back to me saying, "That child is hyperactive. You should take him to a doctor."

"He's just excited. We have a doctor, and she thinks he's fine." I was too tired to play games. "Which room did you put us in?"

While I was there, I didn't see much of my mother. I mostly hung out with my babies. At first, my mother and—when she wasn't in school—my youngest sister would carry Jeremy off so that I could rest, but this caused a certain frantic feeling in both of us, so I started keeping him with me.

I didn't really know my siblings. The younger ones had been children when I left home, and the older ones had lives that were too different from mine. My mother had wanted to keep us apart so I wouldn't infect them, but she needn't have bothered. We had little in common.

Wandering around the house, I felt as though centuries had passed since I had lived there. The memory of those years lurked on the far edge of my consciousness, making me uneasy. Half-forgotten things—pictures in the hallway, the glass-tiled window in the pantry—haunted me with their double exposures of past and present.

I had trouble sleeping and lay awake listening to once-familiar sounds. After the baby's midnight feeding, I leaned against the window patting his back, looking out at the moonlight on the two slim beech trees joined at the base. As a child, I called them the Twins and liked to squeeze in between them, their coarse bark like an embrace.

I visited with some of my Maryland friends, only one of whom had a child, a girl two years older than Jeremy. Jeremy larked about, enjoying the attention, while the baby got passed from one person to another. My friends encouraged me to move back to Maryland, but the thought of leaving Worcester scared me. At least in Worcester, I knew where the junkyards were and the free movies. And how could I manage without Jill?

Grateful as I was for my mother's help and a chance to make peace with her, after a couple of weeks I was eager to get back to my own home and routines.

My older brother came down to visit for a couple of days and then drove me back to Worcester. It was a quiet ride back. We didn't have much to say to each other. He lived in Providence where he had gotten a job after finishing his master's degree at Brown. I wasn't jealous that my parents had paid for his Ivy League education. School seemed like a distant dream to me. I had other concerns.

Remembering how sick I'd gotten after Jeremy was born, when I had gone back to work immediately only to collapse a few weeks later, I decided to take things slowly this time. Now there was no husband to fill in if I should become too ill to care for my boys.

Overcome by lethargy of the mind and my body's cringing exhaustion, I spent many afternoons on the front stoop watching the children. Baby Justin lay in the stroller, smiling when one of the big kids ran over and spoke to him, looking around quietly the rest of the time.

There was still lead paint dust in the yard from when the landlord's workmen had sanded the outside of the house, so Jill and I were afraid to let our kids touch it. I made them play on the sidewalk or the driveway to my right, at least until the grass grew in the side yard. There was usually a group of kids for me to keep an eye on, not only Jeremy and Jill's boys but also the other neighborhood children who came over, like Chance and Teddie.

Lassitude dragged me down as I sat there. I'd been right to expect that I would come down hard after the baby was born. I sat hunched on the hard wooden step, elbows on my knees, chin in my hands. Over the sound of the children calling to each other, I imagined I heard my father's voice complaining about his taxes going to support "lazy welfare slobs sitting on their cans" instead of getting a job.

On the other side of our driveway was a grey house where an old man sat on the top step. When he saw me looking at him, he raised his hat briefly before lapsing back into immobility. He just sat there, hunched forward like me, wearing a buttoned-up, long-sleeved shirt and a brown fedora. On the far side of his house was an empty lot where weeds were already shooting up, ragweed and lamb's quarters, ailanthus with its thick stem and spatulate leaves.

Across the street, I could see Amy seated on her front porch. She was always there, like some primitive stone idol, even late at night when I peeked out from behind my curtains.

Her son Teddie was one of the posse of neighborhood children who turned up in my living room or outside while I sat on the stoop. He usually asked for Michael but would play with Jeremy or any other kids who happened to be there. A bit rambunctious, he was somewhere between Michael's five and Jeremy's almost-two, a round, tough boy with a blond crewcut.

Trying to be a responsible mom, I figured I'd better go across the street and introduce myself to his mother, since Amy never seemed to budge from her front porch.

"Hi," I called out as I mounted the stairs cradling Justin in one arm and holding onto Jeremy with the other.

"Hi." She sat on a mesh lawn chair with a vacant look on her broad face. Surprised, I realized she was very young, perhaps eighteen or nineteen. Next to her was a battered metal TV table with an old portable record player on it, plugged into an extension cord that snaked out under the window screen. There was also an aqua-colored transistor radio.

"Amy?"

She smiled sweetly.

I introduced myself and the boys.

Jeremy asked, "Is Teddie inside?"

Amy's eyes wandered down to fix on Jeremy's face. "I think so."

The screen door opened and a birdlike woman in a flowered housedress and grey cardigan looked out. "Hi, I'm Amy's mother. Teddie's in here. Wait a minute."

She ducked back inside, calling to Teddie. He came out and took Jeremy down into the handkerchief-sized front yard to play.

"That was my ma," Amy said.

I shifted Justin to my other arm and pointed to another lawn chair. "Okay if I sit down?"

"Okay," Amy said. The radio was on and tuned to a pop station that played lots of pop ballads by groups like the Eagles, the Bee Gees, the Carpenters.

"Teddie's a nice boy," I tried.

"Yes," Amy said placidly. She sat without moving, her legs apart, hands on her wide thighs, so still that she might have lived her whole life in that chair. A heavy woman, she filled the chair and bulged a little over the metal arms.

I cuddled Justin, not sure what else to say. Teddie and Jeremy rampaged up and down the steps. "Calm down, guys," I said.

Summer Breeze came on the radio, and she said, "I like that song." Like most of the people on Newbury Street, she had pasty skin. Even the African-Americans who lived there seemed to have dull skin, with a lot of ash on elbows and knuckles. Same with the Puerto Ricans who lived in the small, boxy apartments down toward Pleasant Street, their faces pallid from the long winters and poor diet.

"Me, too." I paused. "So, Justin's a few week's old now. How old were you when you had Teddie?"

"He's my boy," Amy said.

"Yes." I was stumped. Not knowing what else to say, I wondered how she managed. I had found it so difficult to navigate the shoals of the welfare office. I couldn't imagine how someone as simple as Amy could have handled it, if in fact she was on welfare. I shivered, thinking of what would happen to Amy when Teddie started school, as he soon would. According to the current welfare rules, she would have to find work of some kind, yet how could she ever hold a job? What would they live on? I wondered if Amy's mother was old enough to get Social Security and what had happened to Amy's father.

"Well, I guess we'd better get back," I said finally.

"Okay," she said.

One morning Jill came in my back door and caught me with a cup of coffee.

"Is that decaf?"

"No," I said guiltily. Both of us had come to realize that the temporary boost from caffeine wasn't worth the crash later, so had sworn off coffee. "I know. I know."

"Smells good."

"I needed something to get me going. I'm so lazy. I could just sit here all day."

"How can you say that?" Jill demanded.

"What? It's true."

"Here you are nursing a baby with a toddler to run after, both of them in diapers. You're always hanging out laundry."

"I'm so glad I don't have to drag everything to a laundromat. I'm in love with my washing machine, Jill."

She refused to be diverted. "And making your own bread, writing, volunteering at the food co-op—how can you say you're lazy?"

"I don't know. I'm just so tired all the time." I felt that I was no better than Amy, sitting on her porch all day. By late afternoon, I was always tired to the point of dizziness. I couldn't tell Jill what I was really afraid of: that I would always be like this; that I would never be strong enough to work and care for my kids.

"Well, no wonder."

I grinned at Jill. "Want some coffee?"

"Sure."

Later I wrote in my journal: *I think my ambition is to be an invalid. To lie in bed reading while someone brings me pots of tea.*

My family of friends continued to stay in touch with me. Walt's band came to stay a few times, and he always arranged seats for me and my friends whenever they played anywhere close by. So Jill and I took the kids to Boston one night for a concert, and later in the summer, Sherry and I went to New Hampshire for a Bluegrass festival where the band was playing.

Jim came up from New Bedford to visit. Generous as always, he carried me and the boys off for weekend getaways, once to Tanglewood to hear the Boston Symphony Orchestra and once to Fox Hollow, a folk festival in upstate New York.

But in the end, my life was in Worcester, taking care of babies.

Justin was a tiny baby. A normal seven pounds at birth, he didn't thrive as he should, lingering on or below the lowest growth curve on the pediatrician's chart. Worse, he had a heart murmur. That, combined with his obvious frailty, had me hanging over the cradle watching him breathe. However, the pediatrician said that as long as he continued to grow and didn't fall completely off the growth chart for an extended time, then he would be okay. She thought he would grow out of his heart murmur.

Jill called him "the Little Buddha" because of his enigmatic smile. After some crying jags early on, he had settled down into a peaceful undemanding baby who watched us benignly. At the park, I would let down the back of the double stroller Sherry had given me because she no longer needed it for Rora. It was a good sturdy one with one seat behind the other. Justin would lie there for hours, watching the shifting shapes of the leaves as the breeze moved through them, seemingly lost in contemplation of the movement of sun and shade.

At home, he was happy to lie in the cradle, singing little songs to himself, or later sit in the playpen and watch the older children, though delighted when one of them climbed into the playpen to horse around with him.

Jeremy, on the other hand, was a menace. If he wasn't falling off the back porch or teasing one of the neighborhood dogs, he was sprinkling baby powder an inch deep in the bedroom pretending it was snow. He'd become a tyrant about "please" and "thank you", correcting anyone who forgot those magic words.

Any day that wasn't pouring rain, we walked to Elm Park, the stroller packed with rusty toy trucks and cars, sandwiches, fruit and a thermos of milk. We had to go in the morning since I would be too tired by the afternoon. If it was my day to have Rora, or Richard and Michael, they came along too. We'd spend hours there, walking beside the pond and feeding the ducks. Jeremy liked to flop down on the ground and talk to the grass, when he wasn't begging me to push him on the swings or running off to dig in the sandlot. I sat on the bench watching him, feeding the baby when he woke, thinking about this utterly strange and undreamt-of life that I was creating, with park afternoons and long walks to the library and grocery store.

After we trailed home, the children silent in the stroller, I read them a book or two before putting them down for a nap. If it was one of my days to have the other children, I put Justin in the cradle, Rora in Justin's crib, Richard and Michael at either end of the sofa or on my double bed. They didn't have to sleep, but had to be quiet for an hour because I needed a rest. Even with that, I was not able to do much for the rest of the day, but moved mechanically through a haze of exhaustion, changing diapers, nursing, getting the kids ready for bed.

Sometimes at night I puzzled over my being the center of this household, with babies dependent on me. I felt that I had to fill the house, as if its rooms were merely an expansion of myself. I wrote in my journal: *There is so little of me to hold up this great weight. Giving up would be so easy. Just stay in bed and sleep forever. But I'm no Briar Rose or Sleeping Beauty. No prince is going to come and wake me up. If I don't keep this home together, no one will. And then what would happen to the kids?*

By June, Justin was three months old and Jeremy almost two. Jeremy with his fierce intelligence was always pushing me to tell him more, demanding, for example, what made milk turn into yogurt or where exactly people went when they died. Justin, on the other hand, had that enigmatic smile that said he had been born already knowing everything.

I had Rora over for a whole weekend, always an exhausting experience even though I adored her and loved having all these children asleep under my roof. It made me feel like the Great Mother, reaching out my protective arms to touch them and soothe their dreams.

Late Saturday night, Jeremy and Rora were woken up by cats snarling and fighting outside, so I brought them into bed with me. Later, when I got up to nurse Justin, I took him into the living room so as not to disturb them, but they got up anyway and came to stand silently beside the rocking chair like ghosts in the darkness.

After we got in bed again, Rora fell asleep instantly, but Jeremy lay with his chin on his folded hands looking out at the streetlight. He was oddly silent and serious. I didn't say anything—he seemed so self-contained—but I couldn't help wondering what he was thinking.

One afternoon while I sat out on the stoop, Jill came out and sat down with me. "Dan called. He's renting a roto-tiller this weekend to put in a garden out at the farm and wondered if we wanted anything dug up while he had it."

Dan and Fay were friends of ours who lived nearby. I'd known Fay for some years, but only recently had we become friends. Around the time I had Jeremy, she had lost her first baby and couldn't bear to be around babies for a while. Then when Lewis and I split up, she felt caught in the middle, unsure of whose side to take.

A poet and an artist, she was someone I wanted in my life, so I was willing to be patient. Besides, she was such a fireball that being around her was like drinking a whole pot of coffee. She seemed like an Amazon to me, a warrior of a woman. She pushed me to write more and also to get more involved in the community. With her limitless energy, she was active in so many initiatives and co-ops I couldn't keep track of them all.

Now that she had a healthy son, Hamid, born a few weeks before Justin, the time seemed right for us to be friends at last. I never knew who the father of either of her babies was, but clearly they were not a part of her life now. She had gone on welfare when she found out she was pregnant with Hamid, realizing as I had that she could not afford medical care on her own.

They lived right around the corner from us. Dan, Fay, and Fay's sister Linda had bought a run-down Victorian triple-decker together and were working to rehab it. Linda had the first floor; Dan the second, and Fay the third.

Aside from working on the house, Dan did some construction work around town, mostly independent jobs. Tall and gentle, he was always ready to help out a friend or a stranger, and I called on him often for my work exchange. At the same time, though, he had that New England reserve that was like a door closed in your face. So it was Fay—bursting with life like an overripe seedpod—who was my friend.

The farm where they were putting in a garden was in Oxford, a little ways outside of Worcester. It was where Fay and Linda's grandfather and uncle lived.

Jill prompted me. "What about it?"

"Well, we talked about putting in a garden over there in the empty lot," I said reluctantly, not wanting to stand up much less tackle a garden.

All the same, fresh vegetables were an issue. I was a vegetarian, but even without buying meat I had trouble making the food stamps last out the month. I tried to include fresh fruit and vegetables, but they were so expensive that I usually ended up with only the cheapest, like carrots, kale, apples. Bananas were a special treat. For the baby, I didn't buy expensive baby food, but mashed up part of my meals.

Jill nodded. "Let's just do the next thing, get Dan over here, maybe go out to Spag's and get some seeds. I think they have tomato plants on sale this week."

So over the next few days we cleared out trash in the empty lot on the other side of the grey house next door. Then we watched as Dan wrestled the roto-tiller through the hard ground and weeds. I tried to spell him, but wasn't strong enough to handle it. Keeping an eye on the kids playing in the far end of the lot, Jill and I took turns with the shovel, breaking up the clods and digging in some manure.

"I don't know," Jill said as we looked at the ground we had prepared. "Does it look to you like it's ready?"

I eyed the rough ground, still choked with big chunks of clay. "I think it ought to be finer. Maybe we should have gotten a couple of bags of topsoil."

"With what money?"

We stood there scratching our heads, not sure what to do next. Jill picked up a seed packet and started reading the planting directions on the back.

Watching us from his front steps was the old man who lived in the grey house between the lot and our house, the one who always wore a long-sleeved shirt buttoned all the way up. When he saw us looking around the empty lot, he got up with a dry little coughing laugh, and moving slowly, came over to join us. Gaunt, dark-skinned and tough as gristle, he stepped carefully over the rough ground.

"Putting in a garden?" He kicked one of the clods gently. His voice was low and gravelly.

"Trying to," I replied.

"I had a little truck farm down in Carolina," he said slowly. "Back in the day."

"We aren't sure the ground is ready or if we need to break it up more," I said.

"What you need is a hoe."

"We have all this stuff," Jill lifted the seed packet she was holding.

He tipped his fedora back from his forehead a little. "Whatchou got there? Peas? Too late for them."

Jill and I looked at each other.

Turning back to him, she asked, "Would you help us? Not to dig or anything, but with advice?"

He looked at us impassively. Then a gleam started up in his eyes, and I realized he was smiling, just with his eyes. "Get a hoe," he said and headed back to his steps.

It took a while, but he finally told us his name. Mr. John taught us what we needed to know. He showed us how to use a hoe and explained that we had to be out there using it every day to keep down the weeds and give the plants some air.

For ages it seemed as though nothing was going to happen. The straggly tomato plants had adapted to their new home, but the seeds wouldn't come up. I paced the dirt rows looking for any sign of green. Sure that we'd done something wrong, I told Mr. John that I was giving up. I figured I'd go back to sitting on my stoop.

"Keep using the hoe," he said.

"Do you think the birds ate the seeds? Maybe we started too late."

"Takes time," he said, tipping his hat back on his grizzled head.

Then suddenly one day there were seedlings, way too many of them, jumbled against each other: beans, squash, peppers, beets, radishes, lettuce. Jill and I ran from row to row, pointing out the mess of spindly green shoots.

"Gotta thin them," Mr. John said.

I knelt down and reached to pluck one out. I couldn't do it. "They'll die," I said, looking up at him.

His eyes gleamed. "Won't none of them thrive if you don't."

They did thrive, way beyond our expectations. I measured the tiny bean and squash sprouts daily and wielded the hoe the way Mr. John had taught me. Every day I worked in the garden for a while, weeding, planting beans, and replanting onions where they'd washed away or failed to sprout. Instead of exhausting me, working in the garden made me feel stronger.

The day I pulled up my first beets, I cradled the sweet red bulbs in my hand. *Something for nothing*, I thought, *like loaves and fishes or wine from water. Like a baby.*

Inspired by our success with the garden, I decided to try to make progress on the job front and went to talk with the welfare office. I had heard that they would pay for welfare parents to go through one of the trade school programs. Fay, who told me about it, was sure it was some kind of trick. We were all paranoid, such as when we were required to get Social Security numbers for the children in order to continue getting welfare. Everyone was sure that a certain set of numbers had been set aside for welfare children, numbers that would stamp them throughout their lives with the stigma of having received welfare. And there was always the fear that Child Protective Services would arbitrarily decide to take away your kids.

"They make you beg for everything," Fay said.

I decided to try anyway.

The day I went to the welfare office was one of those horribly hot days, with all the windows open and fans clattering on the grey desks. The air smelled of metal and sweat. After the usual wait, I was finally pointed toward a desk halfway down the room. I sat there, holding Justin on my lap and gripping Jeremy with the other hand to keep him from running off.

The man behind the desk was heavy-set and flushed with the heat, his short-sleeved dress shirt unbuttoned at the neck. He wiped his forehead with a handkerchief and looked down at the papers on his desk.

I said, "Send me to automotive trade school. Once I have that certificate, I can get a job and be out of your hair."

He didn't look up at me as he said, "We can send you to beautician school."

There was nothing wrong with being a beautician, but I knew it wasn't a job I was suited for and would not provide enough income to support my family.

"No," I said. "Look, I can tear an engine apart and rebuild it. I can replace brakes."

He looked up at me then, looked at the boys, and then back at me, lifting his chin a little.

"Beautician school or nothing," he said and folded his hands.

I raged all the way home, pushing the heavy stroller uphill in the summer heat.

When I got home, Jill was sympathetic but said that it was probably just as well. "What were you going to do with the kids?"

"I don't know. I figured I'd cross that bridge when I came to it."

"You don't want to be one of those ping-pong welfare moms. Wait for the right moment."

"I don't want to be a welfare mom at all. I want to work."

Jill sighed. "Don't we all. But it's not time for that yet. This is your time to be with your babies."

That night after the children were in bed, I lay awake, too tired to sleep, enervated by the August heat. The curtains hung limply in the discouraged air. On her porch across the street, Amy played the same song over and over, some sad ballad about a horse named Wildfire. I could hear the scratch as the record ended and she picked up the arm, then a second scratch as she placed it at the beginning again. A woman was running after the horse, some dream that she had lost.

I felt like I was running so hard just to stay in one place. When I tried to fight my way out, I got slammed back again. Maybe Amy had the right idea after all: forget about trying and just sit on the front porch listening to sad songs.

In late summer, I was able to get an old VW from some friends of my parents who practically gave it to me. I named the car Patience, because driving it home from Maryland, coaxing it along as it sputtered and popped the whole way, made me realize that was a quality I needed to work on.

I worked on the car pretty steadily, fiddling with the tuning, trying to get it to run better without buying a lot of parts. Sometimes Jill would watch the boys; other times I would take the playpen outside and stick both of them in it, so I didn't have to worry about them wandering off while I was concentrating on the car.

We had heard about these two car guys, Mac and Ben, who worked out of their house and didn't charge very much. Since my "new" car needed a lot of work, I asked them to come take a look at Patience.

As I stood out in the driveway, holding Justin while Jeremy ran around, I felt as though I had known these two men forever. Mac talked and talked. About my height, he looked me right in the eye as he yammered on about various cars they'd worked on, politics, his partner Sarah, their house in Sterling, their blended family of five kids, and anything else that came into his head, like I was a member of the family or something. Ben simply stood there, taller than Mac, with blond hair to his shoulders and a strong chin, looking at the car, then up at the clouds.

Justin started to fuss and I jiggled him on my hip. Ben, who still hadn't said anything, held out his arms, and I passed the baby over. Without even looking at the child, Ben slung him upside down along his arm, a position Justin usually loathed but somehow at this moment quieted him.

Mac interrupted the flow of verbiage for a moment to glance at Ben. "Oh, he's the best. We always give him the baby to hold." Then he was back to telling me about the last job they'd worked on.

Eventually we settled on a straight trade: the engine from my poor wrecked Celia in exchange for the work that the new car needed. That night I wrote in my journal: *Funny mixed-up feelings maybe I'd rather not verbalize. But when you need something, there it is, and generally no more than what you need.*

The garden, on the other hand, was almost too much.

Although we begged him not to, Mr. John was out there most days slowly and steadily moving the hoe among the peppers and squash. He said it made him feel like home to be doing it. He didn't talk much, and always wore his hat and a buttoned-up, long-sleeved shirt, no matter how warm the day.

He showed us how to pinch suckers off tomato plants, and then advised us on how to can the tomatoes that grew in such profusion. Grateful for his help, we gave him as much of the produce as we could convince him to take.

Like many first-time gardeners, we ended up with more squash, peppers and tomatoes than we could handle. We ate collards and chard until I thought we'd turn green. Jill and I gave our vegetables away to friends and to everyone living on Newbury Street. All this abundance came from only part of the lot—Jill and I had only dug up a quarter of it—so we discussed trying to get others to join us next year for a community garden.

"Maybe we could get some funding through Piedmont Center," Jill said, "enough for more seeds."

"What about salaries for us?" I asked.

"For a part-time summer job? They'd just take it out of our checks."

One day, tired of wrestling with the canning kettle and listening to Jeremy fuss about being caged up in the playpen, I decided to take a break. I could hear Amy's radio going, so we went over to visit.

She was on the front porch, of course. I sent Jeremy inside to play with Teddie and sat down.

We talked for a while about the weather. The heavy air of a discouraged summer seemed to hang around us. I told her about our garden and my struggles with Patience.

Then her mother came out on the porch.

"Amy," she said. "I have to go to Iandoli's to pick up a few things. Feed Teddie his lunch."

"Okay," Amy said, struggling out of the chair, still smiling. "Let's go."

As we went through the front room I heard the clank of the metal pushcart as Amy's mother dragged it off the front porch and down the steps. I was impressed with how clean the front room was, knowing how hard it was to keep up with a rambunctious boy. A brown and gold plaid armchair and sofa were arranged in front of a cabinet-style tv. A bowl of plastic flowers, yellow chrysanthemums and white daisies, sat on the coffee table.

I followed Amy into the kitchen. Teddie watched as she spread Marshmallow Fluff on a slice of white bread and handed it to him along with a cream soda. It frustrated me that we could get sodas and Marshmallow Fluff with food stamps, but not soap or sanitary napkins.

Amy had made another marshmallow sandwich and started to hand it to Jeremy.

"Oh," I said. "No, thanks. We have to get back. See you later."

"Okay," she said and followed us back to the porch, still holding the sandwich. As I started down the steps, she settled back into the chair and began eating the sandwich herself.

I thought about Amy as we crossed back to our house. She made me realize for the first time that some people would never be able to get off of welfare. It wasn't a question of laziness, but competence. How would she ever be able to work? The only special work programs I'd heard of were for blind people, and her disability was not so obvious.

I wrote in my journal: *I knew going into welfare that I had advantages many others didn't, like health, nutrition, and education. Hard as it has been for me to find a job that will pay for child care, etc., some people have the added challenge of a physical or mental handicap. No wonder people give up.*

I've been so afraid that I'll spend the rest of my life sitting out front like Amy, not because of any lack of mental ability, but from a lack of physical stamina. It's terrifying to be so weak. Jill says it just takes time to get over having the baby. And I did manage the garden. We have all those gorgeous jars of canned tomatoes in the pantry and containers of beans in the freezer.

All summer I've pursued phantom glimpses of job opportunities, but they haven't led anywhere. At the same time, though, look at the help I've gotten: concerts, a car, a garden. I have to be grateful for that. And for this lovely, plain home of ours.

10
EMERGENCIES

"I can't believe she tried to feed them Marshmallow Fluff on white bread!" Fay threw down her knife. "She's trying to poison them."

"I doubt that," I said, picking up another apple. Jill and I had gone apple-picking the week before and—overwhelmed by the amount of fruit all around me after so many months of doing without—I had made myself sick eating apples as I picked them. Once I got home, I couldn't bear the sight of another apple, and the bulging grocery bags in the corner had been reproaching me for days. When Fay stopped by with Hamid, she offered to help me peel and slice them.

"Marshmallow Fluff!" she raged on. "You have to fight that kind of behavior. Don't just let it go by! Tell her to stop poisoning her child. And don't ever take your children over there again. That's for sure."

I looked at Fay for a moment, enjoying the way sparks seemed to fly off of her. She was as unlike Amy as anyone could be. Restless and fiery, there was no sitting on the stoop for her. She seemed to light up the room. She was so alive, so vibrant, that her body seemed to hum.

I loved her energy and wasn't bothered by her tendency to tell me what to do. After all, I had succeeded in shrugging off my mother's attempts at thought-control over the years.

Through the door to the living room, I could see the playpen. Justin and Hamid were throwing colored plastic rings over the side while Jeremy patiently handed them back.

The sun flickering from behind a cloud drew my eyes back. It lit up Fay's wild hair like a nimbus around her head.

"It's not the end of the world," I said.

Fay shook her head, setting her cloud of hair dancing and glinting. Then she picked up the knife and leaned over the cutting board again. "We need to get these apples on the stove."

I planned to make applesauce and can it, determined not to go through another winter without fruits and vegetables. The canning jars seemed like a huge extravagance, even though Jill and I had found them at Spag's which meant they were a good buy. Spag's was a Worcester institution, a warehouse over the bridge in Shrewsbury with larger-than-life-sized portraits of Spag and his wife over the front windows. It was filled with whatever Spag could find to sell cheaply, an ever-changing bazaar of bargains spilling out into the wooden-floored aisles. I had already used a lot of the jars for tomatoes and wasn't sure if I would have enough for the applesauce.

"Do you think it's safe to use old jars?" I asked. "I have a bunch of old peanut butter jars and some mayonnaise jars."

Fay looked up at me. "Have you thought about drying them? Then you wouldn't need so many jars."

"But the gas to have the oven on that long . . ."

"No." Fay grinned. "We can air-dry them. Here, I'll show you."

It meant that she had to core the apples and cut them carefully into even circles instead of slopping them into the pot any which way. I washed the sticky apple juice off my hands and hammered small nails into the top of the molding for the back door and the door into the living room and we strung a network of bobbing apple rings over our heads. Jeremy came running to see what the excitement was and helped by holding the ball of string. Justin and Hamid clamored to see too and were delighted when we finally brought them into the kitchen, reaching up with their little hands trying to grab the rings.

After Fay and Hamid left, I put the pot of apples on the stove to cook down while I got dinner ready for the boys.

I admired Fay's fighting spirit, even though it was so foreign to my own habitual hiding from confrontation. Aside from rare occasions such as arguing down the manager at The Mart over Justin's crib, I mostly stayed on an even keel.

Near the end of the day, though, when I was tired, it became progressively harder to keep myself together. Once, when the boys started playing with their food, making a game of throwing it on the floor, I spoke sharply, telling them to eat their dinners and barely stopping short of bringing up the starving children in China. Then I felt terrible, remembering my father's towering rages.

On one of my babysitting days, Rora woke up from her nap with her eye swollen shut and a lump on her eyeball. It didn't seem to hurt, but I was frantic, thinking maybe she'd hit it on something. Seeing my fear made Rora start crying which set my boys off as well.

Sherry didn't answer her phone, so I got all three children into their jackets and herded them out to the car.

At the hospital, I found a parking space and got Justin out of his carseat. "Jeremy, hold Rora's hand," I said grabbing her other hand. Her mouth was turned down in a shaky frown but she had stopped crying.

We raced into the emergency room, only to hit a wall at the triage desk.

"Are you the child's mother?" the nurse asked.

I tried to explain.

"We can't treat her without her mother's authorization." The nurse was firm. She tried to call Sherry but the phone rang and rang.

Rora started to cry again, joined quickly by Jeremy and Justin.

Frustrated, I said, "Can't you see this child needs help?"

The nurse lifted her hands in a helpless gesture.

Remembering a strategy Jill had mentioned, I said, "Let me talk to your boss."

We were taken to an office where a middle-aged woman sat behind a desk. Surrounded by crying children, I pulled out all the stops, calling them monsters for letting a child suffer, threatening legal action.

"Wait," the woman said. She laid both hands palm down on her blotter. "Please start over and tell me what the problem is."

I took a deep breath. I showed her Rora's eye and explained that Rora was covered by Medicaid like my children.

"I believe you." Still, she hesitated to let me sign the release.

Rora had stopped crying and simply stood there forlornly, gulping and clutching the tissue I had given her. Jeremy put his arms around her.

The woman sighed. After several more tries to reach Sherry, she finally said, "Okay, I'm going to accept you as the child's temporary guardian."

Having gotten over that hurdle, we were seen pretty quickly. Luckily, it turned out not to be serious. The doctor first asked if she had hit her eye on something, but after he examined her said the swelling and lump were only an allergic reaction, probably to a bug-bite she had gotten in the park.

After that, I made sure that Jill and Sherry had letters from me authorizing them to request medical care for my kids and vice versa.

November brought grey skies and a damp chill. Jill felt the cold more than most people, thin as she was, and had always hated working on cars, so around this time she took her car to a garage on Park Ave for an oil change. They drained out the old oil and changed the filter just fine. Only problem was, they forgot to put in the new oil.

She paid the bill, started up the car, and wham! The engine seized.

Jill was furious, but the manager claimed that since she had paid for the work, it wasn't his responsibility anymore. He must have thought this tiny woman with the ancient VW bug would be easy to intimidate.

Boy, was he wrong.

After all her arguments failed, Jill took the garage manager to Small Claims Court. "No way I was going to let them get away with that," she said. "And once I told the judge what happened and showed her the bill and the statement from Ben and Mac about the damage to the car, there was no question about it."

"Didn't you need a lawyer?" I asked.

"No, only the paperwork."

The judge quickly settled in Jill's favor. The only downside was that she had to let the awful garage fix the car, rather than someone she trusted, like Ben and Mac. We had become friends with them and sometimes went out to Sterling to visit them and Mac's family: Sarah, her four children from an earlier marriage and the baby she'd had with Mac.

The idea of standing up in court terrified me. I told Jill that I would never have been able to persuade the judge to believe me.

"I didn't need to persuade him," Jill said in her matter-of-fact way. "I had the invoice from the garage and a signed statement describing the cause of the damage."

Our second Christmas on Newbury Street was approaching. I had saved my pennies all year in order to buy something for the boys from the Little Brown Toystore on Elm Street, finally settling on the smallest tin of colored pencils for Jeremy and a jingly music maker for Justin.

I wrapped the toys along with some other things I'd found at Goodwill— wooden peg people who went with last year's farm set and a little toy car—using comic sections of the *Telegram and Gazette* and put them on the footlocker in the living room where the tree would go. The boys were excited and tried to guess what was in the mysterious packages.

Then one afternoon a few weeks before Christmas, as I was cleaning up after having all the neighborhood children rampaging through my apartment, I noticed that the presents were gone.

I did not know who to blame. I fumed helplessly. How could this happen? It was so unfair. And after all I'd done to be nice to these children, having them in my house, feeding them, taking them to the park.

I'd worked so hard to save up for these presents, imagining how much the boys would like them. *You have to fight*, Fay had said. But there was no one to fight. It would be impossible for me to accuse any of the children of stealing. Just thinking about it made my anger disappear. Any child needing a present that badly should be allowed to keep it. But I couldn't help feeling miserable about having to disappoint my boys.

Justin didn't really understand what had happened, but Jeremy was distraught. I told him that we could still make Christmas a special day, but he wasn't comforted.

A few days later, there came a knock at the door. It was a young man I didn't know, who apologized for bothering us and came in ducking his head.

"What is all this?" I asked.

"I'm from Toys for Tots," he said. "We had some extras and, well, your name, you know." He shyly held out two packages.

"But who . . . ? Here, take off your coat." I was mortified that anyone thought we needed such a handout.

"Can we open them now?" Jeremy was dancing from one foot to the other, and Justin had come out from behind my legs.

"Okay, I guess," I said.

The young man folded his long limbs like an origami crane to sit on the floor. After he settled himself, he handed a package to each child.

They tore them open with glee to find a small Fisher-Price mailtruck with two clothespin people in one and a baby doll with a plastic head and red-checked flannel body in the other. Neither of the brand-new toys could have cost more than a few dollars, but the boys were delighted.

"They're in boxes," Jeremy said with awe in his voice. Then he set to tearing them open, Justin urging him on.

They traded back and forth several times before deciding that Jeremy would keep the doll and Justin the truck. Jeremy winked at me, a new trick, so I knew he was making sure his brother had what he thought was the better toy.

The young man stood up and put his coat back on. "I'm sorry," he said. "It was what we had."

"No, they're wonderful." My voice was a little shaky.

Thinking about it after he left, I suspected that Fay had submitted our names. Active in every cause in town, she would have known what strings to pull. And she knew about the boys' presents being stolen, knew that it wasn't that I had bungled my finances or ignored the idea of Christmas presents.

Still, to soothe my pride, I suggested to the boys that in the future, we should donate a gift from each of them to Toys for Tots.

Justin didn't understand, but Jeremy asked, "One of our presents?"

"Yes. Say you were getting three presents. Instead, you get two and give the third one to some other child who has none."

Jeremy nodded hard. "That would make kids happy. Like us," he added, looking at Justin, who grinned back at him as he pushed the mailtruck back and forth.

Then my mother called. "You are coming down for Christmas, aren't you?"

"Do you want us to?"

"Of course. It's Christmas. The family should be together."

I didn't have presents for them, but my mother assured me that Christmas was for children, not adults.

Now that I knew my parents would have some presents for the boys, I felt guilty about the mailtruck and doll. But the boys were already attached to them, and I wasn't sure how to give them back.

We only stayed at my parents' house for a few days, but it was time enough for my mother and Jeremy to engage in a battle of wills. Her constant admonitions to Jeremy, an active and mischievous two-and-a-half-year-old, that Santa would give naughty boys and girls nothing but sticks and stones were met with a shrug and an "I don't care."

"He's going to grow up to be an axe-murderer. Mark my words," she told me.

Sometimes my mother would look at my children, shake her head, and say to me, "You could have done so much." My father, as well, kept his distance from the children. Both my parents hated the fuss and bother of small children.

Luckily, my siblings all seemed to adore Jeremy and Justin and enjoyed playing with them.

On the big day, to tease Jeremy, my youngest brother and sister hid his Christmas presents in the hall closet and wrapped up a box of sticks and stones. I went along with it, knowing that Jeremy was a pretty tough customer. He had never been greedy for things, preferring playmates to toys. Too, he had reveled in my siblings' tales of other Christmas "roasts", such as when one brother wrapped up an empty box, pretending it was for my sister, and then one night, saying that she had too many presents already, casually threw it into the fire in front of her horrified eyes.

The box of sticks and stones was the first thing opened. Jeremy's response, when he saw what was in his sole present, startled everyone. "Just what I always wanted," he exclaimed, and busily set about using them and the box itself to build roads and houses for his little cars. After an hour and a half, he had to be persuaded to leave off playing with his cars and open the presents that had been "found".

My mother was convinced he saw through the trick and was merely playing us. But I wasn't sure. I knew how much he preferred digging in the dirt with his battered cars and Tonka trucks. And I remembered how fixated both boys had been on the doll and mailtruck that turned up in such a timely way.

I realized that I didn't need to agonize over not being able to buy the kids expensive presents. Jeremy had shown me what was important and what was not.

One night after I'd put the boys to bed and gone downstairs to make some tea, my father came into the kitchen. We had never been close, so I greeted him a little warily.

"I wanted to give you this," he said, holding out a Christmas card.

The picture was simple, a pencil drawing of a Madonna and child on a Wedgwood blue background. She was so young, no more than a teenager, though her profile looked serene as she cuddled the baby, his head tucked under her chin. Inside, the card was signed by one of my parents' friends.

"When I saw this in the pile of Christmas cards, it reminded me of you," he said awkwardly. "So I wanted you to have it."

"Um, thanks," I said as he turned and left the room.

I shook my head. *And I thought I was bad at relationships. Sheesh.* However, it was obvious that he was trying in his own way to make peace with me.

When I told my mother about the incident, she said, "Oh, he just thinks all women should be barefoot and pregnant."

"He doesn't seem to get angry so much," I said.

"He's changed since he stopped drinking."

My father had not been a big drinker, but it had only taken one beer to loosen the flimsy restraints that held back his temper. However, after a recent bout with hepatitis, he had stopped drinking completely.

My mother's face twisted with resentment. "He's still a monster. Look at the way he's treated me. I've written it all down. Someday the true story will come out." The war between my parents may have changed, but it hadn't gone away.

I couldn't wait to get back to Worcester.

With Christmas over, the dreary New England winter closed in. Cold wind blew through the window frames even with the storm windows closed, and I fretted about heating costs, which were much greater than the rent during these months. I kept the heat turned down low and bundled the three of us into heavy wool sweaters.

Too many days cooped up inside with the kids, without the distraction of going to the park, allowed other fears to come creeping in: the old fear that I would never be strong enough to work again; I would be unable to find a job; and the fear that some hitch in the welfare system would leave us for a spell without resources and me with no savings to fall back on. Then there was always the fear that the landlord would have the house burned down for the insurance, a common problem in neighborhoods like mine. I was still surprised that he hadn't torched the place when the court ordered him to de-lead the apartments.

I worried about the kids. Justin still wobbled on and off the lowest curve on the growth chart. A responsive and loving child, he was clearly intelligent, quick to master new toys. It concerned me, though, that after a few random words he had stopped talking completely.

One day we were having breakfast—me letting the boys splash around with their oatmeal while I read the paper—when I heard "Pass the milk."

Automatically I said, "Pass the milk, *please.*" And then stopped and looked up. Jeremy's mouth hung open as he stared at Justin.

Justin looked at me calmly with his little half-smile and said, "Pass the milk, *peas.*"

Apparently he had been watching and listening until he felt confident that he had mastered this new skill. I put a hand to my forehead. There was no way I could keep up with these guys, or figure out what was going on in their heads.

I devised expeditions for the kids so they (and I) wouldn't go stir crazy, looking for anything free. We went to the library every week for story hour and to exchange our piles of books for new ones. Sometimes I took whatever children I had that day down to Worcester Center, the new mall across from City Hall. Under the arching glass panes, in the sunny warmth, the children could run up and down unburdened by boots and snowsuits. I wished I could afford to sign Jeremy up for classes somewhere, doing anything active, swimming, karate, whatever. I called around trying to find something, but even the children's classes at the Y were beyond my reach.

As a child, I had wished my parents gone, out of my life forever. My ideas of what life would be like without parents were vague but blissful. Now, struggling to make this life work for my boys, I recognized and was grateful for the financial security my parents had given me during my childhood.

Part of my secret life in my parents' house had been writing: poetry, stories, and dreamy little essays. And the journal where I talked with myself, in lieu of anyone else. There were few creative writing programs in the sixties when I was in school, so I struggled to find a way to tell the stories that crowded my head, the stories that I told myself at night, after the light was out.

Jill was the first person to tell me I was a writer. She encouraged me to take my writing seriously, and I began to work at it more steadily, the way Jill worked at her art. A little before Christmas, I started giving readings at the Women's Center and one of the bookstores in town.

I wrote at the breakfast table, while Justin gummed a banana and Jeremy stirred his oatmeal. I wrote during naptime while I rocked the cradle with my foot. I wrote at night when the kids were in bed. Jill always wanted to read my poems and stories, and sometimes I sent them to my friend Christine out in Washington. However, I didn't know anyone else who was a writer. Not till I got to be friends with Fay.

Like me, Fay and her sister Linda both wrote poetry. Fay wrote fiery free verse, angry and political, while Linda's poetry was focused on people. Linda gave a poetry reading at one of the neighborhood centers where she read a poem about a homeless woman named Irene and ended by singing a chorus from the old standard "Goodnight, Irene": *Irene, goodnight*—a love song turned into a threnody.

I was much closer to Fay than Linda, though, and the two of us shared our poetry, critiquing each other's work and suggesting changes.

So I was thrilled when Fay and Hamid showed up at my door. There was a buzz in the air as though we were standing under a power line. As they shed their coats and scarves, we talked about Christmas. Cautiously I told Fay about the toys the kids had gotten from Toys for Tots.

"Really?" she said, not looking at me.

Yeah, she told them about us, I thought. I laid their coats over the back of a chair and gushed about how overwhelmed I was by the kindness. "To think that anyone would go to so much bother to help us out!"

Fay grinned. "Well, that's a happy ending."

"I have another one too." I told Fay about Jill's car and her win in Small Claims Court before the holiday.

"See?" she responded. "That's what you have to do. Don't let them beat you down."

Did nothing scare this woman? If only some of her courage would rub off on me, terrified as I was of everything outside my safe little home. "I'd rather sort things out so that fighting isn't necessary."

"Good luck!"

We were quiet for a minute, watching the children.

Finally I said, "See, this is what I hate about being on welfare. You have to fight and fight for every little thing."

"Why do you think everyone's so desperate to get a job and get away from the welfare office? Anyway, it's not only welfare. It's being poor."

Fay asked why I'd gone on welfare instead of going back to live with my parents, since they had money. I explained how they wouldn't let me.

She snorted. "I would have just camped out on the sidewalk in front of the house."

"In front of all the neighbors? My parents would have been mortified."

"Exactly." Fay grinned triumphantly. "Shame them into taking you in!"

"I never thought of that," I said slowly. My solution had always been to run and hide, pull back under the sofa and put my hands over my head. It had never occurred to me to confront my parents and try to force them to take me in.

"There's this great Lucille Clifton poem I brought you," Fay said. "It's telling children what to say when people ask why their mom is so odd. Wait. I brought it with me." She sat on the floor and began rummaging in her bag.

I looked down at her electric cloud of hair. It seemed to hiss and crackle in the winter light. We were reading a lot of poetry, much of it by women, in slim paperbacks that Fay and I traded back and forth. I shared them with Jill too. We read Adrienne Rich, Anne Sexton, Nikki Giovanni, Denise Levertov, Audrey Lorde.

Fay gave it to me. "She says to tell them she's a poet so she doesn't have any sense. Don't you love it?" She grinned up at me, hair flying, eyes alight.

Later I wrote in my journal: *I wish I had one-tenth of Fay's energy. I'm always trying to wake up from my slow stupor, and Fay is like an alarm clock, bringing me back to life. Even her anger seems like a life-force. It's different from Jill's: Jill's anger is steady and strong and doesn't let up until it gets the job done, but Fay's sparks and sizzles. She's like Sir Galahad—I can see her dressed in white with a great sword chasing off after the Green Knight, keeping her promises. She would be gallant in a fight. I can rely on her to always have my back.*

My own anger seemed like such a paltry thing compared to theirs. It was true I had stood up to the manager at The Mart over Justin's crib and the emergency room nurse about treating Rora, but they had both backed down pretty quickly.

Maybe it was better that it took a lot to get me mad. As I struggled through one exhausting day after another, grinding flour for bread, mending hand-me-down clothes, smearing cream on diaper rash, I sometimes felt like crying from pure tiredness, but never resented my babies and their demands. I was grateful for the structure and meaning they gave my life—my old mantra: the kids come first. I wanted to shape their world into a place where they were safe.

Winter finally faded into spring, allowing the children to play outside once again.

Jeremy was running little metal cars through the dirt to my right. At two, he balanced his mischievous imagination with a grin that beguiled me into forgiving him all his scrapes and escapades. On the rare occasions that I could get him to sit still for a moment, I loved to smooth back the feather-light blond hair that tickled his ears and neck.

Justin had recently learned to walk, and his favorite thing was to climb up the front steps, patting my leg and shoulder as he went, and then stump down them again, putting down one leg and bringing the other to join it before going on.

Justin suddenly lost his balance and tumbled down the steps before I could grab him. He banged his head on the sidewalk, cutting it. Only then did he start hollering. His head was streaming blood.

After a moment of pure panic, I grabbed Justin and ran Jeremy upstairs to Jill, leaving a trail of blood on the stairs. Then back down again, holding a towel to Justin's head, into the car and screeching off to the emergency room.

The triage nurse helped me stop the bleeding. Then, after a long time, we were shown into a small room where we waited a while longer until a doctor finally arrived. A nurse followed him into the room, murmuring *Medicaid* as they came through the door.

The doctor carefully lifted the gauze from Justin's head and probed the edges of the cut. "It doesn't look too bad. Head wounds bleed a lot."

"I know," I said. "I wanted to make sure he was okay, since he hit his head."

Justin sniffled and looked up at me with teary eyes, his lower lip trembling a little.

The doctor put some Steri-strips on the cut. Then he unsnapped Justin's jumpsuit and gently eased his arms and legs out. He examined each limb, turning it like a shopper examining fruit. After that, he lifted Justin's tee shirt and probed his ribs.

"What are you doing?" I asked. "He hit his head, not his ribs."

"Just checking," He let go of the baby and picked up the folder to write something. "Okay, you can dress him again." He clapped the manila folder together and handed it to the nurse. "The nurse will give you discharge instructions."

He and the nurse walked out into the corridor where they spoke for a minute before the nurse came back in. "Wait here," she said.

By the time she finally returned, about twenty minutes later, Justin was starting to fuss.

"Can we go now?" I asked.

"Come through here," she said, ushering us into an oyster-grey office where a solemn man sat behind a metal desk, holding a folder open in his hands.

He looked up over his glasses. "Come in. That's right. Sit there. I'm Mr. French, and I'm a social worker here at the hospital. I just have a few questions to ask you."

"I don't need to talk to a social worker. No offense, but we've been here for a long time and I need to get home."

"This won't take long. Sit. Sit."

I sat, fuming, with Justin on my lap.

"So," Mr. French said, turning over a few pages in the folder. "You have another son, too."

"Yes."

"How often do your children have to come to the emergency room?"

"This is the first time."

"Do you get angry with them a lot?"

"No, of course not. What does that . . ."

"Do you shake them when you get angry? Hit them?"

"I told you, I don't . . ."

Suddenly I realized what was going on. The fear that I'd seen all around me in other women closed tight around my heart. The social worker was the boogeyman, other welfare mothers had cautioned me. Don't ask for too much. Don't cause trouble. They'll take your kids away.

I had thought it was merely paranoia. I had thought I was immune: Surely anyone could see how much I loved my kids. I felt sick. This man had the power, could build himself a story to take my kids away. I knew my panic was irrational. I knew that Children's Protective Services did good work, rescuing children from abusive situations, that the social workers were overworked and underpaid. But I couldn't help it. My babies.

Then the anger began, building up from deep in my gut, rising higher and higher till my face grew hot. How often had my brothers and sisters and I ended up in emergency rooms, with no accusations of child abuse? True, people were only beginning to look for child abuse now, in 1976. But my youngest brother had fallen off a cliff twice, once by accident and the second time showing us what had happened. How had my parents explained that? But of course, they were not on

Medicaid. They didn't have to explain anything.

I felt myself gearing myself up for a fight. What did he think? Just because I was on welfare, I must abuse my kids? I opened my mouth to tell him what I thought of that brilliant idea, but Mr. French's next question stopped me.

"What clinic do you go to?"

"Huh?"

"Which pediatric clinic or clinics do you take the children to?"

What did that have to do with anything? What was he implying? "None. I take them to Dr. Fitzpatrick. She has an office on . . ."

He closed the folder and held up a hand. "That's all right then."

What was all right? What did having a private doctor have to do with child abuse? Maybe he thought that—unlike in a clinic where you saw someone different every time—seeing the same doctor meant that she would notice if something was wrong. We certainly didn't pay any more, not with Medicaid. Maybe he simply thought we must share his middle-class values, though surely he knew that child abuse spanned all social classes.

Mr. French spoke again. "Did the nurse give you discharge instructions? Good. Good." And he gestured toward the door.

Baffled, thankful that I had somehow stumbled across the open sesame that would secure our release, I picked Justin up and left. I was free to go.

But I was never again entirely free of the fear that someone would take away my boys.

11
MUDDY RIVER

"What will it be like? Who's going to be there?" Jeremy asked from the backseat. Almost three, he watched my every move, eager to learn how to operate in the adult world, confidant that he was the equal of any grownup.

I glanced in the rearview mirror to check on his brother. Fourteen-month-old Justin was gazing out of the window, paying no attention to us.

"I don't know," I said, as we left Worcester behind.

It was the Friday of Memorial Day weekend, May 28th, 1976, and we were headed to Marlboro, Vermont, where my morris team would be dancing in the first-ever Marlboro Ale.

I felt like one of the twelve dancing princesses, sneaking off from my real life to go dancing. After everyone was asleep, they opened a trap door and traveled down a long flight of stairs, through trees of silver, gold and diamond to where a boat lay to take them across the lake where music and dancing awaited them. In the morning, everyone wondered why their brand-new shoes had holes in them.

I was like the youngest, the one who hung back going down the stairs. I wasn't at all sure I belonged there with the others. Although I would be dancing in white clothes and ribbons like my teammates, my life was the opposite of theirs and I didn't really fit in. They were young, single, well-off. College students or recent graduates, they were absorbed in boyfriends and careers, while I was just a welfare mom who could recite all of *One Fish, Two Fish, Red Fish, Blue Fish* and give my car a tune-up.

My teammates didn't know I was on welfare. They were friendly and fun to be with, but didn't press me for details when I explained that I had two kids and was separated from my husband. I was reluctant to open up to them, afraid they would look at me differently if they found out I was one of the "greedy needy", as the newspaper tended to refer to us.

Only the day before, I had gone to Stop & Shop to get my assigned share of food for the weekend. When I got to the cashier and pulled out my food stamps, the woman behind me in line eyed the items in my cart and sniffed loudly.

"Mushrooms," she said to no one in particular. "Fresh beans when canned are half the price. Artichoke hearts, for heaven's sake."

I ignored her. I was used to people weighing in on my shopping choices, my judgment open to everyone's criticism. With welfare had come this shocking loss of privacy—not just other shoppers, but also social workers who were allowed to barge in and inspect my apartment whenever they wished.

I didn't much care what my morris team thought of me. We didn't even have to be friends. I was simply there to dance.

I had first seen morris dancing the summer before, shortly after Justin was born, when my friend Jim took us to Fox Hollow, a folk festival in upstate New York. Much as I loved music, I could neither sing nor play an instrument. However, I was drawn to a group of dancers in a clearing in the woods, a musician and six men dressed all in white. On leather pads tied under their knees they wore bells that rang with every step. They sported white handkerchiefs that they waved in the air, bright red vests, green felt hats and long colored ribbons tied to their arms.

I knew what morris dancing was from my reading: a traditional performance dance from the English countryside. It was mentioned in Shakespeare and was part of the traditional village life that Hardy memorialized in his Wessex novels. The dance predated written records, so no one knew its exact origin. It was thought that the name derived from the term for Moors, due to the ancient custom of dancers blacking their faces, a custom that had almost completely died out before Hardy's time.

Surprising as it was to see morris dancing in upstate New York, it seemed appropriate there under the trees, just the single violin weaving a tune and these strong, silent men in white.

Circling, intertwining, handkerchiefs waving overhead, catching the sunlight, they seemed to have stepped out of a legendary past. Not speaking, not touching, but totally connected, they moved through the intricate figures. And I too felt like a part of their magic circle.

When the dance ended with a great flourish and shout of *Hey!*, I came to, my mouth hanging open. I took a deep shuddering breath, not knowing if I had breathed at all for the last few minutes, and felt again Justin's weight on my arm and hip, Jeremy's hand gripping my jeans.

The men circled and began another dance. Their movements were like a cross between basketball and ballet: the strength and grace of basketball players interweaving in their complex patterns, and then jumping, hanging in the air like Nureyev, seemingly without effort, almost forever. And behind the dance, the music framing it, supporting it, driving it.

In that moment, I knew I had to be a part of this dance. Although I lived in a run-down apartment in the city, I dreamed of being among the trees. The men's dancing—so strong, so sure—belonged there. It seemed to speak the same language as the trees, a language I had to learn.

In school, I had been the most unathletic person, but now I decided to take a chance that I, too, could do this. Perhaps it could be a way to be involved with music despite my inability even to pick out a tune on a recorder.

After we got back from Fox Hollow, I jumped at a friend's suggestion that I come to her dance series in Worcester where she taught contra dances and folk dances from around the world. The evening series offered reduced admission for people with tight budgets and the opportunity to attend for free if you volunteered to sit at the admission desk for a while. I tried to get Jill to come too but she preferred free-form dance, where she could better express herself. Since she took care of the boys while I danced, I didn't stay out late. I expected any moment that midnight would sound and my horses turn back into mice.

In December, I went to a contra dance at the Scout House in Concord, Massachusetts. As I took hands in a ladies' chain, I recognized one of the morris dancers I'd seen in New York. Older than the others, he had seemed to be the leader of the group.

As the evening ended and people were starting to collect their coats, I pushed aside my nervousness and approached him. Roger Cartwright was a trim elfin man with laugh crinkles around his eyes.

I introduced myself and told him how much I admired his dancing at Fox Hollow.

"Why, thank you," he said, twinkling at me.

I took a deep breath. "Are there any groups of women doing morris dancing?"

"A women's team?" Roger said. "You don't ask for much, do you?"

"What?"

"You have to meet this woman," he went on briskly. "She's starting one right now." He took me by the arm and led me over to a tall woman talking at breakneck speed to a group of people as she buttoned a Navy pea coat. "Cynthia, this woman wants to join a morris team."

She turned with a distracted look and said, "Okay, give me a minute." She rummaged in a coat pocket and pulled out a scrap of paper and a pen. "Here, hold on; let me write this down for you."

I thanked Roger as he turned away, and then said to the woman, "My name's Barbara."

She held out the paper. "Cynthia. Here's my phone number. Give me a call. We'll probably have our next meeting in January at Wheelock College. Have you done any dancing?"

"Not morris. Contra and some international dancing."

"Great. We'll be in touch."

As I drove home, I was excited but determined to be practical. I gave myself a year; if at the end of that time I was still clumsy and felt ridiculous, then I would stop. There was the drive to Boston for practice and the problem of babysitting. I would have to see if Jill would be willing to watch the kids one night a week. But dancing with a performing group seemed like a perfect opportunity: I could get exercise and socialize and it wouldn't cost me anything but gas for the car. Morris dancers passed the hat when they danced out, like any other street performer, so I could make a little extra money. Most of all, it would let me forget—however briefly—that I was just a welfare mom.

Roger didn't look much like a fairy godmother, but he turned out to be mine. I loved dancing morris and quickly forgot my self-imposed deadline. I didn't care how ridiculous I looked; I was going to keep dancing.

The new team was named Muddy River Morris, derived from the original name for Brookline, where we practiced: Muddy River Town. Cynthia turned out to be a natural teacher. From a family of professional musicians and a violist herself, she worked us hard in practice, obsessing over details, drilling us over and over on beginnings and endings to dances.

She invited Shag to help teach us at first. Tall and thin, with a dry wit and short pointed beard, Shag made me think of Don Quixote. He danced with the Pinewoods Morris Men and the Black Jokers, the other two men's teams in the Boston area, besides the New Cambridge Morris Men, the team I'd seen at Fox Hollow.

Shag was taking a great risk in teaching us. Morris was considered by most people to be a dance for men, completely inappropriate for women. 1976 was still early days for the women's movement. The ink was barely dry on Title IX, which mandated equality for women's athletics. Believing that women were incapable of strenuous physical exertion, many dismissed Billie Jean King's "Battle of the Sexes" win over Bobby Riggs on the tennis court as a fluke.

Shag simply said that when he looked at us, he didn't see women; he saw dancers.

He and Cynthia taught us an assortment of morris dances, encouraging us to dance strong, which meant keeping your body up and up into the air continually. My teammates loved learning the "hankie" dances, but a few objected to the "stick" dances. Clashing the yard-long sticks together caused vibrations that hurt their arms, they complained. However, the rest of us swung our sticks fiercely, enjoying the power they added to the dance.

It was a hankie dance, though, that finally caught me. We were running through a chorus of sidesteps and double steps, when suddenly I found that I no longer had to count in my head to keep my steps in time to the music. It was true what people always said, that the music told you what to do, because it was as if I was a puppet being pulled here and there by the tune.

The notes flowed through my body into my feet, resonating through the core of me, and I moved almost without conscious volition, lifted out of myself. I felt each movement through my whole body, a rush of warmth. My feet had springs. I floated, barely tapping the ground occasionally to stay aloft, buoyed by the music and the connection with the other dancers.

They sensed it too; I saw it in their eyes, felt it in their hot breath, heard it in the ringing of their bells and the snap of their hankies. We looked at each other, breathing hard, tasting salt sweat, and there was something between us, some glowing ball that we all held up, some interconnecting web as though we were holding hands without actually touching.

I was hooked. I was willing to drill figures for hours for those few transcendent moments. I felt as though I, unmusical, unathletic, had been given a great gift. Dancing became my secret life, my hard-won joy.

Jill continued to babysit for Jeremy and Justin so that I could go to practice one night a week. Living upstairs, it was mostly a matter of putting the boys to bed and then leaving both front doors open so she could hear if they awoke.

I tried to get her to come with me, but she wasn't interested. "I'd rather learn African dancing," she said.

Nor could I convince any of my other friends. Sherry claimed she was too klutzy and anyway couldn't be away from Rora that much. Fay said she was only interested in modern dance. So I went off week after week by myself, except for the rare occasions when Jill couldn't watch the kids. Then I brought them to practice with me, which turned out to be the best thing I could have done.

The other members of the morris team hadn't known what to make of me, showing up as I did and not sharing anything about myself. But when Jeremy and Justin appeared, my teammates' faces lit up, and they opened their arms. Many of them were studying Early Childhood Education at Wheelock with Roger Cartwright, and had been steered to Muddy River by him, as I had been.

Those who were out of school seemed to have stepped effortlessly into careers, mostly as teachers. So they loved children and spoiled my boys terribly.

During one dance, I heard Justin start to cry from his stroller and then stop. Looking around, I saw Shag, an inveterate bachelor, holding baby Justin competently in his arms while he continued to call out instructions to us.

From January till April we practiced every week and then began to dance out in public. We mostly toured with the other local morris teams and danced at places like the Arboretum and Roger's Mayday celebrations on the Charles River.

When we danced out, Muddy River wore white shirts and pants topped by a teal-colored tabard lined with green. We made the tabards ourselves; they were designed to minimize the differences in our body types so that we would look like a team. I wore a white oxford shirt from high school and an old pair of white pants that Cynthia gave me because they were too short for her. Flashing under our white pants, our matching green socks added a whimsical touch. Long ribbons were tied to our arms and flew around us as we danced. I put ribbons in my hair too. I always brought the boys with me, and they would run about imitating our movements, their blond hair bright in the sunlight, charming dancers and audience alike.

My original hope of making money didn't pan out. In fact, dancing with Muddy River was a continual expense, not only the initial outlay for bells and other kit materials, but also the gas to travel to practice and tours. The little money we collected went into the team treasury or paid for the day's lunch.

Most of the women on my team hated to pass the hat—"It feels like begging!"—and didn't need the money. Several argued that we shouldn't pass the hat at all.

I kept quiet. There was no way they could understand what a couple of extra dollars might mean to me.

Everyone on Muddy River was excited about the ale. For most of us, it was our first chance to see morris teams other than our four Boston teams. The Marlboro Ale was the brainchild of Tony Barrand, who had started the Marlboro Morris Men. Morris was still pretty new in the U.S. Of the dozen or so teams in the country, all but two—Pinewoods and the now-defunct Village Men in New York—were only a few years old.

Tony was on the faculty of Marlboro College and had persuaded the school to let him use the college grounds to host the ale, a convocation of morris teams. All teams were invited, and twelve accepted, including Muddy River and the other Boston teams. He chose Memorial Day weekend for practical reasons, such as the three-day weekend, and whimsical ones, such as the note in the Marlboro town charter giving permission from the English King in 1751 for the town to have a fair on the last weekend of May.

There would be show dances performed for each other on Saturday, and then on Sunday we'd break into smaller groups to tour around the nearby Vermont towns. The ale was not a competition but a chance to present our best dances and learn from each other.

Although we were eager to show off to the other teams, we were also apprehensive.

"A lot of people are violently opposed to women dancing morris," Cynthia warned us as we prepared for the ale. "They will be looking for us to mess up, so we have to be twice as good as the men's teams."

The first women's morris team in the U.S was Ring o' Bells in New York City, founded by Jody Evans in 1974. The following year, Cynthia started Muddy River and Tony's wife, Andy, formed the Marlboro Women in Marlboro, Vermont. Women dancing morris was a new and controversial development.

The earliest references to morris dancing go back to the 16th century, but the dances as we know them were first collected in the early 20th century by folklorists Cecil Sharp and Mary Neal. At that time the few village teams still performing were made up of men, although women had sometimes participated in the past.

Both Mary Neal and Cecil Sharp taught morris dancing to groups of women. However, as the revival gathered strength, the Morris Ring, an umbrella organization in England, took the stance that women should not dance morris. It was a male thing, they declared; only men could and should do it. Women simply weren't strong enough. Women could do other traditional dances—clog or garland—but morris was for men.

Initially most morris men in the U.S. took their cue from the Ring and refused to teach women or to dance on tours where women's teams were present. One influential teacher had even refused to bring his team to that first Marlboro Ale because women's teams were invited.

So Muddy River faced a fight for recognition, even for parity. Cynthia saw our struggle as a microcosm of what was going on in the larger society in the mid-seventies: women trying to liberate themselves from old roles, and men resisting their incursions.

"It's about getting in touch with our bodies," she said, echoing the new book, *Our Bodies, Ourselves.* "We have to learn to feel the music in our muscles and dance through our entire bodies."

I didn't want to get involved in the politics. I had battles enough with the welfare office and didn't need any more antagonists. Anyway, most of the men in the Boston area were supportive. There, men and women knew each other, not only from morris, but from the weekly social dances: New England contras and English Country dancing. Many of them sang together in John Langstaff's new production, the Christmas Revels, or in other singing groups. The dance community in Boston was tight, and no one wanted to start a civil war by taking sides against the women who wanted to do morris. Not that I felt part of the community. I came to practice and sometimes to a contra or English Country dance, but didn't have the time or money to socialize with these folks.

We were among the first to arrive at Marlboro, the boys tumbling out of the car and running around in the grass. My teammates trickled in, selected an area, and set up their tents. Having no tent, I had decided that the boys and I would sleep in the back of the car, a VW square-back, like a miniature station wagon. With the box of tools and spare parts on the front seat and the back seat down, there was just enough room for me to lie down if I bent my knees a bit.

My team cooked a festive dinner of couscous and vegetables on a Coleman stove. The boys, excited, ran from one woman to another, who all cooed and cuddled them.

Saturday morning the boys and I woke up first. Toddlers didn't understand the concept of sleeping in, especially when there were so many thrilling new adventures to be had. I tried to keep them quiet so they wouldn't wake the others.

After my teammates emerged from their tents, I tried to find someone to watch the boys while I took a shower. Only Cynthia, the one person who had no experience with young children, agreed. She did fine, having quickly learned the fine art of dispensing graham crackers to keep the boys quiet.

The morning was supposed to be spent in teaching sessions to review the massed dances. Tony had selected seven dances, along with a processional and recessional, which all the teams had learned so we could do them as massed dances between individual teams' show dances.

Most of my team skipped the review sessions, feeling that we knew the dances pretty well. Too, I was a little intimidated by all the people milling around, dancers from other teams and their partners. My secret life had suddenly filled up with strangers. I was still coming to terms with the people I had met in Boston—my teammates and dancers from other Boston teams—and now here were people from all over. I felt so different from everyone, being almost the only one with children and certainly the only welfare mother.

Instead of hanging out with my teammates or going to the review session, I spent the morning with the kids, walking around, exploring the campus and the nearby woods. This was what I knew best: being a mom.

After lunch, while a crowd of friends, parents, and townspeople gathered around the soccer field, the twelve teams assembled at the top of the hill by the college buildings, a milling mass of dancers, energized and ready to go. With his bullhorn and whistle, Tony marshaled us into one long line ready to process down the hill, a grand parade to the soccer field where a huge maypole had been erected. The boys were waiting at the bottom with the mother of one of my teammates.

The music started, ragged at first, and then strong and loud: fiddles, accordions, whistles and drums.

"This time!" Tony yelled.

And down the hill we came, a tumbling, jostling crowd of musicians and dancers, ribbons flying, catching the sunlight, white hankies rising in unison on the upbeat of every phrase. It was a glorious jumble, my teammates grinning in the sunlight as we danced the Winster Processional.

At the bottom of the hill, we circled the maypole and—after a blast from Tony's whistle and the command "All out!"—ended in unison with four capers.

We stood there, nearly a hundred strong, one foot raised in front of us, hands thrown up in the air. The wind snapped our hankies and the long ribbons of the maypole.

Then the crowd began to applaud. At another blast from the whistle, we walked off, each team staking out a piece of turf. Jeremy ran skipping across the center of the field, while behind him, my teammate's mother guided Justin's stroller.

"That was great!" Jeremy said, clutching my knees briefly before dashing off again.

I had scoured Goodwill for white clothes for the boys, finally sewing a smock shirt for Jeremy out of an old sheet. In their whites, blond hair curling out from under cotton sailor hats, trailing streamers of colored ribbons, the boys ran and tumbled around the field. They waved borrowed hankies and imitated the dancers as best they could. Almost the only children there, they got lots of attention.

Our show dances were Abingdon Princess Royal and Adderbury Bluebells of Scotland for eight. Dances were referred to by the name of the village as well as the name of the dance because villages often had different versions of the same dances. Morris dances were for sets of six people, except for jigs which were for one or two dancers. Most people at the ale had never seen a dance for eight people, so we hoped to amaze and astound them with our Bluebells.

We were the second to last to do our two show dances and lobbying for places had gone on all day, since there were too many of us for everyone to perform. Cynthia wanted to field our best dancers in both show dances, in order prove once and for all that women could do morris. However, many of the women argued that their boyfriends or parents had come all this way to see them dance, so they should be included. Not having a boyfriend to show off for and certainly not one of the best dancers, I told Cynthia to leave me out of the show dances; I'd be dancing in our show dance at Newfane—the last stop on Sunday—and that was enough for me.

I knew Shag and Cynthia had taught us well. Watching my team take its place on the field beside the rippling ribbons of the maypole, their teal tabards bright in the sunlight, I thought they were on a par with the teams that had come before. And the dances *were* beautiful: the parallel lines of Princess Royal moving in unison, white hankies making a brave show, and the exhilaration of the final double-time sticking chorus of Bluebells, ending with a flourish and a shout. Surely we had banished any doubt about women being able to dance morris.

By Saturday night, the dancing over and everyone gathering for the feast, the kids were overtired. The large room packed with long tables rang with talk and laughter. Dust swam in the yellow lights, the air hot and thick with food and people and the scrape of chairs against the floor. People were jammed together at the tables, some still in kit, sweaty from dancing, others in fresh clothes, all a little bleary from exhaustion and beer. Periodically someone would get up and go outside to the keg for a refill.

One table at a time was invited up to get food. My teammates were off flirting with their boyfriends, so—juggling three plates, trying not to spill food on my whites—I ushered Jeremy and Justin through the buffet line, their small steps slowing everyone down.

After they'd eaten, Justin almost falling asleep in his plate of spaghetti, I realized I would have to put the kids to bed. It would mean missing the contra dance and other merriment, the singing and skits, but I had no choice.

As we stepped outside the hall into the Vermont night, a man loomed up in front of us, tankard in hand. He was short and stocky, with reddish hair and beard. He swayed a bit, his shirt-tail half out.

"Damn kids," he said, waving his tankard at Jeremy and Justin and barring the way with his other arm.

I pulled the boys behind me.

He still had on his whites—grass-stained and dirty by now—but no vest or sash to identify his team. "Who do you think you are, bringing kids here? Don't belong here. Not a place for women unless they're ready to party, and you go bringing kids here like it's a kindergarten or something. How can we have fun with that one looking at me?" He pointed at Jeremy whose steady, scornful gaze hadn't wavered.

He pushed his face close to mine. "You shouldn't be here. You don't belong."

I picked up both boys and walked around him, making for the car. Justin clung to my neck, but Jeremy wriggled to get down.

"What did he mean?" Jeremy asked.

"Don't worry about it. He's just tired and cranky. He'll be sorry tomorrow."

I got them into their pajamas and all of us into the car where I had made a bed for the three of us with the sleeping bag and quilt. I lay there in the darkness, a sleeping child on either side of me.

The boys breathed slowly and evenly. It had taken a long time to calm them down. Crickets whirred a steady song.

I heard the music for the contra dance start up, faintly. If I had felt like the youngest princess before, now I was hearing a branch crack behind me, a thief discovering and ruining my secret life. It was time to stop kidding myself. The man had been awful, probably drunk, but he'd been right. I didn't belong here. This wasn't my world. It was useless to try to break out of my circle of welfare mothers. I couldn't wait for Monday when the boys and I could go home to Worcester.

First one up again the next morning, I had lit the Coleman stove and heated water for tea by the time my teammates emerged from their tents.

Jeremy tugged on my hand. "Will the bad man be there today?"

"Hush," I said. I didn't want to say anything to the others. It wasn't any of their business.

"What bad man?" Cynthia asked.

Justin held up his arms to Cynthia to be picked up. Her mouth opened slightly, as if to say *Who? Me?* and then slowly, carefully, as if handling a Ming vase, she reached down and picked him up. He settled himself on her hip and beamed up at her.

"It was nothing," I said.

"He yelled at us," Jeremy maintained, scowling, his fists planted on his hips.

"Tell me," Cynthia said.

So I did. "He was right," I added. "I shouldn't have come and shouldn't have brought the kids. This isn't a place for kids."

The response was not what I expected.

"Of course it is! How can you say that? Don't let one jerk ruin it for you." In her indignation, Cynthia turned and drew in the rest of the team. "You have as much right to be here as he does," she concluded.

Madeleine said, "Did he hurt you? I would have been terrified."

"That jerk!" Cathy said. "Point him out to me."

Judy fulminated about men in general, but Robin said, "They're not all bad."

"That's right," Cynthia said. "Look at Shag, teaching us, and Roger. And of course we all love John."

Robin blushed, but it was true that her boyfriend John, who danced with New Cambridge, had always supported our team.

"It won't happen again," Margie said.

Diane nodded. "One of us will always be nearby."

"And if one of them is rude to you, we'll get him," Judy said.

"Group hug!" Skylar cried.

Squished in their embrace, I looked around at my teammates, my protectors, my friends. I felt something give in me, some deep breath released. Like the dancing princesses, I would have to go back to the real world, where shoes wear out and trees have plain green leaves. On Monday, I'd return to my Worcester apartment, my battles with the welfare office, and the endless juggling of pennies. But this was different. I could let down my guard with these people. At last I was beginning to feel a part of their circle.

12

MOTHERLESS CHILDREN

I gave Fay a call before stuffing my latest poems in the diaper bag and both kids in the stroller. As we rumbled down the sidewalk, the pale summer sun tried to escape the clouds, but the air had a damp chill to it that set Jeremy coughing. Luckily it wasn't far to Fay's house.

Every time I walked up her street and entered Fay's yard through the wall of dark hemlock trees, I felt that I was entering a secret garden. Shielded from the street by overgrown privet arching over the sidewalk and tall feathery hemlock trees, the yard seemed a mysterious, untended place. The house was different from every other house in the neighborhood. It was quite run-down— had actually been condemned—but Fay and her housemates were working to fix it up. The house, a grey Victorian triple-decker with interesting angles, was an oddity in Worcester with its streets of plain frame houses. The house had tall windows and gingerbread trim under the eaves, carved into graceful curves and circles like the moon over waves. The front porch wrapped around the side of the house, and it too was decorated with gingerbread trim, this time curlicues with Celtic crosses.

The house would be gorgeous when they finished restoring it.

The two sets of front doors were of dark wood with long narrow windows. Inside the front hall was a curving staircase in dark wood. The newel post at the bottom was topped with a white globe lamp that didn't work. Leaving the stroller in the hall, we headed up to Fay's third-floor apartment.

"What can I get you?" Fay asked as we got settled.

"How about some tea? Jeremy was coughing on the way over."

"Sure." Fay whirled around to put the kettle on the stove.

We could hear Jeremy in the living room, talking to Hamid and Justin who were in the playpen together.

"Jeremy, stay away from the tools," I called.

"He should have some peppermint with honey. What kind of tea do you want?" Fay pointed to the shelves of glass jars over the table. "I have chamomile, verbena, St. John's wort. Well, you can see for yourself."

Gathering wild plants for tea was how we first connected, back when I was pregnant with Jeremy and Fay with the child she eventually lost. A friend of Lewis's and Jill's, Fay had invited me to join the evening class she was taking with a man she admired, an authority on edible wild plants.

I asked her if she still saw him.

"No. I was telling him he needed to change his diet, explaining about food combining, and he told me there was no medical evidence. Medical evidence!"

I sipped my tea.

"You're still doing that Adelle Davis thing, aren't you?," Fay went on. "Combining food for protein. That is so wrong. You should never eat protein and grain in the same meal. Wait, I'm going to give you a book." Fay raced out of the kitchen, her untouched tea left cooling on the table. I could hear her speak to the boys as she went through the living room I followed her more slowly, carrying Jeremy's tea.

Fay's living room was still under construction. The floor had been sanded but not yet varnished. Lumber and tools were piled by the wall, awaiting the next onslaught—replacing the window molding, by the look of things. The room had great potential: a spacious rectangular corner room with tall windows on two sides that looked out into the treetops. Fay wanted to put mirrors on one of the other walls and use it as a dance and yoga studio, maybe give lessons. For now, besides construction supplies, it held only a playpen and the mattress where she and Hamid slept. She hadn't tackled the bedrooms yet. They were stuffed with boxes, a few chairs, a bureau.

By the time I caught up with her, she was pulling boxes out of one of the bedrooms and rummaging through them. Although slight, she had a tomboy's wiry strength. The boys watched in awe as the jumble of boxes and piles of books began to spread.

Suddenly Fay sat back on her heels. "Here," she cried holding up a dog-eared paperback. "Read this! It explains everything."

I took the book to humor her, knowing I would probably never read it. A mutual friend at the food co-op had complained about Fay, saying that she was too bossy. To me, she simply seemed strong, sure of herself, unlike me.

"I have something for you too," I said. "Let me get some of this tea down Jeremy, and I'll dig it out. It's an old Ms magazine with an essay by Adrienne Rich."

One of my favorite poets, Adrienne Rich had come to speak at my high school, her alma mater. I didn't remember anything that she said, only my realization that if she had survived the stifling atmosphere of Roland Park, then I could too. I drew not just comfort but fire from her poems.

As in the bartering scheme I had set up, my main concern in my poetry was to make connections, or at least create a space where they could be made. I loved the way a haiku by Bashō set up a vivid image of something from nature and then turned it upside down.

Fay curled up on the mattress, leaning back against the wall. I sat on the edge of the mattress and helped Jeremy with his tea while she read Rich's essay.

It was about Jane Eyre as a motherless woman, and the temptations she faced while trying to remain independent. The orphan Jane had been placed in the care of her unfeeling stepmother who cruelly shut Jane in the Red Room for an imagined infraction and then sent her off to an abusive school where Jane had to learn to tame her passion for affection and fair play. As an adult, Jane refused to be drawn into an illicit relationship with Mr. Rochester despite her love for him or a licit relationship with Mr. Rivers despite her respect for him.

I had always liked the book because of Brontë's refusal of the romantic, as Rich pointed out, but her essay also gave me a different perspective on the story.

"Yes!" Fay cried and pointed to the paragraph referring to Phyllis Chesler's description of women as motherless children because our mothers have no power or wealth to pass on to us.

"Motherless children," I said, setting down the mug and spoon. Jeremy went across the room and climbed into the playpen, where he soon had the younger boys acting out some story they seemed to be making up as they went along.

We talked about Jane Eyre and the way all of us lacked the mothers who would teach us how to be the kind of women we wanted to be, women who defined themselves, who fought back. That led us into talking about the women's movement, what mothers could be teaching their daughters, and what that meant for us, raising sons as we were.

"We have to believe that it's possible," Fay said, throwing down the magazine and jumping up. She strode back and forth in front of me, gesturing as she spoke. "We have to believe that there is a way for them to be men without being monsters."

"Strong men," I agreed.

The boys' game had gotten progressively rowdier, and they began to roar like lions, rattling the crib railing.

"What are you doing?" I called. "I can't hear myself think."

Hamid let out his deep belly laugh, legs collapsing under him. Justin sat down in sympathy, giving us what Jill called his Buddha smile.

Jeremy said, "We're being Wild Things."

"I see," I said, thinking they must have heard us talking about monsters. They all three loved Sendak's book. "Do you want to be tamed? I have the secret tickling weapon."

"No," all three roared.

"Okay. Well, try to be wild a little more quietly."

Fay plumped down next to me and picked up the magazine again. She turned a page and then glanced up at me.

"What about your mother?"

When I first read *Jane Eyre* for school, I had been staggered by the opening scene: Jane hiding from her family in a curtained window, trying to look at her book in peace. Recognition had flowed through me. That image summed up my entire childhood.

I twisted my hands together. "Maybe it was my fault for shutting her out."

One of the tenets of the women's movement was to recognize our mothers and grandmothers for their struggles against the constraints society put on them. I had tried hard to feel sorry for my mother. Certainly she would have been far happier continuing her career as a nurse instead of being stuck at home with six kids. She would no doubt have ended up head of nursing if not running the whole hospital.

But the old habit of shrugging off her complaints was too strong. Why was it so easy to forgive my friends for their faults and not my mother? Maybe because of all her melodrama and posturing. Maybe because she never seemed to care about me.

Fay fingered the corner of the magazine's page. "My parents are both dead, but I wish my mother had warned me what it would be like. I always thought I could be whoever I wanted to be."

At the thought of leaving my own kids motherless, my eyes burned and a hard knotted pain gripped my chest. I thought about Fay and her sister. No matter how isolated I felt, they were truly without a mother or father. Their only relatives were an uncle and a grandfather who lived together on a farm outside town. Much as I was independent of my family, I was still shocked at how alone in the world Fay and her sister were.

I said, "What is that like? Without your parents?"

"You know how many children in stories don't have parents?" she said. "Cinderella, Snow White."

"Or they have evil stepparents."

"It's as if the story couldn't happen, they wouldn't be in danger if they had real parents."

There was that pain again. I wanted to protect Jeremy and Justin. Keep anything from ever harming or hurting them. It wasn't just what a mother ought to do; it was what I was compelled to do.

"She talks in here about Jane Eyre looking for other mothers, like in Miss Temple and Helen Burns," Fay said, lifting the magazine. "I don't think I do that."

"Me either." I was convinced that independence was the only way to protect myself. "Not another mother. Sisters, maybe."

Fay raised a fist. "'Sisterhood is powerful!'" she intoned and then started to laugh.

Jill's words came back to me: *This must be what it is like to have a sister.* Thinking of my own biological sisters—one too young and the other too different—I had said no. Yet, here were Jill, Sherry, Fay. In the same way that my Maryland friends were my surrogate family, these women had become my sisters. We exchanged advice and information, helped each other out when necessary, as when they had cleaned my house while I was in the hospital.

I didn't actually trust parents, even surrogate ones. There always seemed to be a power struggle sooner or later which usually ended with the "child" breaking free, like the person at the food co-op who initiated the split with his former mentor, or Fay with the man who taught her about wild plants. I didn't want us to outgrow each other.

Fay said, "Do you hear from your sisters?"

I shrugged. "Oh, well, younger sisters—you know, they want to do everything you do but better."

"Linda's not like that."

"I heard a press in Boston was going to publish her book."

"Yes. She's going to include that poem about the Main Street fire." Several people whom Jill, Fay and Linda had known had died in that fire.

I looked for signs of jealousy, the copycat younger sister trying to steal her older sister's dreams, but saw none. Then Fay spoke again.

"Linda wants to include poems by other people too, you, me. You should give her some to pick from."

"I will."

I left my new poems with Fay and took away a pile of hers to critique. Later that night, having put Jeremy and Justin down, I sat on the couch folding the laundry that I had brought in before dinner. Even in summer, if there was no wind, the clothes dried stiff and scratchy. I rubbed Justin's little terrycloth jumpsuits to soften them up a little, then folded them. A pair of Jeremy's overalls were set aside for mending—he had gone through the knees—and two of my socks that had holes in the toes.

After I finished folding the clothes, I picked up my sewing basket and got out the wooden egg and darning needle. As I wove the needle in and out, creating a webbed patch across the toe, I thought about the conversation with Fay.

Jeremy called out, but he must have been dreaming because when I went to check on him, he had gone back to sleep with the blanket rucked down around his ankles. I straightened it, pulling it up to his chin. Justin had crawled out from under his blanket and turned himself around so that he lay across the top of the crib mattress, his "color blankey" clutched in one hand. I eased him back down under the blanket.

I had switched bedrooms with the boys, giving them the big room at the front of the house and taking the tiny room off the side of the living room for myself. My double bed took up most of the space, along with a table by the bed. The bureau was still in the front room along with the boys' cribs and their things.

It was late, so I put away my sewing things. I liked the small room. Even with its white walls, it felt like a cave, an outlaw's hideout. Sitting down at the table, I picked up my journal.

Without parents, I wrote, *whether through death or neglect, we have no choice but to mother ourselves. We tell ourselves stories that explain the world and teach us how to behave. We tell ourselves stories that comfort us and help us to sleep.*

Less than a week later I heard about the fire at the farm where Fay and Linda had put in a garden the summer before, where the last remnants of their family lived. Jill came down to tell me late one afternoon.

I had been peeling potatoes for dinner. Once a week I tried to have a special dinner that was more than just beans and rice. Jill automatically picked up the peeler and the half-done potato and described the fire while I washed and cut up broccoli. No one knew how it started. The land was untouched, but the house utterly destroyed. I knew from fires in the neighborhood how the stink lingered for days, weeks.

While Jill sliced the potatoes, put them in a pot of water and turned on the burner, I got out a saucepan and heated butter and flour, gradually stirred in milk.

"And that's not the worst of it," Jill said.

I stopped stirring.

Fay and Linda's uncle and grandfather had both died in the fire, she told me. Now the sisters really were the last of their family. They had only each other. And us, of course. I thought about Fay, so feisty, so strong.

"Fay is so brave," I said. I understood that she had to carry it all. No matter how distant I might feel from my parents, they were still there, like some kind of skin, some extra protection between me and the sky. But Fay stood alone, the big sister, with Linda sheltering behind her.

I thought about Fay's chaotic house, full of wood and tools and half-finished projects. She put so much effort into her hard shell, her intricate and indestructible exterior—Fay, with her strong nose, clear eyes, and wiry tomboy strength, daring the world to hit her again.

Jill, washing the cutting board and peeler, looked over at me. "I don't know how close they were to the uncle and grandfather, but it's got to be hard."

I cut up cheese into the white sauce and added a little red pepper.

"Yum," Jill said, looking over my shoulder at the potatoes. "I have to get back upstairs to the kids."

I could hear my boys in the living room whispering under the tent they had made by draping a sheet over the furniture. I couldn't help worrying a little for my boys; I was so afraid for them. What would become of them if something happened to me? Feminism's call to be your real self—not sacrificing who you could be in service to someone else—resonated with me. But my boys were already here. They didn't ask to be born. And they had only me.

The bubbling of the pot drew me back. I stepped into the bathroom to blow my nose and wash my face.

I drained the potatoes, dumped them into a baking dish, added the cheese sauce, and set the whole thing in the oven. I put the broccoli on to steam and went to get the boys for dinner.

A week later I heard a noise at the front door. When Sherry brought Jeremy home, she usually came around to the back, like everyone else, but she had borrowed the stroller and knew that I kept it in the front hall.

I crossed the dank hallway to let them in. It had been a chilly, grey day, not like summer at all.

Jeremy and Rora with their matching red cheeks grabbed my legs in a quick hug.

"The park was great!" Jeremy said, and the two of them were off to the bedroom. I could hear them pulling toys out of the cardboard box.

I lifted Justin out of the stroller, and he snuggled against me. Sherry set the stroller by the staircase and followed us inside.

"How are you feeling?" she asked.

"Much better." My head was still stuffed up, but a nap had helped.

"Summer colds are the worst."

Divested of his jacket, Justin gave me a strangling hug and then toddled off to see what the big kids were doing. I collapsed into the chair.

Sherry folded up onto the sofa, long legs crossed under her. She leaned forward, a grin on her broad face. "I met the nicest person in the park. She was telling me about this new health food store that's going to open."

Her voice seemed to come from far away. Everyone she met was wonderful. Why was I so prickly? So afraid of everyone?

There was a knock at the back door. I went to open it and found Fay and Hamid.

"We called to you from down the street," Fay said to Sherry. "Guess you didn't hear us."

"How are you?" I said. It was the first time I'd seen her since the fire.

"Fine." She wrestled Hamid's jacket off, and he ran to find the other kids.

I put on water for tea. We sat around the kitchen table while Fay and Sherry talked about the new health food store. I asked if it was going to take food stamps.

Sherry turned to me with a look of concern. "You still sound really congested. Do you want me to take the boys overnight?"

"No, I'll be alright, but thanks."

Fay started reeling off cold remedies, asking me if I had hyssop and offering to splurge on a lemon for me.

"No chicken soup?" I teased.

"Motherless children," Fay reminded me. "Someone's got to take care of you."

"I don't understand," Sherry said.

So Fay explained about the Adrienne Rich essay we'd read. "You really need to read it," she finished, as Rora ran into the room and started pulling on Sherry.

"At least we're not childrenless mothers," Sherry said, hugging Rora briefly before the child ran off again.

The light went out of Fay's eyes, and she looked out of the window with desolation in her face.

Sherry and Rora left soon after that, but Fay lingered. Hamid and Justin were playing quietly in the living room with Jeremy, building something with blocks.

It was disconcerting to see Fay so silent. She seemed so slight, sitting there, pale as a wraith. I thought about the baby, the one she'd lost. How did you survive an intolerable loss like that?

"Remember when I was pregnant with Jeremy, and you were too? You never told me what happened with the baby," I said warily, ready to back away if she didn't want to talk about it.

Fay wrapped her arms around herself. "No, I guess not."

"Are you cold? I can turn on some heat." I gestured toward the stove.

She sighed. "No, it's okay." Her face seemed to empty. "You remember how we were both going to that clinic on Main Street?"

"That place!" I said. "I was so unhappy with them that I decided to go somewhere else, thinking I had another month before Jeremy would pop out. When I started labor two days later, Lewis and I had to go to the ER and take whoever was there. I wasn't letting anyone from that place touch me again."

"You did the right thing."

"Well, it was partly knowing you were so mad at them, even though I didn't know the details. It was a month before Jeremy was born, wasn't it?"

"Yes," Fay said, looking out the window again. "I went into the clinic with contractions. I knew my labor was starting but they left me sitting there. By the time someone saw me, hours it was, hours." Fay sat up a little straighter. "By that time, the contractions had stopped."

"I heard they can come and go."

"Well, I demanded that the doctor—he was really only a physician's assistant—give me something to start them up again, or do some tests or something, but he said it was just false labor and sent me home." She paused, her shoulders tensing up.

"But you knew something was wrong," I prompted.

"She wasn't moving anymore. All that night. And she had been so active. I couldn't feel anything. I kept touching my stomach, feeling for a kicking foot, like maybe I simply hadn't noticed. Maybe she was moving and I just couldn't feel it—too scared, too used to it, too looking for it."

I thought of that long night, lying there in the darkness, the fear seeping in, growing. I thought of Fay wondering if something was wrong, thinking it must be, then sure it couldn't be, but gradually becoming convinced that, yes, something was seriously wrong with the baby.

She looked at me. Her sadness fell away as her eyes grew hard. "I went back to the clinic in the morning, and they said the baby was dead."

"They induced you then? You still had to go through labor, all that pain, knowing the baby was dead?"

"Yes." She smacked her fist on the table. "They should have done it when I told them to. Doctors! They think they know everything. It was my body. I *knew*. I should have made them. If I hadn't given up, if I'd had the money for a real doctor, my baby would still be alive."

I leaned forward and put an arm around her tight shoulders. She didn't shake it off. I remembered my mother saying *I danced with boys who went off to The War the next day*, and began to understand about needing to be in control.

Hamid and Justin came running in, holding hands and laughing. I lifted my arm from Fay's shoulder as they let go of each other and collapsed against our knees.

"Ma," Hamid said, looking up with the grin that transformed his face, "come see what we made."

She ruffled his dark curly hair. "Sure, honey. Show me."

13
SMALL CLAIMS

During the day I was too busy to think, but night was a different matter. Back when Lewis and I were splitting up, he had threatened to go to court to get custody of Jeremy, sure that the judge would see him as the better parent, being employed and all. He could then deny being Justin's father and avoid any question of child support. Though I never believed he would actually go through with any of these threats, I was still afraid to go anywhere near a courtroom. During the year we had been apart, I had not taken any steps to formalize our separation. Sometimes in the darkness, I lay awake arguing with him in my head, but didn't get any further than that.

One day I got an angry letter from Lewis. He'd heard about Celia being wrecked—over a year ago at that point—and not only berated me for being irresponsible but accused me and Alan, the man to whom I'd loaned the car, of being lovers. I tore up the letter. I decided that enough was enough and made an appointment with a Legal Aid lawyer to talk about getting a divorce.

I was nervous about going, even though several of my friends had gotten excellent help from Legal Aid. In addition to everything I'd heard about how dishonest lawyers were, I was nearly paralyzed by the fear that getting involved with the legal system would somehow end up with my kids being taken away. But then, thinking of Fay's courage, I felt ashamed of my cowardice.

When the day came, I bundled the kids into the stroller and walked downtown. Whatever other fears I might have, I was never afraid to walk around my neighborhood. The houses may have been shabby and the cars pitted with rust, but there was very little crime. People often left their houses unlocked. As far as I could tell, there wasn't much in the way of drugs, some marijuana and speed but little else. Also, we had a motorcycle gang—based in an abandoned warehouse around the corner from us—who seemed to keep the peace.

Once inside the Legal Aid building, my boys enjoyed the ride up the elevator with its heavy brass doors. Ushered into a small, stuffy office with dingy windows, we found a man in his thirties impatiently tapping a pen on a legal pad.

"Come in. Let's go. Divorce, huh?" he said.

I sat on a chair facing the desk, Justin on my lap. Jeremy set off to explore the room, running his hand over the spines of the books.

"Don't touch anything," the man said to him. Then he smiled at me. "Okay, we'll get this taken care of, no problem."

"Great," I said.

"Now, we're really going to put the screws on this guy. Don't worry! We'll get him."

"No," I said sharply, making Justin wriggle to get down. I leaned over and set him on the rug. "No, I don't want to get him. I just want to undo the legal tie with the least amount of hassle for everyone."

"Marriage: easy to get into, hard to get out of. People should look at the divorce laws before they get married. Now, he can divorce you for not keeping the house clean, or you can divorce him for not providing financial support, but not vice versa."

"That's not right."

"Doesn't matter. We can get him for non-support."

"You're not listening. I don't want to get him." I explained about Kevin, and Lewis's fear that court-ordered child support could lead to Kevin's being taken away from him.

The lawyer threw down the pen and leaned forward. "Look here, we have to go after these deadbeat dads. They're scum. We have to make an example out of them whenever we can, dumping their brats for society to support."

Jeremy tugged at my arm. "Why is he so angry? Who's scum?"

"Hush. I'll tell you later," I said and turned back to the lawyer, struggling to keep from getting angry myself. "You don't understand. He doesn't have any money. There's no point in going after him. Even if I wanted to, and I don't."

"Doesn't matter what you want. Anyway, these guys always have money," he said, picking up his pen again and tapping it.

"But he doesn't . . ."

"You!" He looked at me angrily. "You welfare moms are too lazy to fight when you can sit back and get a check without doing anything. Then it comes out of my paycheck instead of his."

Justin started to cry.

The man sighed. "Look I'll make it easy for you. Sign these papers, and I'll take care of everything."

"Okay, that's enough." I stood up. "You know what? Just forget it!"

"No sweat. Less work for me." The lawyer smiled and sat back, as I stormed out with the kids.

The boys were the center of my life. They woke me up in the morning, and as soon as I got them settled at night I fell into bed myself. They played around me while I worked in the garden—Jill and I had planted peas and radishes as soon as it got warm—and came with us when we went out to Spag's to get scraggly on-sale tomato plants whose overgrown branches trailed along the ground and shot out their sharp odor whenever someone brushed by them.

The garden was easier the second summer. While still hoping to give much of it away, I insisted that we plant less squash and chard. Jill wanted to try corn and cucumbers. Jeremy begged for pumpkins.

It was the Bicentennial year, 1976, so there were lots of activities in town. I walked the kids to Institute Park for the band concerts and watched them dance around to Sousa marches. I wheeled the stroller downtown for the Fourth of July parade, and bought the boys little American flags to wave.

Wherever we went, we ran into other welfare moms I had gotten to know over the past year, all of us taking advantage of the free activities. We all struggled—there was no doubt about that—but in Worcester I didn't see the kind of grinding poverty I had glimpsed from car windows back in Baltimore, nor the kind of crime that dominated the newscasts there. Worcester was still small and isolated. Drugs hadn't really taken hold.

Also, Worcester had a lot to offer even if you didn't have money: parks, college campuses, trees on every street. Even the poorest streets had lilacs and mountain laurels, sometimes an apricot or pear tree.

But the main difference was that welfare moms could actually survive on the Massachusetts welfare allotment, because it was one of the highest in the country. This was surely thanks, in part, to Jill and Melinda and the Welfare Rights Organization. What little I knew about poverty in Baltimore may have been exaggerated as it filtered through the media, but perhaps not, given how much smaller the checks were there.

Worcester was small, more manageable somehow than Baltimore or Boston, although I had gotten to know several welfare moms in Roxbury when I had been thinking about moving there, and they seemed much like me: just trying to get by and keep their families together, hoping their kids didn't grow out of their shoes too fast.

It helped that we lived in a mixed community rather than the projects. Aside from a few of us welfare moms, our neighborhood consisted mostly of people who went off to work every day, even if only in their rusted-out trucks with rakes and shovels sticking up in back.

And then too, I had a lot of advantages starting out: I was healthy and educated. I was accustomed to the world of work, and knew I could fit in if I could only solve the child care conundrum. I could sew and cook and knew a lot about nutrition, which gave me some options. Most of all I had Jill, whose advice and support carried me over the rough times.

As we had the previous summer, the kids and I spent a lot of time at Elm Park. Situated amid middle-class and upper-middle-class neighborhoods, it drew families from all socio-economic levels. I liked it because it gave the boys a chance to run around and play with other children. In between watching the boys play in the sand pit, pushing them on the swings and chatting with the other moms, I soaked up the peaceful scenery: wide green lawns dotted with oak trees, clusters of rhododendrons and azaleas. There was a string of ponds with little islands where ducks and white swans nested, connected by wooden footbridges where the boys liked to play Pooh-sticks, throwing sticks off one side of the bridge and then racing to the other in time to see the sticks float out from under the bridge.

One day, Jeremy climbed onto a blue plastic fish that was set on a spring, and started rocking back and forth. He had on shorts and strappy sandals like Christopher Robin's. Imaginative in his mischief, he was always getting into scrapes, like persuading some big kid to sit on the other end of the see-saw and then not understanding why he couldn't get his end back down to the ground.

Justin asked if he could feed the ducks. I gave him some bread and watched him walk to the edge of the pond. He was a tiny little thing with blond hair sticking up all over reminding me of the Little Prince. Like that character, he seemed untouched by the world, yet seeing everything so clearly. The large white swans paddled over and scooped up the bread crumbs he threw into the water.

Then Jeremy ran over to Justin, yelling for bread. When Justin held up his empty hands, Jeremy started saying something. I couldn't hear what it was because his back was towards me, but I could tell from Justin's face that it was not pleasant.

I stood up, but before I could say anything, Jeremy started backing up. Behind Justin, the swans had started to come up out of the water. Craning their necks high, they were almost as tall as Justin as they surrounded him and continued forward towards Jeremy. Two of them suddenly stretched their wings out and reached forward with their long necks.

Letting out a yelp, Jeremy turned and ran towards me.

Then the swans settled down onto the grass, preening their feathers. Justin stood among them, his back very straight, looking at us with his little half-smile. Then he walked through them to where Jeremy and I stood.

"Did that just happen?" Jeremy asked.

"I don't know," I said.

It was a long time before Jeremy teased his brother again.

I wrote a poem about the swans and how baffled I was by this strange child. I was working on several stories too. I never stopped dreaming of getting off of welfare but knew writing would never pay the bills. And what would I do with the boys? How would I find the time or energy to work?

My check and food stamps were late again, which meant another trip to the welfare office. I packed up some toys and books, stowed the boys in the double stroller, and set off to walk downtown.

It took a couple of hours to get there on foot, and the waiting area was already full when we arrived. Nothing could be done over the phone, and the office was understaffed. We weren't allowed to make an appointment in advance; instead, we had to wait in a corner of the room next to the staircase where there were a row of folding metal chairs. With no play area for the children, it was a constant struggle to keep them occupied and away from the open stairs. I ended up getting out all the toys I'd packed to keep the boys entertained, which they shared with the other children.

The social worker we finally saw tracked down the problem and said I'd get my check in a week. I pointed out that it was already one week late, and I was almost out of food stamps and cash, having only a few dollars left from the previous month. She told me that I should have budgeted better.

It was mid-afternoon by the time I wrestled the stroller down the stairs and back out onto the street. The sun was ferocious. Jeremy complained about being hot so I got him to sing Old MacDonald with me to distract him.

On the way home, we stopped at Goodwill, where I found a pair of corduroy overalls with snaps that worked and knees that weren't even worn out. But they cost a dollar. I wheeled the boys over to the counter and explained about my check being late.

"What do you have?" the young woman asked.

I emptied my purse: eighty-three cents. After some negotiating, we settled on thirty-five cents.

Then I went to Stop and Shop to get an onion and two carrots to go with the beans. Catching sight of his favorite fruit, Jeremy said, "Bee-nay! Please? We want bee-nays." He could say *banana* perfectly well but preferred his own word.

I had only five dollars in food stamps left and another week to get through, but the boys had been good, and we still had a long walk home. "Okay," I said, breaking off two. "A special treat."

At the checkout counter, I set down the bananas, onion and carrots. A woman with a cart piled high with food nudged into line behind me. When I got out my food stamps, I heard her snort.

"Lazy welfare mothers," she said to no one in particular. "They should get a job."

The morris team had stopped practices for the summer, but I hadn't forgotten our new-found friendship. Meeting up with Cynthia or Janet at contra dances, I made an effort to talk more about my life. I realized that I had to make myself pervious in order to connect.

Cynthia was surprised to see me flirting with my partners. "We thought you were a lesbian," she said.

"I was married, you know."

She waved that away and pointed out that I never talked about boyfriends or seemed attracted to men. "Of course," she added, "we don't know very much about you."

I conceded that it was my fault for not telling them more about myself. However, there was still nothing I could say when they started talking about boyfriends. For all Lewis had another girlfriend, I myself didn't expect to meet someone else. If I couldn't make marriage to this man I loved so much work, then I never could. I figured I had stood alone my whole life, even in the midst of a large family and a crowd of college friends. That was just the way it was going to be.

Also, having two children seemed very different from having one. With Jeremy, I had tried to fit him into my life (*our lives*, I thought sadly), but with two children I knew that I had to organize my life around theirs. The things that I wanted to do—read, talk with Jill about politics, write poetry, listen to music without distractions—had to be squeezed into the furtive corners of a baby-centered life.

Sherry sometimes teased me about Ben, calling him my boyfriend. It was true that we had become friends. I liked the house he shared with Mac and Mac's family out in Sterling. Ben often helped me with my car, showing me how to fix things, lending me his tools, but I wasn't sure what I felt or really what was going on between us. His reticence seemed impenetrable and my own heart still frozen.

One day in July, Fay brought Hamid over to play. Jill was there too, having come down to let me know that Jeremy was upstairs with Richard and Michael. Fay joined us at the kitchen table, as Hamid ran to Justin.

Hamid looked like a cherub with his round cheeks and dark, curly hair, but he had his mother's passionate nature. When angry or puzzled, he had a scowl that twisted his whole face and made you want to do anything to make him laugh again. Laughing transformed him. Scrunching up his face, he radiated an infectious and irresistible joy. He attached himself to Justin with a loyalty that never wavered. They didn't argue, as Jeremy and Rora sometimes did. Hamid shared all his toys with Justin, as Justin did with him.

Hamid wasn't jealous when other children came to play with them, readily including them in any games. Adults were another matter. He was always pulling Justin away from us, the women sitting at the kitchen table or park bench. Justin let us cuddle him, but Hamid would squirm away and refuse to be hugged, pulling on Justin, saying, "Come on. Let's go play."

While the one-year-olds pulled pots out of the cupboards and banged them on the floor, stacking them up and pushing them over, we talked about fires. Fay read aloud her sister Linda's poem about her six friends who died in the Main Street fire the year before. I didn't know them, but Jill and Fay did. I had seen the photos. After reading the poem, Fay sat there with the papers in her lap, absently tracing the words with one finger. The anger that usually drove her fell away for a moment.

I asked if the Main Street fire had been caused by arson, but Jill said that it was because there were some other tenants living there who had no fire safety awareness; they threw lit cigarettes on the floor. "There was this one woman," Jill said. "I know where she's living now. And she's still doing the same things. She punched a fireman who tried to reason with her."

I was shocked. "Punched him?"

"That's right. It's the landlord I blame," Jill said, speaking deliberately, as she always did when she was truly angry, her voice cold. "He kept renting to them. He knew what they were like, and he kept renting to them."

Fay agreed. "It wasn't like he hadn't been warned." She slid the papers into her bag and sat up, pushing her heavy blond hair out of her face. Hamid abandoned the pots to come over and lean against her leg. She put an arm around him absently.

Justin too left the pots and ran over to us. He climbed onto Jill's lap and sat there quietly watching us as we talked about Jill's old landlord on Piedmont Street who had threatened to torch the house, and another house up near Main where there were so many fires that people were afraid to rent the apartments no matter how cheap they were.

Fay lifted her head and seemed to regain her confidence, along with the fierce conviction that she knew what was best, not only for herself and Hamid, but for everyone. "I wouldn't be surprised if your landlord burned this house down," she said. "You should move."

"Usually," Jill said, "the landlord will come by to warn people, you know, to get their stuff out and go somewhere else."

"I wouldn't count on that," Fay said. "Those scumbags don't care what happens to you."

I wrote in my journal: *I would hate to leave this place, the first home that is really mine. It's been my fort against the world, but fire could easily breach it. We hold our lives in our hands. Our decisions—and those made without our knowledge or consent—could mean life or death.*

I started dreaming about fires and would wake up hour after hour to smell the air. It was 1976, when almost no one had smoke alarms, certainly no one in poor neighborhoods like mine. I was vividly aware of the number of empty lots I could see with my own eyes, the scorch marks on buildings, and the photos of the Main Street fire, especially the one showing a woman's body dangling upside down, being lowered by a crane, ropes tied to splayed feet, dark hair hanging wild over her face.

I didn't trust our landlord. Friendly when we first met him, he had become invisible, refusing to respond to maintenance requests. The garage that was on the verge of tumbling down had never been fixed, as he'd promised, so we couldn't use it and had to constantly caution the children to stay away from it. I knew I ought to throw off the lethargy of what was familiar and move someplace safer. It was hard, though, to make the change.

Jill, Erica and I debated holding back our rent until the repairs were made. Before we could decide, though, we all received registered letters.

I knew a registered letter couldn't be anything but bad news. My mind flashed to Lewis's custody threats, the social worker at the hospital, the welfare office. But it concerned none of these.

The letter was from a local bank saying that it had repossessed the house, and henceforward we should send our rent checks to them. As it turned out, our landlord simply hadn't bothered to pay the mortgage, a not uncommon practice for absentee landlords in poor neighborhoods: pocketing the rents while not investing anything in either maintenance or the mortgage. It was all profit, at least until the bank took over the house. And, oh by the way, the bank's letter went on, when our leases ran out we'd have to leave.

I didn't understand. "Why wouldn't they want three good tenants who keep the place up and pay the rent on time?" I asked Jill.

"It's easier to sell an empty house. They can do a few cosmetic fixes and then sell it to someone who can choose his own tenants and set his own rents."

"They aren't going to get anybody better than us in a neighborhood like this," I stubbornly maintained.

"What I'm more worried about," said Jill, "is our security deposits."

The bottom dropped out of my stomach. "But if they've taken on the leases, they have to honor the whole thing."

"You'd think. But I don't trust them."

And she was right not to. The bank admitted that there was no damage to the apartments but claimed that as they had never received our security deposits, they couldn't give them back. After prolonged arguments with several people at the bank, we realized that we were in trouble.

"Jill, I don't have another hundred dollars for a security deposit," I said. "I'm not going to be able to get another apartment when they kick us out of here."

"Me either," she said, looking down at her coffee mug. We'd both fallen off the no-caffeine wagon during this crisis. "Or Erica, I'm sure."

"What do they expect us to do? Live in a cardboard box?"

"They don't care what happens to us."

I thought for a minute. "Without an apartment, welfare will cut us off. Then we'll never be able to get together the money for a security deposit on another place."

"That's true. And it's not like we can ask someone to loan us the money. Who would we ask? How would we ever pay it back? My mother barely scrapes by on her Social Security."

Jill's mention of her mother made me think of my own. The money would be nothing to her, a fraction of what she spent in a single shopping trip to Hecht's or Hoschild Kohn, but she had never offered to help me financially, so I hadn't asked. Our relationship was tenuous enough, and she would surely refuse anyway, claiming her own "poverty". Our last phone conversation had been devoted to my mother's complaints about how poor they were, so poor that they could not afford to buy a summer home on the Chesapeake Bay.

An even harder task would be to break through my mother's refusal to admit that I was on welfare. She continued to maintain a fiction that I was living some splendid middle-class life similar to hers.

"You know," Jill said, "it's risky, but we could refuse to leave. Be squatters. People do it all the time. Stay an extra month and use the rent we would have paid as a security deposit for the next place. The only problem would be if welfare found out."

I looked around my kitchen, the white walls, the windows out to the side yard and beyond it to the grey house where our gardening friend lived. "I don't want to leave."

Jill tilted her head and smiled sympathetically. "Me either. Another possibility is to withhold the rent till they agree, put it in a separate account, escrow. But then they might come and toss us out on the street. Pile up all our stuff on the curb and bolt the doors."

I sighed. "I'm with you that we have to fight this thing. I just wish there were some way to do it legally, so we don't put ourselves in the wrong or find ourselves out in the street."

Jill grinned wickedly. "Well, we could try Small Claims Court. After all, it worked for me with that garage."

So the three of us went down and filed our claim against the bank. As the court date approached, we began scouring our friends' closets for proper clothing to wear. Jill wanted to go in our normal clothes to show how poor we were, dressed in castoffs dredged out of the sour-smelling racks at Goodwill. But I argued that the judge might see informal attire as disrespectful.

Our friends responded quickly. We did this all the time: assembling a reasonably formal outfit for someone who had to go to court or a job interview. None of us had a full set of good clothes, but Sherry had a nice skirt, Fay a blouse, and so on.

Come the day, Jill, Erica and I were formally, if uncomfortably, dressed as we rode up the brass elevator in the courthouse. Our kids had remained at home with Sherry, which added to the uneasy feeling in my gut. I couldn't think of a time when the three of us had ever gone out together without the children.

The courtroom smelled of dust. There were tall windows filmed with dirt and drooping flags that looked like they'd never been moved. When it was our turn, the three of us stood by our table with no legal pads or pens, only a manila folder with copies of our leases, rent receipts, and the letters from the bank. I was dismayed to see that at the other table there were four lawyers in expensive-looking suits clustered around the man from the bank.

I whispered to Jill that we didn't have a chance.

Jill whispered back, "They're spending more money on one minute of those lawyers' time than it would have cost them to give us back our security deposits."

Erica leaned over from Jill's far side. "At least we have that satisfaction," she said grimly. "Even if we lose, we're costing them an arm and a leg."

The bang of the gavel shut us up. The judge, a tired-looking heavyset man in his fifties had us all approach. I was too nervous to open my mouth and Erica too angry, so we let Jill speak for us. When she handed over the paperwork, the nearest lawyer shrank away from her arm as though he might catch something.

The judge then turned to the lawyers and let them state the bank's case. I thought we were doomed. They were so polished. They spoke the lingo. Who were we, a trio of poor women, to think that we could take them on? We didn't know anything about the law.

Clearly they thought the same thing, speaking with self-confidence bordering on arrogance. The man from the bank smirked at us triumphantly.

When they were finished, the judge shuffled the papers in front of him and tapped them into an even pile. Then he frowned at the group of men in their fancy suits and said, "You know perfectly well that when you took over the house, you took over the debts as well. You ought to be ashamed of yourselves for trying to trick these women." Not only did they have to give us our security deposits, he went on, but they also had to pay all the court costs.

The three of us looked at each other in shock for a long minute before thanking the judge so effusively that he had to wave us off in order to move on to the next case.

We celebrated with hot fudge sundaes at Friendly's. Seeing the three of us all dressed up in borrowed court clothes, the waitress asked what the occasion was. When we told her, gleefully repeating the judge's words, she laughed out loud. When she brought us our sundaes—the cheapest ones on the menu—we found that she had slipped in an extra half-scoop of ice cream and put a second cherry on top.

14

APPEARANCES

The next step was to find somewhere else to live. It was hard for me to imagine leaving my garden and the white rooms where Jeremy and I had welcomed Justin into our lives. Like a snail whose shell has been ripped away, I trembled, afraid of losing the fragile happiness I had found here. It had been a year and nine months since that winter night when I had finally accepted that I would have to go on welfare, holding Jeremy while the darkness closed in. Orphans of the storm, babes in the wood . . . I had grown up a lot since then. Not only had I created a home, but opened it to out-of-town friends—Jim, Walt, Christine—and to Worcester friends whose children had come to seem like my own.

Sweeping the kitchen floor after lunch made me wonder how many more times I would clean that speckled linoleum, but by the time I had finished, I had shaken off my premature nostalgia. After all, we had taken on the lawyers and won. We could make another garden. I was no longer sitting like a lump on the stoop, but standing up to people who threatened us.

Erica and Andrew found another place to live and moved out. Jill and I wanted to live in the same building, which made our search more difficult. Finally, in August of 1976 we found a house with three apartments for rent on West Street, only a few blocks away.

West Street ran between Pleasant and Highland streets. When Jill and I first turned onto it from Pleasant's crowded lanes and dreary shopfronts, West Street stunned us with its beauty. Many of the houses belonged to Becker Junior College, identified by discreet signs next to the front steps. Becker was a commuter school, hidden away in a few square blocks of side streets.

All of the houses looked freshly painted. The small yards were planted with azaleas and chrysanthemums that even in late August were well-tended. Although the houses were mostly triple-deckers, there was one large apartment building made of yellow brick about halfway down the street, and across from it a farm store with a free-standing metal sign advertising Polar soft drinks. Maple trees lined both sides of the street, casting a welcome shade over the asphalt.

Predictably, though, the house we came to see—the one in our price range— was the most unattractive and dilapidated one. A plain wooden house with peeling grey paint, it squatted on a brick foundation, surrounded by a narrow frame of ground, not more than a couple of feet wide and full of plantains and dandelions gone to seed. At the front of the house, the first two floors had small porches and bay windows. The third floor had a deep gable, while other gables continued around the sides, each with a double window. In the back, all three floors had dark enclosed porches with a round spiderweb of clothesline hanging off each one.

On the plus side, though, the house was on the corner, providing a little extra privacy. The back of Elm Park Community School was right across the street, which promised an easy walk for Richard and Michael and a view of playing fields for us.

Also, the houses around it were well-kept. The house next door boasted a clipped privet hedge, pear and quince trees, and forsythia bushes. Fruit trees were not uncommon in the back yards of Worcester's triple-deckers, a legacy of the immigrant families who had settled there.

When I entered the first floor apartment, dismay filled me. It felt like a cave, the air dank and musty. What was clearly the original wallpaper—mauve gone to brown with faint tracings of taupe flowers—hung off the walls in sheets, revealing pock-marked plaster beneath. The floors were hardwood, though, and the windows fitted with storms.

It was larger than the Newbury Street apartment, with a double living room, the large one at the front of the house with the bay window across its width, and then an archway leading to the small parlor where the space heater crouched. On one side of that room was a large bedroom, while a door in the far wall led to the kitchen. Off the kitchen were the bathroom, a smaller bedroom, a minuscule pantry, and the door to the back hall.

Clearly the place had never been renovated. It looked like something out of the Forties. The kitchen floor had never seen linoleum; it was plain bare wood, the varnish mostly worn away. The moldings throughout the apartment were unpainted, still stained a dark brown.

For all its windows, the apartment seemed dark, but I hoped that white walls might change that. And anyway, we were running out of time to get out of Newbury Street, so I took the first floor; Jill the second; and my friend Gloria and her husband the third.

I had met Gloria at Elm Park. Her son Nathan was the same age as Justin and the two of them had fallen immediately into a natural companionship, pursuing their endless construction games in the sandbox, sharing bread to feed to the ducks and swans, demanding simultaneously to be pushed on the swings.

Next to me on the park bench, Gloria sat up very straight, her lips compressed, one arm curved protectively around the slight swelling of her abdomen. Six-months pregnant, she was strung very tightly. She kept her eyes on Nathan and her limbs still, one elegant hand with long tapered fingers resting lightly on her thigh.

"You have the most beautiful hands," I said.

There was an appealing vulnerability in the way she ducked her chin and looked up sideways before speaking. "I used to work as a hand model for commercials," she said apologetically. She gave a short, self-deprecating laugh and held up one hand, examining its reddened knuckles. "No one would hire me now, would they? Too much dishwater, too many diapers."

Despite her complaints, she seemed to me to have it easy: married, able to stay home with Nathan while Wayne worked. I could never keep straight what he did. It seemed as though he had a different job every time I talked with Gloria, working with a friend's construction company one month, at an auto parts store another.

When I told her I was on welfare, she didn't say anything, just sat on the park bench with her mouth tightly closed, hands folded. I explained about separating from Lewis and my parents' refusal to help me, leaving me with no other choice.

"I would never go on welfare," she said. But then she smiled and opened one hand, palm up. "I understand, though. It's not easy."

She and I initially became friends because of Nathan and Justin, but then discovered that we shared an interest in the music of words. Gloria had grown up in Boston, frequenting the clubs and coffeeshops, and she dreamed of being the girl with a guitar singing onstage. She wrote songs that she would not sing for me, saying they weren't finished yet. I gave her my poetry to read, but all she would say was that the poems were good; I was never sure what that meant. Still, Gloria and I shared our favorite books and records with each other, and talked non-stop whenever we met in the park.

When an argument broke out in the sandbox, Gloria rose in a single graceful movement and went over to the children where she knelt down and kissed Nathan on the top of his head.

"Nathan, you must not take other children's toys," she articulated carefully as she took the contested Tonka truck away and restored it to its owner.

I watched Gloria walk back. Tall and slim—aside from the bulge of her pregnancy—she moved with the careful precision of royalty. Her beauty was intimidating, to be sure, those long legs in jeans, the slim neck rising out of her frilly blouse, the exuberantly curling black hair that cascaded down to her shoulders. But her regal carriage was at odds with her accent, the way her vowels opened up and overwhelmed the nearby consonants.

Jeremy planted himself in front of her. "Are you a countess?" he demanded.

She let out a spurt of laughter, and her long fingers moved as if to grab it back. "No," she said. "I'm not any kind of royalty. I grew up in South Boston. We didn't have money, much less tiaras."

"Okay," Jeremy said and turned back to the other children.

Gloria's eyes still gleamed with amusement as she turned toward me. "What an imagination!"

I shrugged. I thought she had dramatic beauty of Eustacia Vye from Thomas Hardy's *Return of the Native*.

She looked back to the sandpit where the children were playing. "Zack called me last night and talked for hours. I didn't turn out the light until two o'clock." Zack was an old friend of Wayne and Gloria's. Obese to start with, he had grown so huge in recent years that he was no longer able to leave the house. He called Gloria often to talk about his problems. She seemed to like taking care of people.

I didn't want to be taken care of, but I did want to get to know her better, so I was glad she and Wayne were moving in upstairs.

There was a painting at the Worcester Art Museum by Childe Hassam that fascinated me. A woman in a deep turquoise Chinese robe sat on a chair peeling an orange from a bowl of fruit on a round wooden table. Behind her stretched large windows veiled by filmy curtains, pale in color, but deepening to blue in their folds. Beyond the curtains, barely visible, you could discern the outlines of skyscrapers and dark boxy buildings.

Given a view of the dark machinery of the city, the woman had created her own world. She had hidden the brutal ugliness with light wisps of curtains, curtains like dreams, like Corot's wash of grey-green leaves on slender silver trees.

Inside her world were the brilliant turquoise of her robe, the warm brown of the wood, the spicy smell of orange peel, the filtered light. There was no sound of cars or sirens; of that I was sure. Perhaps the delicate counterpoint of a trio sonata.

Still buoyed by our victory over the bank, I was determined to make another home for us. After stripping off the old wallpaper, which came away in long sheets without even needing a steamer, I painted the apartment walls white. The move itself went smoothly, with the help of our friends, including Dan and his truck. The kids got the big bedroom off the parlor and I took the little back room for my own.

Gloria and I did some reciprocal child care. It was not a bad thing for my sons to have multiple parents, though I wondered how they would react to having Wayne upstairs. There weren't many men in our world, not many married couples. Wayne mostly left the childcare to Gloria, he explained with his wide friendly grin, glasses slipping so he had to tilt his head up to see me.

"It's not that I'm against women's rights, but this works out better for us," he said, pushing his glasses back up. "I'd rather be staying at home all day lazing around with the kids, but somebody has to work."

I liked his openness and decided to leave it at that; it was none of my business how they worked out their marriage. I was relieved to find that Jeremy and Justin busied themselves with their games and ignored Wayne. I wanted them to know more men, but wasn't sure he was the role model I would have picked for them.

I was conscious that my choices affected their lives too, a responsibility that unnerved me. I felt safe in my world of women, so although I met men through dancing, I didn't get involved with anyone. Cynthia had said they thought I was a lesbian. Christine believed I was still heartsore about Lewis. They were both wrong. It was simply easier for me to be on my own. A boyfriend would just be someone else to take care of, I told myself. To Christine, I joked that when I wanted to get married again, I'd find some rich guy who could support us.

Jill said that statistically marriage was the most common way for women with kids too young for school to get off of welfare, though she herself didn't expect she would ever marry. Marriage and my kids being old enough for school seemed equally far away. I wanted a job, impossible as that sometimes seemed.

Ben started coming over fairly often, at first to work on my car or Jill's and then simply to visit. There was a stillness about him as he sat over a cup of tea at the kitchen table that was at odds with his relentless work ethic. When he worked on Patience, I tried to work alongside him, hoping to learn more about car repair.

Once, the screwdriver kept slipping off a screw buried deep in the engine, and I complained, "If I could only see it!"

Ben, imperturbable, said, "Do it by feel."

"I can't."

"Sure you can. Close your eyes. Take your time."

The screw turned easily. "Are you always right?" I asked.

He grinned.

Although I did learn a lot, it was hard to keep up with him as he worked on and on without a break. I had to keep stopping to see to the kids.

Jeremy was disappointed that Ben never wanted to roughhouse with him, the kind of physical, rolling-on-the-floor play that he couldn't get me to do. Jeremy had come to expect that all male visitors would be willing participants in these wild wrestling games. However, both he and Justin adored Ben who treated them with a gentle courtesy that made them respond in kind, with a maturity that surprised me.

Soon after moving to West Street Jill and I found out that our applications for Section 8 housing assistance were finally being processed. It had been almost two years since we had applied, but Jill said even this waiting period was short. She thought that some kind social worker must have gotten things moving.

If we could get Section 8, we would really be on easy street: the government would pay our rent, freeing up a big chunk of our checks that we could then use for something else. Rent was our biggest expense—except for heat, which in the winter was almost half again as much as the rent each month—so the stakes were high. The only hitch was the inspection. Of course we couldn't be trusted to create a home ourselves; we had to have someone check up on us.

When your name came up for housing assistance, they sent an inspector, ostensibly to make sure that the building itself was safe and up to code, but really (I'd been warned) to see if you deserved it. You had to be "good" poor to qualify. You had to be both humble (no backtalk) and proud (meaning clean).

Angry as I was over the stereotypes that fueled this intrusion into our privacy, I knew there was no point in trying to argue. We needed the money too badly.

The inspection was simply one more obstacle. Seething inside, I scrubbed every surface and stashed stuff at friends' houses. One of the things that had surprised me about being poor was how much stuff we accumulated. I was afraid to throw anything out. It wasn't as though I could replace it, especially if it was something that food stamps didn't cover. Even cheap hand lotion had become an extravagance.

So the corners of the apartment filled up, not only with the garbage bags of hand-me-down clothes intended for the kids as they got bigger, but also tins of old nails and bolts, torn sheets that I could mend or use to make curtains, and of course the piles of paper: used envelopes, old flyers. In those days, when I walked through department stores and drugstores too poor to buy anything, I reused every scrap of paper. A pad of paper, a whole pad completely fresh and new, was a luxury I couldn't afford.

Gloria helped me sort and clean, taking some things upstairs to store for me. One afternoon as we sat over tea in her kitchen, with the children running in and out, I complained about the necessity of prettying up our lives for these intruders.

"That's what happens," Gloria said, her long fingers wrapped around the warm mug. "If you take their money, they have the right to tell you how to live."

"Their money?" I said. "It's our money. From the taxes I've already paid and will be paying for the rest of my life."

"That's not how they see it."

I sighed. "I know, but we do what we need to do to survive."

"I would never go on welfare," Gloria said.

"Well, you have Wayne. You don't need to."

"Even so." Her mouth settled into a tight line as she shook her head, making her luxuriant dark curls ripple and sway.

I didn't get the sense that she was criticizing me. I knew she'd grown up in near-poverty, her father a writer for one of the tabloids found in supermarket checkout lines, her mother a housewife. No matter how strained their finances, her family had never asked for public assistance. Gloria and Wayne certainly qualified for food stamps, but she had refused to apply. Of course, they did have Wayne's paycheck, and each other to help with child care.

I changed the subject. "Any new songs?"

She shook her head. "I wanted to write one for the new baby, but it isn't finished."

I glanced around her kitchen. With winter coming, the dark closed in earlier each day. "Isn't your brother coming to visit?"

She closed her eyes to think for a moment. "Yes. It's this weekend."

"That'll be good, to see him, won't it? It's been a while."

"He's . . ." She hesitated, looked down at her mug and then up at me again, sideways, with her head turned slightly away. "I was like a mother to him and my little sister. I basically raised them. As a result—at least I believe that's why—they rebelled against me when they were teenagers instead of our parents."

"Maybe that'll be over by now."

She pressed her lips together and looked out the window.

I didn't meet Gloria's brother that weekend. Jill did, and reported that he acted like an unruly teenager, despite being twenty-one. He was rough with the children, rude to Jill, and mean to Gloria, making cutting remarks about her cooking, her looks, and her marriage. He criticized her for getting pregnant again, saying that it was a crime to bring another child into the world. Gloria didn't respond to any of his remarks.

"I don't know why she lets him in her front door," Jill said. "I'm certainly keeping my kids away from now on."

Gloria's need to take care of people puzzled me too. "I guess it's because he's family." Although that didn't explain Zack.

Jill shivered. "Glad I'm an only child. How's the cleaning coming?" Jill's inspection had occurred the week before.

"I'll be ready. I'll even put on my nice face for them."

The inspector turned out to be a woman in her forties, with permed hair and heavy shoes. Her handshake was just three cold fingers in my palm.

I nervously introduced myself and the two children, who had come to stand next to me.

She didn't look at the boys, but simply said, "Let's get started, shall we?"

She held a clipboard crooked in one arm and moved from room to room with me and the children straggling after her.

"The space heaters give off plenty of heat," I offered.

When I saw her eying the living room windows and marking something on her clipboard, I said, "The storm windows are in good condition."

She didn't say anything.

As we went into the kitchen, I began to babble about the stove and refrigerator being only a couple of years old, but trailed off when I realized she wasn't paying any attention to me.

She nodded at the clean stove and the borrowed set of dishes in the cupboard (my own mismatched china from Goodwill was hidden in a box at Gloria's), and moved on to the bedrooms. She raised an eyebrow at my having the small, dark room off the kitchen and shook her head at the two cribs in the larger bedroom.

Finally we stood by the front door again, the children still silently holding onto my legs.

She finished writing something on her clipboard and said, "Overall, not bad."

"If there's something wrong, I can fix it."

She consulted the clipboard. "I marked you down because the living room windows lack curtains. And the bedrooms are not in good order: the furniture in one isn't a set—how hard is it to get a bedroom suite instead of random bits and pieces?—and the crib blankets and curtains in the other don't match." She frowned at me. "It's not a real home unless care is taken."

I started to protest about unnecessary expenses for appearance's sake, but then realized that what she wanted to see was a parody of a middle-class home. There was no point in arguing with her. Sometimes you just get tired of fighting. You have to fight and fight for every little thing.

"Did we pass?"

"You'll get a letter from the office."

I was never so glad to show someone out of my house. I resented being judged, and that such a judgment could affect everything in our lives. But the important thing was passing. I couldn't be sure until the letter arrived a few weeks later. I tore it open and scanned the paragraphs. I had to read it twice to be sure: it said that we qualified for housing assistance.

The extra money eased my ever-frantic worry about getting by. One of the first things I did was buy new underwear for myself. Since going on welfare almost two years earlier, I hadn't bought any clothes for myself, not even from Goodwill. I darned holes in my socks and underwear, patched and repatched my jeans, wore bras past the point where they'd lost their elastic. The boys' clothes came out of the hand-me-down bags that circulated among the people we knew, supplemented by the occasional pair of pants from Goodwill. I bought their underwear and shoes new, but nothing for myself, so I felt almost decadent going into Zayre's and looking for the cheapest package of ladies' underwear.

At Thanksgiving, our first in the West Street house, I invited Jill, Gloria and Wayne for dinner. As soon as the cold weather hit, I had hung a heavy curtain in the archway, closing off the big front room with its many windows, abandoning it to the cold. But for Thanksgiving dinner, I opened it up and pulled tables together for my extended family.

I worked all morning fixing a variety of dishes. Around noon, as I was closing the oven door, Wayne showed up with Nathan in tow.

"Gloria's in labor," he said. "Can you take Nathan? We have to get to the hospital."

"Sure," I said, taking Nathan's hand. The corners of his eyes drooped, making him look sad even when he laughed.

I set Nathan to helping Jeremy and Justin color pictures of turkeys and corn to hang on the wall while I finished cooking.

Later, Jill and I sat down to dinner with the five boys like stepping stones: Nathan and Justin were a year and a half, Jeremy three, Michael six and Richard nine.

"Soon we'll have another little one," I said to the boys. "Aren't you excited?"

"May I have another roll?" Nathan asked.

At that moment the phone rang. It was Wayne to say that it was all over; baby and mom were fine; and could I put Nathan on.

"Wait!" I said. "Boy or girl?"

I ran into the front room. "It's a girl!"

"Finally," Richard said.

Nathan quickly set down his glass and ran to talk to his father.

We spent a few days with my family in Baltimore at Christmas. Ben gave Patience a special tune-up, and she made the trip easily. I brought my parents a photo of the boys in a nice frame I'd found at Goodwill.

The boys spent a lot of time with my youngest sister. She and her friends played Candyland with them. Justin in particular didn't have to make a special effort to get along with anyone; he simply beamed happily at everyone and everyone adored him.

Jeremy's antics continued to tease my mother. Half in fun, she threatened to swat him with the yardstick, but it broke in two before it reached his bum. After that, she left the disciplining to me. Justin, equally mischievous but much quieter, flew under her radar, the same way I had as a child. Both of them were completely unafraid of their grandparents.

My father seemed happy to have the boys there. I had prepared them for his occasional bouts of temper, so they just looked at each other when he snapped out some sarcastic remark or when he marched into the room and changed the channel away from Mr. Rogers to the news as though they weren't sitting right there.

Jeremy informed me that it was up to him—Jeremy—to make whatever concessions were necessary. "Grandfather isn't used to having little kids around," he explained.

I was surprised one evening to find Justin in his pajamas snuggled next to my father on the couch in front of the tv, watching a news program. As I hustled him off to bed, I asked Justin what he'd been doing.

"Grandfather needed a cuddle," he said, as though it were obvious.

"Did he say so?"

Tilting his head to one side to look up at me, Justin said, "No. Course not."

My father—who had never once bought a toy for any of the six of us— suddenly decided that Justin had to have the plastic Snoopy train the child had seen on television. Since he didn't even know where to find a toy store much less how to navigate in one during the holiday rush, my father dragged me or my sister around with him for two days until he finally found one. On Christmas morning, as he got down on the floor to help the delighted Justin play with it, I realized that he was not the same man who had terrorized my childhood. Hard as it was for me to let go of the past, I had to accept that he had changed.

The boys and I drove back to Worcester in a snowstorm, and the following day was devoted to laundry and shoveling the walk. That night, after the boys were asleep, I went up to Gloria's apartment on the top floor, leaving the doors open so I could listen for the boys.

I called her my friend, but I was a little afraid of her. Sometimes her temper lashed out, and there was some tension that never left her. Despite that, something about her gripped me; like a tune you can't forget, it kept me sitting next to her wanting to hear more.

Wayne wasn't home, Gloria told me as we moved into the kitchen. I sat at the table by the window while she fixed chamomile tea. Outside, everything was quiet. The deep snow had been pushed around, plowed, and criss-crossed with boot prints, but still conferred that eerie winter silence on the neighborhood.

Gloria brought the mugs of tea and sat across from me. She seemed frail, as if she'd been ill. Her dark eyes were huge in her pale face, her body attenuated.

"Have you lost weight?" I asked.

"I don't know. We don't have a scale."

I wondered if she had an eating disorder; she was that thin. "My sister used to make herself throw up after she ate anything."

"Waste," Gloria murmured.

"Then she tried all these weird diets trying to lose weight."

"I'm not trying to lose weight. Far from it. It's just that I feed the kids first."

"Oh." I felt stupid. "Do you need anything? I have some vegetables and those bags of rice and beans from our last wholesale order. Not fancy, but there's plenty of it."

"No. Thank you. Everything will be fine. We got a little behind when Wayne couldn't work during the blizzard."

"Okay." I told her about driving back from my parents' house in the snow.

She looked up from her tea. "Why don't they support you or have you live with them? Don't they know what your life is like here?"

"Probably not."

Her eyes burned like dark coals in her face. "They must be monsters to let you live in poverty when they have plenty of money. You shouldn't have anything more to do with them."

I shifted in my chair. "Don't worry about me."

Gloria gripped her mug, and some tea sloshed onto the table. "No, I mean it."

"Everybody has scars from childhood," I said. "You try to forgive your parents and move on, don't you?"

She stiffened. "Some parents don't deserve to be forgiven."

Startled, I asked her what she meant.

"Just because they had you doesn't mean you have to keep them in your life."

"I think it means you give it an extra try. They can change."

She shook her head and said I didn't understand.

I touched her hand. "What is it?"

She jerked her hand away and, in a tight voice, began to describe the physical and emotional abuse that she and her brother and sister had suffered from their alcoholic parents. "He hit her, and then she hit us. She hit us with anything she could lay her hands on, an ashtray, a pan, once my brother with a big knife. He was lucky not to lose an eye."

I thought about Gloria's tense relationship with her brother, and the sister who never came to visit.

The abuse was so bad that Gloria had moved out in her mid-teens and gotten her own apartment. So bad that a judge actually gave her custody of her younger siblings, and Gloria only a minor herself.

She described her high school years: working minimum-wage jobs after school to pay the rent, scraping money together to buy food for her brother and sister.

"I took speed for a while. I wasn't doing it to lose weight—I just didn't want to fall asleep in class. There was so much to do when I got home. I never got more than a couple of hours of sleep."

Her hands were shaking, so I took them in mine. They were cold as a handful of snow.

"Then one day," Gloria said, "I got scared about what I was doing to myself and flushed it all down the toilet."

"Cold turkey," I said.

"After that, well, you know. I just went on."

I thought of her piling one day on another, and each day she held on—each day she survived—a victory.

"I'm not stupid," she said. "I know what all the studies say, that an abused child will grow up to abuse her own children. But I will not let that happen; I will not hurt my children."

That was where the tightness and over-control came from. She was the bulwark of her fragile family, then and now. I saw the courage as well as the fear that dogged her as she patrolled unceasingly the paper-thin wall she had erected to protect her children. As she went, she sang to keep up her courage, a song that was at once strange and utterly familiar.

15

BLIZZARDS

I didn't use the extra money to buy a bedroom suite or matching curtains. Instead, I put it aside, hoping to use it to go back to school. Jill had said that school was a priority, her ticket to somewhere else. That was how I saw it too: a way to get a job and a better life for my kids. Jill and I had both been to college, but her art degree and my English degree were not much use in the job market. If anything, they were a hindrance, making managers who wanted minimum-wage workers look at us askance.

Every morning, I pushed my coffee cup aside to spread out the newspaper, the Worcester *Telegram and Gazette.* Pen in hand, I read each want ad carefully but found none to circle. They all called for training or experience that I didn't have.

My job experience was pretty limited. While in school I had worked part-time in the library and during the summer as a waitress: jobs that didn't pay much. After I graduated, along with the other baby boomers flooding the job market, I worked briefly in the envelope factory before going to work as a secretary. With so many factories closing down, jobs were hard to come by and paid very little. As for getting another secretarial job, I didn't know where to look for one other than the Classifieds.

And even if I found a job, I still didn't know where to find child care for kids as young as mine, or how to pay for it if I did. I felt trapped.

With Richard and Michael both in school, Jill found herself in a kind of in-between time. According to the rules, she should have been looking for a job. Unfortunately, like me, her lack of qualifications and excess of education combined with a tight job market to keep jobs out of her reach.

Jill didn't waste time being discouraged. She took stock of her skills and experience, and set herself the goal of becoming a social worker. The only problem was that social work required a master's degree. Refusing to give up, she eventually found a one-year, low-residency program that she could pursue from home and pay for herself out of the savings she'd scraped together, supplemented by grants, student loans and the extra cash she now had a result of getting Section 8. Unfortunately, the welfare office considered her student loans as income and cut her check accordingly, a decision she appealed and won.

I, too, needed credentials or some kind of training if I was going to get a job. I didn't think that another degree would help me; I needed something more immediate. But without any clear idea of what that would be, I decided to go ahead and take the Graduate Record Exams (GREs), which you needed before applying to graduate schools. I did pretty well, but still didn't know what to do next. However, I posted the scores on the refrigerator to remind myself that I still had a brain.

I regretted not having taken courses that would have trained me for a specific job when I had the chance. I considered becoming a medical secretary. Also, I thought about taking the trade school courses that the welfare office had refused to pay for.

One day, while I watched Ben adjust Patience's timing, something I never seemed to be able to get right, I talked about trying to get a job. "It'll be another year and a half till Justin's old enough for day care but maybe I can start getting ready. Reading the want ads is so depressing; I don't seem to be qualified for anything."

"What do you want to do?" he asked, not looking up from the light flashing on the belt.

"Maybe I could be a mechanic."

Ben slanted a look at me. "Don't know of any place around here that's hired a woman."

"But it's not impossible. And it must pay well."

He chuckled. "Better than McDonald's but not by much."

Jeremy and Justin came whooping off the front porch. They knew better than to grab Ben while he was bent over the engine, but felt no compunction about pulling on me, demanding their lunch. I invited Ben to stay and eat with us.

Ben brought up the subject again over lunch, asking me why I had taken the college courses I had.

I explained that at the time I had hoped to go to graduate school and eventually become a college professor.

"So?" he asked.

"You need a master's, really a PhD." I said. I wasn't sure I had the luxury of the years it would take to get a degree and do enough research to gain a teaching position at a college. Even if I did somehow manage that, I didn't think the salary would be enough to support the three of us. Plus, I was limited to Massachusetts; I couldn't afford to move to another state where welfare allotments were much less than what I was getting.

"What about teaching high school?" Ben asked, looking up through the blond hair that had fallen across his face.

I thought about it. "I have taken a few courses that would count towards certification, like Child Psychology." I couldn't dismiss the idea simply because it was the career my mother had planned for me.

After lunch I walked Ben to the door. Normally I was nervous around tall men—a leftover from my childhood fear of my father's rages—but Ben was so gentle that I didn't mind him looming over me in the doorway. He put his hands on my shoulders, and I caught my breath. But he only smiled.

"You'll think of something," he said.

I wanted to make the apartment fun for the kids. Their bedroom had a deep, narrow closet with a window. I built a platform in it, which became Jeremy's bed, his private hide-away. The boys used the dark space under the platform for games: one day it was the hold of a ship, the next a cave for hiding from bears.

Justin wanted to sleep in a tent, so I put his crib mattress under a table and covered everything with a large sheet. I bought another sheet to hang on the wall. The design was of trees piled upon trees, with little animals peering out of the branches, like one of those puzzles where you have to find a hidden shape.

My little back room had its charms, too. It was so small that I had to push my bed up against the wall, and dark as a cave for most of the day. There was one hour, and one hour only, at the very end of the day, when the sun came sneaking in the window and touched the wooden back of the chair. Then, stronger, it slanted across the table I used for a desk, and the room suddenly brimmed with light, the white walls brilliant and warm.

At night both boys lay on their stomachs looking at picture books in front of the space heater. The heater was large, three feet tall, with glass blocks in the front so you could see the flames. The boys pretended to be Abe Lincoln reading in front of the fireplace. "Maybe I'll be president someday," Jeremy said once.

My aspirations were much smaller. I just wanted to give them a comfortable home like the picture on the box of Sleepytime tea. Someplace simple and warm. It didn't seem like so much to ask.

Although I'd hoped to avoid it forever, I finally bought a used television set, a small red plastic portable from a rental place. The boys loved Mr. Rogers and Captain Kangaroo, the only shows that I allowed them to watch regularly.

One of the local stations started showing Shirley Temple films at dinnertime on Sundays, so watching them became a family ritual. Jeremy called her "the goodest girl" and pretended to do the tap steps with her. I made pizza as a special treat, mixing up the dough in the morning along with the week's bread, and splurging on mozzarella to go over my homemade tomato sauce.

I signed up for courses in German and Anthropology at Quinsigamond Community College, thinking I might leverage what I'd learned about morris dancing into a master's degree in folklore. Then I holed up over the winter, studying whenever the kids would let me. As February closed in, with cold winds blowing through the cracks around the windows, I sometimes even closed off the parlor and kept the kids in the kitchen where I could use the space heater in the stove to keep that room and the bathroom livable. I would make a batch of play-dough from flour, salt and water and let the kids go wild with it at the table while I sat in a corner doing my homework.

I didn't see as much of Gloria and Jill as I had before. Both were busy with their own things, Gloria with the new baby and Jill with her own schoolwork, although we still helped each other out with child care sometimes, which was the only way I could go to classes. Other friends drifted away also while I was occupied with school. Jim had a new job that took up a lot of his time. Sherry had moved to a nearby town with a boyfriend, and I had no new poems to show Fay. Jill's kids being in school meant that we discontinued our weekly child care swap; no more writing day. I had stopped writing and barely even touched my journal.

I didn't want to meet anyone new. Some days it felt as though my compassion had all been used up. There were just so many sad stories: Gloria's abusive parents, Sherry's cruel mother, Fay's lost baby. It seemed as though everyone I knew had a secret sorrow. I began to understand why some social workers behaved so coldly and marveled all over again at the few whose enthusiasm and concern had survived.

Too, I began to steer clear of my activist friends and the community organizations with which I'd been involved. They didn't want me to bring my kids, considering them a disruption at our earnest meetings. The others either didn't have young children or were wealthy enough to have child care. Not wanting to impose further on Jill or Gloria to babysit, I retreated to my studies.

But even my classes were discouraging. I doubted that they would ever really lead to a job. I was overwhelmed by the whole process of choosing a career and collecting the necessary credentials. Every day I had to force myself to push on and not drift back into the life that had become so familiar.

If by some chance I did manage to get a job and trade my welfare existence for a nine-to-five world of work, my life would surely change in ways that at this point seemed dark and mysterious to me. I feared failure, which seemed inevitable. I feared losing my friends, as I moved into a different world. Worst of all, I feared my going off to work would damage the children.

The boys were old enough to play on their own now and then while I studied. Justin made up endless stories that he acted out with little wooden people, banana peels, or even just his fingers. Jeremy loved to be read to, usually preferring new books to old favorites. If no one was available to read, he would sometimes sit turning over the pages of a book, murmuring a story to himself or to Justin who would come and sit beside him, peering over his arm to look at the pictures or looking up at his brother's face trustingly.

Jeremy began to have nightmares about monsters, being trapped by a monster. When he woke up yelling, Justin woke up and cried too. I couldn't make out what Jeremy was afraid of and hoped it was simply cabin fever from being shut inside so long or perhaps too many readings of *Where the Wild Things Are.*

To compensate, Jeremy and Justin made up an elaborate game about the monsters living far away in a tunnel somewhere. Sometimes I took them for a wild ride in the car careening through every tunnel I could find, mostly under the expressway that bisected the city.

As we entered each tunnel, the boys would scream, "Look out! Here we come, Mr. Monster!"

Every time we saw a door in the wall of a tunnel, always shut and locked, we would all yell at the monster inside.

"Nyah, nyah, you can't get out!"

"Stay there, bad monster!"

"Woo-hoo, boo-hoo, Tunnel Monster!"

In one of my now-rare journal entries, I wrote: *Justin woke up with a fever and came into bed with me this morning. He made himself so* small. *It is pathetic how tiny he is. He became a baby again, my poor silent baby. I ignore him and his brother too much. It was a shock to look at dosages and realize Justin is still only two.*

Had another in a long series of talks with Gloria about school: my time in school deprives the kids but it's only to make life better for them in the future. Is the future worth it? Isn't this the most important time to be with them?

I wonder if it is this withdrawal (that began when I started studying for GREs) that makes Jeremy so sad and afraid to be alone. The one thing that I wanted for him was that he wouldn't be afraid. I miss my writing too, but without that day per week Jill used to guarantee me, it's hard. Jill says Jeremy's thing is a normal stage.

Despite my attempts to make it fun, the house was dark and dismal. And cold. Everything seemed so hard. Seeing me preoccupied with school, the boys were unhappy, and I didn't even know if it would ever help me get a job. I wanted to draw my own gauze curtains against the city and live in a private world with oranges and turquoise dresses.

I thought about Fay with her inexhaustible energy that stimulated me to get moving, not only with my writing, but with my life. And Jill's angry refusal to give in that kept me fighting. But when the fighting failed, when I was beaten down, then it was Gloria who came to mind, and her tenacity that inspired me. Jeremy still thought she must be a countess, trapped in this Worcester life by some evil fairy or jealous stepmother.

But I recognized something in her of my own stoic philosophy, the belief that persistence itself, just going on was sometimes the only thing you could do, and doing it counted as a success.

One thing I persisted with was morris dancing. Dancing was my other life, one that had nothing to do with Worcester or welfare or poverty.

I continued to go to practice every Monday night, driving into Cambridge no matter how bad the weather. Dancing had become an addiction. I longed for those moments when we were all in synch, our bells chiming together, when the earth let go of me, and leaping into the air became effortless. The strict grace of the dances freed me in a way that nothing else could.

I loved when we danced rounds, a figure when all six of us pulled out into a wide circle, linked by a band of intangible energy. Dancing around in the circle, we suddenly swept into the center, as if the band holding us had been suddenly pulled tight, hankies thrown up over our heads in a great burst of white cotton. Then we gently stepped back into place.

I had vowed the previous May at Marlboro that I would try to become friends with these women, but I had little in common with them. As I had begun to feel an outsider with the community groups, so I felt like an interloper among these people I once might have called my peers. We may have started out in similar circumstances, but now they were concerned with boyfriends and finals and their jobs, while I worried about toilet training and how to make three dollars last till the end of the month.

Also, they had a self-confidence, a certainty that they were on the right track. For sure, I had made some bad choices, but they didn't seem afraid of losing their way. Maybe these young women had families they could fall back on if they made equally bad choices.

I leaked out information about myself slowly, not wanting to share anything about my Worcester life. I didn't believe there was any way to explain. They would never understand what was in my heart when I had to take the boys to the library on the bus because the car wouldn't start, or tell the kids they couldn't have a banana because we were low on food stamps. I feared that if Cynthia and the others really understood what my life was like, they wouldn't want me on the team; they would shrink from me the same way the bank's lawyers had recoiled from Jill, as though our poverty were contagious. Not that my teammates ever gave me any reason to fear such a thing; logic didn't really enter into it.

At least being with my teammates was a relief from the ever-present sense of being watched and judged, whether it was the Section 8 inspector or the woman behind me at the grocery store. I could never figure out why being poor meant that my doings were everybody's business. Why should they care if I bought mushrooms or whether my bedspreads matched my curtains?

Knowing I was being unfair to lump my teammates together, I listened to them talk, tried to smile and be friendly. As spring drew near, Cynthia stepped up our practices to prepare for Marlboro. I was determined to be in our show set for this second ale, pushing myself during practice. By the end of the night we were all collapsed on the floor, limp as dishrags with exhaustion.

"My legs are like rubber," Cathy said. "Look at me—I'm Gumby."

Propped against the wall beside me, Robin asked why I never came out to the pub with them after practice. "Everyone's there," she said. "It's fun. The guys from Newtowne go there after their practice, so it's like a party every week." Newtowne was a men's morris team that had grown out of the New Cambridge Men, the team I had seen at Fox Hollow.

From my other side, Diane joined in. "Yes, you should come with us." Her face was red from exertion.

I pleaded the long drive back to Worcester. "I really have to get going."

Diane pushed her hair back from her face and lifted it off her neck. "Oh, I know. If I had kids like yours, I'd rush home too. Give that Justin a kiss for me."

As I drove home under the stars, I thought of them laughing together in the pub. Perhaps if I stayed I would get to know some of them better. But it was out of the question. The truth was that I couldn't spare any cash for beer.

Hoping for the miracle of a fellowship that would let me go to graduate school, I did interview at a few schools. However, as one man explained to me, I was hopelessly naive about how colleges—graduate programs at least—worked. One of the things that had attracted me to Clark, where I did my undergraduate work, was that you had the option of doing away with grades altogether. Called Pass/No Record, the option meant that courses you failed were ignored and others only recorded as a Pass. Looking over my transcript, the man shook his head. The sixties, he gently reminded me, were over.

I was wasting my time. I felt as though every way I turned was blocked off. I would never get out.

I wrote in my journal: *The future tantalizes me. I'm afraid to reach for it. I've learned to live day by day and am afraid of the other.*

All I could do was hang on and hope things would get better. I settled back into a kitchen complacency, making soup and kneading warm balls of bread dough.

Then things did get better. Jill brought me the news that a friend of hers at the Mayor's Office of Cultural Affairs was submitting an umbrella proposal under the Comprehensive Education and Training Act (CETA), and we could apply for grants if we could come up with a proposal for something that would train us for a career and also benefit the community.

Jill was going to propose to teach art classes at the neighborhood centers around town, and get her students to paint murals on the sides of buildings. Jill had already done a number of murals around town. She suggested I do something similar with creative writing classes at the neighborhood centers. So we wrote up proposals for CETA grants and turned them in. I didn't really expect anything to come of it.

With the fall weather, Muddy River started dancing again. In October, I was sick a lot, one cold following another, so I missed some practices which only worsened my isolation.

That winter of 1977-1978 was unusually cold, or maybe it was the way heat escaped from the West Street house. The walls might as well have been made of paper. The storm windows were useless when the cold air just sieved in around them. We hadn't thought to ask if the walls were insulated.

As January closed in, I grew depressed looking at the bleak monochrome of the snow. Reading fairy tales to the kids at naptime reminded me of the hobgoblin's mirror that made even the most pleasant landscapes look like boiled spinach. I felt sometimes as if, like Kay in the story, I had a grain of that glass in my eye and a sliver in my heart, turning it to ice like the world outside our windows. There was no way out. I wrote in my journal: *Winter, moonlight on crusty snow; I am hard now and cold and very still.*

Jeremy complained about the cold, saying that it was like Narnia: always winter and never Christmas.

I reminded him that we had just had a Christmas.

"That was forever ago," he moaned.

Another journal entry after I had lost my temper with Jill over something completely trivial: *A day of blizzard, shut in with myself and the other people in the house by snow and wind. Jill forgives me everything. The things I would be angry with someone about for months she ignores, or quickly forgets. I admire and am grateful to her for that*

One night Jill and I decided to go to a Mike Seeger concert at Worcester Polytechnic Institute. With their sliding scale, we could afford it. The only trick was getting there. My car was out of commission, the carburetor arm having fallen off. I hadn't been able to get to the auto parts store yet to replace the screw that was supposed to hold the arm on. Jill's car, always finicky in the cold, refused to start.

After some discussion, we decided to walk. There was snow on the ground but the streets and sidewalks were clear. It was only a little over a mile away. I packed my boys in the stroller with lots of blankets. Jill bundled her sons up, and we set off.

The night air was cold, but we were in good spirits. The boys and I sang *Jim Along Josie,* a counting song called *The Tree in the Wood,* and *Puff the Magic Dragon* as we walked along. Jill didn't sing but looked up at the sharp sparkle of the stars in the indigo sky.

The concert was wonderful but when we came out into the lobby afterwards, the stroller was nowhere to be seen. Puzzled, we stepped outside. There was the stroller, by the steps, a tangled heap of metal and torn fabric.

A student lounging nearby peeled himself off the railing and stepped up to us. "I saw what happened. It was a bunch of guys."

"What in the world did they want with a stroller?" Jill demanded.

The boy shrugged. "They were using it as a sled, but they were too heavy for it."

"Obviously." Jill turned to me. "What are we going to do?"

"We'll have to walk. I don't have money for a cab."

So we walked, slowly, at a pace Jeremy's little legs could manage. Jill and I took turns carrying Justin who—sleepy—was a dead weight. Jill's angry denunciations of selfish students with more money than brains tapered off as she tired. When Jeremy got too weary to go on, Richard carried him piggyback for a while.

We walked in silence, absorbed in our own thoughts and the necessity of putting one foot in front of the other.

Eventually Michael lifted his mouth free of his ice-encrusted scarf and said, "I'm cold, Ma."

"I know, honey," Jill said. "We all are. Hang on. We'll be there soon."

As we finally neared the house, Jill said, "You know, the weird thing is that I wasn't surprised about them wrecking the stroller and having to walk home without it. I think being poor dulls your expectations. Of course you're going to be mistreated; you're everybody's scapegoat."

"It does sometimes seem like I'm wearing a sign that says 'Kick Me'. But we'll feel better once we get inside."

Jill shook her head. "The whole thing just wears you down. You rise to the occasion and you rise to the occasion and after a while you just can't do it anymore."

"We did, though," I said. "We're home now. It'll be okay."

I described the night in my journal and added: *You have to fight and fight for every little thing, but when you can't fight anymore, you just hold on. Sometimes simply not giving up is enough.*

In February of 1978, a powerful northeaster blew down, rattling the windows. Jeremy and Justin knelt on the sofa in the cold front room, watching the fine dry snow flowing almost horizontally, completely hiding the brick school building across the street. The boys were excited and a little scared. I made them hot chocolate and let them pretend to be Eskimos and make igloos out of blankets draped precariously between chairs.

By the next day the drifts were so high they covered the lower half of the windows. All the children were wild to go outside, but we were afraid to let them out with the snow well over even Richard's head. Jill heard on the radio about a child in Auburn who had fallen into a drift and suffocated before they found him.

The city closed down. I had bragged to my family that Worcester—unlike Baltimore which was famous for panicking at the first rumor of a snowflake—could handle snow and never had to shut down, but that blizzard proved me wrong. Everything was immobilized; the plows couldn't get through; no one was going anywhere. The phones were out, and the stores were closed, but at least we had heat and enough food.

When the snow finally stopped, Jill and I took turns digging out the front walk so the boys would have a place to play. We debated waiting for Wayne and Gloria, who were sleeping in, but decided to just go ahead and get it done.

When I finally reached the curb, I leaned on the shovel and turned around to Jill who was resting on the front porch. "Do you remember where we parked the cars?"

Aghast, Jill looked at the sparkling surface of the snow. There wasn't even a slight undulation to show where our VWs were.

Richard, who had come out on the porch to check our progress, said, "I have an idea." He raced into the house and came back bearing a broom.

"I don't understand," I said as he came down the walk and handed it to me.

Jill started laughing. "He's right. We'll have to poke around in the snow to find the cars before we can dig them out!"

And that's what we did. A few days later, when the street was finally plowed and the alternating sunny days and cold nights had formed a crust on the snow, we sent Michael out prospecting with the broom. He was light enough to balance on top of the snow's crust, but we still watched him carefully, ready to dig like maniacs if he fell in.

As we got the second car dug out, Jill and me taking turns with the shovel, the plow came through again, heaving a great ridge of ice and snow up against the cars. Jill groaned from the curb where she was resting. Exasperated, I stood up, one hand on my lower back.

Then I heard a toot and Ben's car pulled up alongside us. Unwinding himself from the VW bug, Ben said he wanted to make sure we were all right.

"The Iandoli's on Park Ave was open when I went by," he went on. "Are you okay for food, or would you like a ride down there?"

"Food's not a problem," I replied. "We were digging out the cars so we wouldn't feel so trapped."

"Here." Ben held out his hand for the shovel which I gladly surrendered. "I'll dig out a spot for my car too while I'm at it."

"You're an angel," Jill said. "We didn't want to let the kids out today till we were done and could keep an eye on them."

Ben glanced up without varying his rhythm. "How much trouble can they get into? It's not like there's any traffic to speak of."

Jill shook her head. "You have no idea. Michael wants to jump out his bedroom window, or even better, one of Gloria's. He's convinced the snow is deep enough to cushion him."

"If he's going to do that, then I'm getting the camera," I said. "Will he really jump?"

"Not if I have any say in it," Jill maintained.

Ben stayed for dinner with me and the boys. He and I talked a little bit about our dreams, what we wanted our lives to be someday. I told of my dream of a farmhouse with a quilt-covered bed under the rafters and a huge kitchen with a stone fireplace. He talked about wanting to get some land for a farm, build a house himself.

"It ought to have a big kitchen," he said, with his slow grin.

The kids, wild with excitement over having Ben there, kept interrupting our conversation. It took forever to get them settled down and into bed.

"I think they're asleep," I said as I came into the parlor from checking on them. Ben was standing up. I wondered if he was getting ready to leave. I moved closer to him.

"Maybe I should stay over," he said.

A thousand things went through my mind, apprehension, consternation, and a deep warmth. Was I really going to do this? Oh, yes. I felt the sliver in my heart shift and begin to melt.

Inarticulate as he was in the daylight, Ben's reserve vanished when I turned off the light. His big mechanic's hands ran over me, as he might search through a hidden part of an engine, touching me, taking me apart and putting me back together, learning me by feel. Enveloped, entwined in the long bulk of him, I couldn't stop touching him, the planes of his shoulders, the bones and hollows of his hips.

Afterwards, we lay without talking, still tangled up together, sweaty in the cold night. There would be no whispered secret-sharings with this man, but I cherished our closeness. After a while, he moved away long enough to rescue the quilt from the floor and, settling back alongside me, he tucked the quilt around us. With the wall on one side and Ben's long body on the other, I felt safe. I could let down my guard. Silently we watched the blue snow-light glow on the walls.

16
CRYSTAL PARK

Suddenly everything seemed to change. When Wayne and Gloria's financial crisis eased after the blizzard was over, they put in a down payment on a house in the Main South neighborhood. It was even more rundown than the West Street house, but Wayne and Gloria planned to fix it up and resell it.

After they moved out, Jill warned the landlord to shut off the water to the third floor apartment. That winter of 1977-78 was unusually cold, and the little heat that drifted up from the second floor would not be enough to keep the pipes from freezing.

He didn't shut off the water, and eventually the pipes in Jill's ceiling cracked, not all at once but in small leaking slivers. She didn't know anything was wrong until the water had finally saturated the fiberglass panels and the drop ceiling in the kitchen fell, bringing down plaster and a terrible smell with it. When she notified the landlord, he yelled at her for damaging the ceiling and threatened to take the cost of the repairs out of her security deposit.

Jill tried to reason with him, but finally got so mad that she gave notice on impulse.

"I don't care what happens anymore—homeless, whatever—as long as I can get away from him," she raged. "What does he think? That he can bully me just because I'm poor and a woman?"

That meant we both had to find a place because I didn't want to stay there without her and certainly didn't want to be left alone to fight with the landlord. Jill couldn't seem to find a place. Most landlords didn't want to have to deal with the welfare office over Section 8, or they were afraid that Section 8 recipients would be bad tenants.

Finally she found an apartment on Montague Street, near Webster Square, that she fell in love with. She was waiting to hear from the owner, a woman who hadn't been very encouraging. Then her car broke down.

"Even if I get the apartment, how will I move?" she cried. "Why does everything go wrong at once?"

The snow dumped by the blizzard had not even melted halfway before being topped with subsequent snowstorms. There was no way for anyone to work on her car, even if she could spare the money for parts. We were both frustrated, hampered by the icy streets.

Then, a few days later, the woman who owned the house on Montague Street called to say Jill could have the apartment.

And we learned that our CETA proposals had been accepted.

I found an apartment on Gates Street. Even though it was right across Main Street from Clark University, no students lived on Gates Street; they lived on the other side of the campus. Only two blocks long, Gates Street had some factories at the far end near the railroad tracks and a small park across the street from us. Otherwise, the street was lined with triple-deckers, one side mostly Irish families and the other mostly Puerto Rican. I was neither, but it didn't seem to matter to my Irish landlord, who lived with his family on the second floor. He said he'd rather have Section 8 tenants because he knew the rent would always be paid on time. I didn't mention how often my check was late. Maybe the welfare office was more diligent about paying landlords.

Crystal Park was one of many parks that studded Worcester. One block wide and two blocks long, it boasted a steep hill at the end farthest from us, with lots of beech trees and a small playground at the very top. At the base of the hill was a pond, and then a wide, sweeping lawn with a few maple trees made up our end of the park.

Our house was up on a hill, so our third-floor apartment got sun all day. It was larger than I was looking for, six rooms. The two front rooms were side by side and looked out over the park. I put the furniture in the smaller room where the space heater was, and left the other mostly empty for the boys to scamper around in. Jeremy used the space to run and tumble and roll, but Justin loved to put on a sleeveless lace dress that came to his ankles, salvaged from the dress-up box. Holding it out, he would twirl slowly in the sunlight, creating patterns of light and shade on the hardwood floor.

I put the rocking chair in the bay window under shelves of plants—Swedish ivy, purple passion, spider plants, all from cuttings Jill and Fay had given me—and called it my sunset window. As the day fell away, I could sit and rock there, watching the sun go down over the bare trees of Crystal Park.

There were three bedrooms off the large kitchen. I took the tiny back bedroom that caught the sunrise. I slept on a single bed mattress on the floor; there wasn't room for anything else. I gave the boys the master bedroom and turned the medium-sized room into a guest room and study by putting in my double bed and my writing table. Having a guest room made sense, since friends like Jim and Christine still came to visit regularly.

Even such a large apartment was cheap given Worcester's depressed economy. Both sides of the street, Irish and Puerto Rican, struggled to get by. Having my landlord living downstairs made a huge difference. We didn't become friends, but he treated me fairly. After our struggles on Newbury and West Streets—with landlords cheating us out of money, carelessly spreading lead paint dust, refusing to make even the most essential repairs—simply being treated fairly was like heaven.

Scared and sad about not living with Jill, I hid my feelings from the kids and made the best of it. I was consumed with preparing for my CETA job, reading every book I could find on teaching creative writing, and searching for day care for the kids, in between settling into the new apartment.

I threw a housewarming party one Sunday afternoon and invited all of my Worcester friends. Most came and brought food, wine and beer turning it into a feast. The sun poured into the crowded rooms where we talked over the children's chatter. The party lasted well into the evening and several people stayed over, including Mac and Sarah's family and Ben. The house was completely cleaned up by departing guests, so we were able to collapse without guilt.

The next day, everyone except Ben left by midmorning. He and I sat at the kitchen table relaxing over tea.

"That was a great party," he said. "You should move more often."

"Sarah mentioned that she and Mac were moving soon themselves."

"That's right."

I waited but he didn't say anymore. "Well, when they do, are you, I mean, do you know what you're going to do?"

He looked at me ruefully and then ducked his head to run a hand through his hair, pushing it back off his forehead. "I don't know."

I thought about that for a minute.

An argument erupted in the living room, and Ben went to sort out the boys. He didn't hurry, just eased off, arms relaxed at his sides. There was a looseness in the way his limbs hung together.

When he returned, he put a hand on the back of his chair and stood looking at me for a moment. Then he slid into the seat.

"I guess I was wondering if I could stay here for a while," he said hesitantly.

I swallowed. The sun picked out gold highlights in his hair and lit up the mossy softness of his flannel shirt. "I'd like that," I said.

So Ben moved in. We swapped my little back room for the larger room I'd planned to use as a guest room. He fit so easily into our lives that it seemed as if he had always been there. His quiet presence filled the apartment like the sun which moved through the rooms during the day, from the back bedroom, through the kitchen, to fill the front room with a rosy glow before disappearing.

Jill was fighting with her new social worker, who demanded that she get a job, as she was required to do now that her children were in school. She explained to him that she was finishing up a graduate program and was about to start a job funded by the CETA grant. Her previous social worker had kindly agreed to "lose" her file for a year so that she could finish her degree. But this new social worker could not believe that a welfare mother could possibly succeed in a graduate program, and insisted that she get a job immediately, even it was in a factory or Friendly's.

She felt that what she was doing, between the degree and the CETA grant, had more long-term promise than a job at Friendly's. Once she made it off of welfare, she never wanted to have to get public assistance again. She didn't understand why her social worker couldn't see that.

When he finally understood that the grant meant she would have a job, he called the woman in the Mayor's Office of Cultural Affairs to try to hurry up the grant.

Jill was furious. "He could have lost me the job!"

"Maybe he thinks you're lying, trying to trick him into letting you stay on welfare," I offered.

"He can't. He knows the grant is coming." Jill moved papers around on my table. "It's so frustrating. I don't even know what to do."

Our CETA grants finally started in February. The stipend was enough that we didn't get welfare checks anymore but we were still officially on the rolls and got food stamps and housing assistance. I also got day care assistance, part of an incentive plan to encourage people to get off of welfare. If any one of those pieces had been missing, I could not have afforded to accept the grant.

Jeremy was supposed to start half-day kindergarten in the fall, but I didn't see how I could shuttle him to day care for the rest of the day if I was working. To complicate matters further, the few day care centers in Worcester refused to take children until they were three. Justin still had a few weeks to go, but I couldn't put off starting my job.

I worried about leaving them. Jeremy would love having other children to play with, but Justin would miss his special friends, Nathan and Hamid. Also, he preferred to play by himself, absorbed in his own quiet games, much to Jeremy's frustration. Every now and then, though, playing in the other room, he would suddenly start crying, a heart-broken cry, as though he'd woken up and realized he was alone. How could I stand not being there to comfort him?

Finally I found a day care center to take the boys. They offered a kindergarten program for Jeremy and agreed to bend the rules by taking Justin even though he wasn't quite three yet.

Meanwhile I had to figure out how I was actually going to teach my classes. Writing was important to me. As a solitary child, naïve and confused by a world I didn't understand, I had taken refuge in books. Books were easy; it was people who were hard. In books, life's chaos was tamed to a narrative. Even more than reading, though, writing was the way I made sense of the world: stories, poetry and the journal in which I kept track of what I thought I had learned.

Never having taken a writing class myself, I had no idea how to go about teaching one. The CETA program was supposed to fund on-the-job training, but I would have to teach myself. *What have I gotten myself into?* I wondered, but it was too late to back out, so I headed for the library to learn what I could about leading small groups and teaching creative writing.

I put together a syllabus and some rough lesson plans, using books like Andrew Elbow's *Writing Without Teachers*, Robert Bly's *Leaping Poetry*, and Kenneth Koch's *I Never Told Anybody: Teaching Poetry Writing in a Nursing Home*. I planned for each session to combine a writing skill, such as setting or character description, with a topic, like childhood or gardens. Since most of my participants would be new to writing, each session would start with freewriting: all of us writing for ten minutes about anything, the only rule being that you couldn't stop writing, even if it was only a word or phrase over and over. I would provide a topic or a photo as a jumpstart, but they would be free to write whatever they wanted and could choose whether to share what they'd written with the group. Then we would discuss the day's topic to brainstorm ideas, go over the basics of the selected writing skill, and do a writing assignment. Finally volunteers would read their work aloud and critique each other. It seemed like a workable plan.

In addition to preparing for my classes, I found time to go dancing. By the time I moved to Gates Street and started my CETA job in February of 1978, I had been dancing with Muddy River Morris for two years.

One night we had a team meeting and pot luck dinner. We had recently spent a weekend in Binghamton, New York at a gathering of morris teams.

"What happened, Barbara?" Cynthia asked. "There were all kinds of stories about what you did Saturday night."

"Well, it was no big deal." I remembered waking up to the sound of pleading out in the hall, a woman's voice—*Please don't hit me*—and a man's angry reply—*Then quit fucking around with me, you fucking cock-teaser.* I lay there hoping they would work it out or someone who knew them would intervene, but then there came the sound of a blow and the woman again—*Won't anybody help me?*

I looked around at my teammates and said, "There was an argument out in the hall. The woman seemed afraid, so I went out and brought her into the bedroom. I didn't want them to wake up the kids."

"But what about the chair?" Cathy asked.

"Well, the guy—I don't know what team he was from; didn't recognize him—followed us in, so I picked up a wooden chair and threatened to break it over his head if he didn't get out."

The other women looked at me, eyes wide. Diane finally said, "I couldn't have done that."

"I gave her my bed and crawled in with the kids. He apologized the next day, said he'd had too much beer. But later I heard another man saying that this was why women's teams shouldn't be invited to morris ales."

Later, after we'd finished with the team business, we had a potluck dinner. As we talked, I mentioned my CETA grant to teach writing.

"You might consider teaching as a career," said Robin, who was herself a teacher in a private school. "You're used to dealing with children, and you would have the same schedule as the boys."

Diane, who had a soft heart for any underdog, asked why I didn't just go home to my parents.

Not wanting to go into detail, I simply said that it wasn't an option.

"But welfare!" Diane protested. "You know what the statistics are for children who grow up in poverty."

Cathy snorted. "We know about being poor. We've all lived in nasty apartments and most of us got food stamps while we were in college. It's no big deal."

I didn't respond, letting the conversation move off of me and onto the perennial topic of boyfriends.

While the others talked, Cynthia leaned over to me and said, "But it's different for you, isn't it? We were only playing at being poor."

I thought of the temporary poverty of college students, almost a pride in living a bohemian life, knowing that a career waited at the end of the four years. At least it did for these graduates of Middlebury, Wellesley, and Harvard. "Yes. It's different."

I was surprised that Cynthia understood. Unlike the other women on the team, she wasn't on a traditional career path. She had dropped out of college and was working temp jobs as a secretary so she could devote her time to dancing. She managed easily on her salary, but of course she didn't have kids to support or child care to worry about.

I was moved too at the way the others had accepted me in spite of how different I was. I knew that they were on my side.

Though busy with dancing and my writing workshops, I didn't want to lose touch with my Worcester friends. One day I walked the boys over to Wayne and Gloria's.

They hadn't made much progress on fixing up the house yet, Gloria explained as she showed me into the chilly rooms. Indeed, it looked like a bomb site, with a huge gaping hole in the wall between the hall and the front room.

Gloria followed my glance and let out a spurt of laughter. "I got frustrated one day and just started whacking away with a crowbar."

"I'll bet that felt good!"

"Yes, it did. I want to open this whole space up." Gloria gestured around the front room.

"You're lucky it's not a load-bearing wall," I said.

"I guess we'll find out. Wayne made me stop when I hit these wires."

"I think Eddie has a friend who's an electrician. Do you want me to . . . "

"Oh, no," Gloria said, cutting me off. "No, no, we'll take care of it. That's okay."

I eyed the nest of black wires hanging out of the bottom of the hole and cautioned Jeremy and Justin to stay away from it. When I was a child, our cat had found its way into the space between the walls from a hole in the basement and crawled up to the second floor before panicking and getting stuck. We could hear it crying inside the wall. My mother had my brother take a hammer to the wall in order to reach in and drag the cat out. My mother called a construction company to come immediately and repair the wall. As I looked at Gloria's wall, I thought of how what seemed like a catastrophe in our world became merely a minor inconvenience when you had the money to fix it.

While Nathan and Chanté took my boys upstairs to play, we went into the kitchen where a ball of dough sat on the flour-smeared table.

"Did I interrupt you?" I said.

Gloria said, "No, not at all. I wanted you to show me know to knead bread. I think I'm doing something wrong."

I found it hard to imagine myself as the expert at anything, but I did make pretty good bread, so I went over to the sink to wash my hands, noticing that bits of food crusted the dishes piled there and a sour smell of mold hung over them.

After we finished with the bread and set it to rise on the pilot light, Gloria offered me some tea. As she handed me the mug, I noticed that her hands were red and chapped, the skin over her knuckles cracked open in a web of angry welts.

"How's it going?" I asked.

"Okay. We still have a lot of debts, but Wayne's working."

As we finished our tea, we exchanged news about my writing groups, her song-writing, new things our kids had learned to do. Without the warmth of the tea, a chill ran through me.

"I know," Gloria said, noticing my involuntary shiver. "We're trying to be careful and make the fuel oil last, but I worry about the kids. They always seem to have runny noses."

"Mine too. And chapped cheeks from wiping their sleeves across their faces. I put Chapstick on their cheeks now too," I volunteered.

Gloria hid her hands in her lap. "I know."

"And I seem to use gallons of hand lotion."

She looked out the window. "Lotion is way down on the list. Food is more important."

She got up and took our mugs over to the sink. If she couldn't afford hand lotion, things must be pretty grim. I wished she trusted me enough to let me help her more. She seemed to me like an enchanted princess, trapped in her own reflection in the mirror, trying to be who she thought she should be, unable to break free.

"I'm worried about her," I said to Ben as we did the dishes that night. The sink was in the little pantry off the kitchen, which was barely wide enough for Ben to sidle past me to put away the dishes he'd dried.

When he picked up another wet plate, still not having answered, I glanced over at him. His long hair fell forward around his face as he rubbed the plate with a towel.

I asked, "Do you think she would be offended if I got her some lotion?"

"You know her better than I do," Ben said, lifting one shoulder and looking at me sadly, "but I can tell by looking at you what the answer is."

I plunged another plate in the soapy water. Over the steam from the sink, I could feel the warmth that radiated off him, a wave of sympathy that washed over me. We continued to work together on the dishes, gently bumping against each other like a canoe against the dock as the water changes underneath.

17

TOUCHSTONES

"Justin, stop playing with your food and go get dressed," I said, stuffing books in my bag for work.

Justin looked up from swirling his oatmeal into patterns and smiled at me, his eyes crinkling under the blond hair that was spiky in front where his older brother had cut his bangs for him, ignoring the rule about using the sharp scissors. I hadn't thought to make a rule about not cutting each other's hair. Anyway, Jeremy, at four already a philosopher in the making, could argue his way around any rules I made. Justin, who simply ignored the ones he didn't like, had gone back to playing with his oatmeal.

"Move," I said. "I'll be late. I have to go to the jail and then with Jill to meet a new client." Ben had already left, so it was up to me to get the boys to day care. Barely a few months into my first job in over three years, I was still nervous about work.

I took the milk off the table to put it away. On the refrigerator was a quote:

Why work if you don't have to? the interviewer asked some fabulously wealthy heiress who had actually gotten a job. *Oh, because it's so wonderful to have something to do when I get up in the morning!* she gushed.

I'd cut the quote out of the paper when I was first on welfare, frantically trying to adjust to my new life: keeping up with two babies, washing endless piles of diapers, and fighting with the welfare office over lost checks and shorted food stamps. I had never lacked for something to do in the morning, but now, after three years of struggling to find a way to get by on welfare and a way to get off of it, I finally had a job.

I put the milk in and turned away from the refrigerator. For now, my only concern was getting to the jail.

The writing group at the Worcester County Jail had been in my grant proposal, so I felt that I had to follow through, but the truth was that I was terrified. All I knew about jail was what I had read about in books. I pictured rats scurrying across the filthy cells in *The Count of Monte Cristo.*

Jill thought the idea hilarious. "We're talking about the Worcester County Jail, not the Bastille."

"But the prisoners? I know there are guards and all; that's not it. And not the people who are in for drugs or robbery—I can understand that."

"What then?"

"Well . . . what if there are people who are in for abusing children? I don't think I can even be in the same room with someone who's hurt a child like that."

"They're just people," Jill said. "You remember what it's like in the middle of the night when the baby won't stop crying. I may not lose control like an abuser does, but I can certainly understand it."

I did remember. Nights in the rocking chair, crying because I was so tired.

The first time I went to the jail, I almost walked back out again. It wasn't the women, though I had been warned many of them only had a third grade education at best. It was everything else about the place.

I had to put my possessions in a locker that was like something out of high school, with ill-fitting grey metal doors that had to be wrestled shut. Then, with only my books, I had to go over to where one set of guards waited behind scratched bulletproof plastic shielding and put my driver's license in the heavy steel drawer. I caught my finger, cutting it deeply, the raw unfinished edge of the drawer slicing through the flesh of my too-slow finger.

Then into the airlock—a double door—one set of bars clanging shut behind me and a long delay while another set of guards inspected me from behind their window before the inner bars slowly slid open. I stood there for a full five minutes, feeling humiliated, not daring to look at the guards after one such glance revealed the three men, double chins bulging over their tight collars, nudging each other and miming the shape of my breasts.

I was already terrified about meeting the prisoners and having to be alone in a room with them, but now I was also furious. If they treated me, an outsider, with such contemptuous disrespect, I could only imagine how they treated the female inmates I was coming to see.

That first time, we met in one of the classrooms. Only two women showed up. Rhonda lumbered in first and sat in the middle of the front row, enveloped by a deep calm and air of being at home. Right behind her came Iris. Thin and nervous, Iris walked around the room a few times, looking at the blackboard and running her hand over the dull cement block walls before coming to sit next to Rhonda. They compared nail polish, hands spread out in the air in front of them, while we waited to see if anyone else was coming.

Rhonda and Iris seemed like anyone I might have met on my street or in the tot lot. I talked a little bit about the class and asked what they wanted to get out of it. Rhonda said she wrote poetry, and Iris that she wanted to write a memoir. I suggested a writing exercise but they politely refused, saying that they had to wait for inspiration before they could write anything.

Afterwards I talked with Jill about giving up since there didn't seem to be much interest, but she encouraged me to keep at it.

"Just show up," she said.

The following week the room was filled with silent, surly women. *What have I gotten myself into?* I thought. Then I remembered the touchstone Miss Smith had given me back in college: *Pay attention; each person has value.*

After much prodding, one woman said that they had been told their furloughs would be affected if they didn't take my class.

Frustrated and angry, I adjourned the class to the common area in the women's cellblock. It looked like a lunchroom with six or seven long tables, orange molded-plastic chairs, a television tuned to soap operas, and a window with a view of a high wall. By meeting there, I figured that the women who were not interested in the group could do what they normally did while still officially being in my class. The black women sat at one table, the white women at another.

A handful stuck with me, week after week. Maybe they felt sorry for me or were simply bored. We sat at the table farthest from the television. Rhonda had written some poetry, and wanted advice on publishing it. Iris, a recent arrival, wanted to write about her stint in a Mexican prison. "People think Mexico is *hot*," she said, banging on the table, "but the prison was in the mountains and it was *cold*. I'm telling you. No glass in the windows and only one thin blanket each."

The other three women claimed they had never written anything and didn't know how. I found that they were happy to talk, however, and figured I had to start where I could and work from there. I had arranged for pads of paper and pencils to be available, since I wasn't allowed to bring them in. That day they wrote character descriptions of each other: Iris getting people in trouble; Linda strutting out to meet her hated lawyer with one hand on her hip; Toots trying to clean a window by holding the bottom of her sweatshirt against it and jumping up and down "right in front of the damn camera"; and Rhonda always willing to help the girls with their hair but bitchy right after she woke up.

Rhonda took me to see her cell. All the cells, though tiny, were clean and decorated with photos and pictures cut out of magazines.

"You all don't stay in your cells?" I asked. "Everyone always seems to be out in the common room."

"Yeah, we're only locked in at night or if there's something going on," she said.

A young African-American woman about my age named Charelle showed me a photo of her two children. I showed her a picture of Jeremy and Justin.

"It tears me up," she said. "Not seeing them. I don't want them to come on visiting day, see me like this."

I asked her what she was in for.

"Prostitution, like most everyone else. It's that or drugs. Sometimes both. I've been in before. It comes with the job."

"If you hate it so much, why don't you do something else?"

"Like what? Welfare?" She looked at me coolly. I had told them my background, figuring it might be common ground for us. "Don't make no money on welfare. I can make more money in a night than you get in a year."

"Three thousand? Every night?" It seemed like a lot to me.

"Well, maybe not every night."

It was sometimes hard to get them to concentrate. One day they were playing gin rummy and counting down the minutes till Rhonda got out of lockup, where she'd been for a week. We talked a little but they jumped from subject to subject, coming back to Rhonda every few minutes. When she finally walked in, however, everyone acted blasé and played cards furiously.

Without looking up from her cards, Iris said, "Welcome home." That prompted an old woman in the corner to start up her usual rant about wanting to go home. The other women ignored her and continued their gin rummy game.

The women in my small group did some of my writing exercises, such as describing their ideal man or a house they would like to live in. Iris described a house with heavy Spanish furniture and black wrought-iron balconies, while Donna yearned for something filled with early American antiques. I expected that most of them—the lucky ones who didn't live in projects such as Great Brook Valley—lived in neighborhoods like mine and Jill's, where the buildings were pretty rundown, with hallways that smelled of damp plaster and stale exhaust from the gas space heaters.

I wanted to move on to poetry since that was Rhonda's area of interest. The others agreed, but when the time came, there was no way I could coax them into writing poetry. I read some Nzotake Shange and Audre Lorde, and we talked a little about what we liked about the poems. They looked through the books that I brought and picked out poems to read aloud themselves. They even wrote a collaborative poem, passing it around and around the circle, each woman contributing a line at a time or passing it on:

Dirty floors & dirty ceilings; keep the walls clean
Sacred broom, sacred mop; I mean
Believe in yourself because if you dont than nobody Else Will
I only believe in the clean walls.
Walls are clean enough when they disappear
Speaking of walls, I need to do two rooms in wallpaper.

People wont let be live the way I want to. so I'll Have to make them
Santos is leaving his walls to melt into the sands of Puerto Rico
walls, walls, walls, walls, walls, is that all?
It's always good to be 3 steps ahead because someone is going to push you
2 back.
I can recall a fall past the walls and that's not all, it was good for me
Pizza Pizza on the wall, what's the best pizza of all?

That was as far as they would go in terms of writing a poem. I tried reading them a working draft of one of my own poems and asking for their advice. They seemed to enjoy talking about which parts worked and which did not, and we had a lively discussion that started out to be about possible images that might be effective in the poem, but then took on a life of its own and migrated to scatological metaphors for certain guards.

Sometimes I helped them write letters to their lawyers in proper business-letter format. I also worked with them on writing letters to their children that sounded more like the way these mothers actually talked, instead of stilted formal notes.

I told Jill things were getting better, though it was always a struggle to get them to write anything. "I would kill for an empty room and all that free time," I said. "You know, Lewis Carroll once said that he thought being in prison, if he had access to books and paper and didn't have to do hard labor, would be perfectly delightful."

"What was he complaining about?" Jill asked. "No kids to take care of. Servants too probably."

On this day, despite all my rushing around, I was late. I hustled the kids out of the house with shoelaces untied and hair uncombed. Then my old junker wouldn't start until I took off the distributor cap and dried the points. At the day care center on Edward Street, I just dumped Jeremy and Justin instead of staying for a few minutes to ease the transition as I usually did. But I was still late for the jail.

Rhonda and Iris were sitting at our table. "Where's everyone else?" I asked.

"Donna's in the laundry room. Linda's in her cell putting on nail polish. Don't know where Princess got to." Rhonda yawned. "I'm gonna take a nap." She plodded out of the room.

I looked at Iris.

"I don't think I want to do this anymore," she said.

"What about your book about Mexico?" I asked.

"What difference does it make? It don't matter." She turned to look out of the window.

"I think it does matter," I said. "Remember how you were going to warn people not to go to Mexico and do drugs because jail there wasn't like here?"

"So I'll do it when I get out. Don't worry; I won't forget. I have everybody's name."

"But why not work on it now while you have all this time?" I persisted.

Iris looked at me. "Because I don't exist," she said bluntly. "Not till I get out. I got myself turned off. Not thinking. Not feeling."

Chastened, I said, "What do you want to do, then?"

"Watch the stories, I guess." So we watched tv together till it was time for me to go pick up Jill.

As we drove, I told Jill that I was going to give up on the jail. "They're just trying to get through their time without ever waking up, and waking up was exactly what I was trying to get them to do."

"Well, you tried," Jill said. "It'll be different with Arlene."

Arlene was the new client Jill wanted me to meet. One of the public art projects supported by Jill's CETA grant was a mural at a neighborhood center called Friendly House. As part of the Model Cities piece of the War on Poverty, the neighborhood centers were designed to bring the city and federal services closer to the people who needed them—anyone who needed them, not only welfare recipients.

Arlene showed up to help with the mural and ended up talking with Jill about her dreams. Arlene had two: to go back to high school and to write a book about her family. Jill roped me in to help with the book but also thought it would be cool for the two of us to make some of it into a film with Arlene. The public library had recently gotten some video equipment we could borrow.

I thought the book was a great idea, but it seemed to me that there was no point in making a film unless there was something in Arlene's family history that would interest other people.

Genealogy didn't interest me very much. My mother had busied herself for years with tracing her family tree, proud that she could trace it back to the earliest days of the colonies. But I didn't see the point. What did it matter if your ancestors were royalty or farmers or pickpockets? Once a person's life was over, it was over. It didn't matter anymore.

What mattered was doing the best you could with the life you had. And families couldn't help you much with that, I thought, cut off from my own as I had been. Perhaps I had abandoned them first, choosing to spend my childhood hidden in a tree with a book. Certainly my mother had shut the door in my face when my marriage ended, leaving me holding Jeremy's hand, our trail of breadcrumbs eaten by birds and the dark woods all around.

However, I trusted Jill, and certainly her description of Arlene aroused my curiosity.

We got out of the car under the budding maple trees in front of Friendly House. Jill said, "There she is," and waved to a plump African-American woman coming down the steps, grinning at us and waving her arm in great sweeps over her head.

As the three of us left Friendly House and walked down the broken sidewalk toward Arlene's house, I said how much I'd looked forward to meeting her because of what Jill had told me about her.

"It was the fish, right?" Arlene said, her eyes bright as she looked up at me. She grinned, revealing a gap between her front teeth. "Jill loves my fish."

It was not the fish that made me eager to meet her, but the math. The woman walking beside me was the same age I was, 27, yet she had seven children and two grandchildren. In 1978, people were still saying I had a babyface, but Arlene, with her rounded cheeks and breathy voice, seemed no more than a teenager. Jill had explained to me that the babies Arlene had at thirteen and fourteen had both gone on to have babies themselves when they each turned thirteen.

She had dropped out of school when she got pregnant with her first child, but fourteen years later she was still happily married to the father of her seven children. Theirs was a biracial marriage that had succeeded despite all the odds. They struggled financially of course, with so large a family living on a policeman's salary, but if it was a strain, it didn't show on Arlene's merry face.

Jill, Arlene and I came from different backgrounds: blue-collar, no-collar and white-collar. Although, of the three of us, Arlene was statistically the most likely to end up on welfare, in fact she never had. Jill and I were the welfare moms.

Jill, walking behind us, said, "Get ready to be amazed. Arlene's apartment is more than the fish. It's incredible."

"We'll be there in a minute," Arlene said stepping carefully over the uneven sidewalk.

In the April sunshine, Wall Street's cracks and potholes showed clearly. A few trees might have helped buffer the light, but there weren't any. As we approached the corner, a city bus pulled away from the curb leaving a cloud of exhaust hanging in the air. The sidewalk was bounded by chainlink fencing that sagged in one corner and showed streaks of rust. Behind the fencing, shabby triple-deckers crouched sullenly in small, grassless lots.

The apartment being a little below street-level, we had to go down a few steps. Inside, the windows would have let in plenty of light, but they were covered with ocean-colored drapes. The greenish-blue light made me feel like we were underwater. Dark shapes lurking on the edge of my vision turned out to be chairs and a couch pushed back against the wall. The only other light in the room came from an enormous aquarium bubbling eerily in the corner. It had colored pebbles and ferns and more fish than I'd ever seen, some with long flowing tails, some with wide fins. There were some that were jet black till they'd dart into a turn and suddenly glint bright blue all down their sides.

"Aren't they cool?" Jill said.

"Gorgeous," I said, but thought: *mysterious*. These silent, brilliant fish swimming around and around in this dark, undersea room on Wall Street.

Arlene moved around the room turning on a few lamps. When I saw what emerged from the dimness, I was stunned into silence.

"Ha!" Jill said. "Told you! This is such a fun room, Arlene."

We were surrounded by animals. Huge rugs imprinted with lions, pandas, leopards, and tigers hung on the walls, overpowering the family photos. Behind the rugs, the wallpaper was a cheerful busy pattern of pandas and giraffes. The sofa was covered by a throw printed with lions, pumas, and zebras, and on the floor at one end sat a life-sized china tiger cub.

It was fun. "The children must love this room," I said, thinking of the pictures of lions and giraffes that filled my sons' room.

"We all do," Arlene said proudly. She opened a door in the far wall, saying, "Here are the kids."

Daylight poured through the doorway from a kitchen where a tall slim young woman with her mother's big grin was making peanut butter sandwiches for a swarm of children.

After introductions all round, the three of us returned to the living room with its cheerful collage of animals. We could hear the buzz of the children's voices in the kitchen and the bubbling of the tank where the fish swam in a mesmerizing pattern.

Arlene's ambitions were for her family. Arlene, who had dropped out of school to marry her sweetie, was determined to go back and finish high school in order to show her children and grandchildren the value of an education. We talked about getting a GED, but she said it wouldn't feel real unless she went back and sat in a classroom.

Then she leaned forward on her chair, gripping her hands tightly together as if to keep them from reaching out and grabbing at the air. Startled by her intensity, I realized that I had been taken in by her gentle manner and breathy voice.

"Before I go back to school, to get ready for it, I'm writing a book," she said. "And Jill thinks we can make a film about it."

I looked at Arlene, her round serious face and hair pulled back tightly into a little ponytail, and asked her what the book was about.

"It's my family," she said. "They've lived around Fitchburg for generations, you know, Shirley, Leominster. My family's part of the history there, and somebody needs to write it all down before everyone dies." She told me about a relative who had been an herb doctor. Arrested for practicing medicine without a license, he had been bailed out by his wealthy patients and went on to send his son to medical school.

But the story that made her decide to write the book was the one about her grandfather's grandfather, Gardiner Hazzard, who fought in the Civil War in the 53rd Regiment and was wounded at Honey Hill. His photograph hung in the Shirley Town Hall. It was his story Arlene most wanted to tell, what happened to him before the war, in 1839, when he was only nine years old.

Knowing Shirley as a sleepy little New England town with a white church and brick town hall anchoring the common, I tried to imagine what it must have been like in 1839: even quieter perhaps, with nothing interrupting the steady birdsong but the rattle of wagon wheels and the clopping of horses as farmers plodded into town to get coffee and sugar at the general store.

I didn't know much about that period, right before the Civil War, and wasn't sure how active Abolitionists were then. I was more familiar with the civil rights struggles of the decade just past, the 1960s, with its long hot summers of riots and Malcolm X preaching about white people all being devils.

By 1978, when I sat with Jill in Arlene's living room, the riots were long past, but the anger and fear had not disappeared. Racial tensions ran high everywhere, as white families protested court-ordered busing, while those who could afford it fled to the suburbs to avoid integrated schools.

This story about Gardiner, the one that Arlene most wanted to write down for her children, turned that anger and fear upside down.

In 1839 this man, a Mr. Little, convinced Gardiner's mother to let him take the boy, saying that he had a good job for him at a hotel in Little Washington. Instead, Mr. Little took nine-year-old Gardiner to Richmond and sold him to a Mr. Wiggins as a slave.

Mr. Wiggins intended to resell Gardiner immediately and shut him up in a pen with other slaves until the sale started. I thought about the pen and the child locked up in it, like Hansel sticking out a chicken bone for a finger.

Gardiner must have been pretty resilient, though, because it wasn't long before he was playing marbles with another boy. Then, tiring of that, he asked one of the guards if he could have a book to read.

How shocked the guard must have been! Slaves couldn't read. Yet here was this little boy, his dark skin covered with dust, asking for a book.

Gardiner was taken before the authorities and questioned closely. Mr. Wiggins had ordered him to lie, but Gardiner told them the truth about his family back in Shirley and the hotel job Mr. Little had promised him. Realizing that the boy was not a slave, the authorities wrote to Mr. Barrett who owned the store in Shirley Center.

What's the value of a life? What does one little boy matter? A lot, apparently. When the white townspeople of Shirley heard about Gardiner's being kidnapped and sold as a slave, they were so wrought up that they commissioned Major Brown, a local man who happened to be traveling in the South selling palm leaf hats, to go get Gardiner.

"Imagine that," Arlene said, her eyes shining, gripping her hands together even more tightly. "They got together and had Major Brown go all the way to Richmond and bring that boy back home. White people did that."

I understood why Gardiner's story had become a touchstone for Arlene and her family. All white people weren't devils, any more than all prisoners were animals, or all welfare mothers teen-aged African-Americans.

Arlene, herself, had already become a touchstone for me. We all want someone to swoop in and rescue us the way the townspeople had rescued Gardiner. But Arlene rescued herself. Like those who made art out of found objects, Arlene was the artist of her own life. With her fish and her magic room, she showed me that it was possible to live an enchanted life even on the broken streets of Worcester.

And her dreams stretched beyond her small home. She wanted to help heal America's racial divide, the legacy of slavery, Jim Crow, the busing riots in South Boston. She saw a middle way, a way to trust each other and see a child as, not a dog in a cage, but a real person to be cherished and nurtured and for Heaven's sake freed.

I thought about the quote on my refrigerator. *Why work if you don't have to?* If I could help get a story like Arlene and Gardiner's out to a wider audience, then I would have done something truly worthwhile.

18

JANUS

One Saturday morning I was sitting at the kitchen table. I set aside the morning paper to admire the daffodils on the table, their deep yellow petals catching the sunlight and reflecting off the wooden surface. Ben was drinking a cup of tea very slowly and looking out the window.

"What are you thinking about?" I asked.

"Nothing," he answered, distracted, as if listening to something that only he could hear.

I sometimes thought our minds ran on different circuits altogether. "What's on for you today?" I asked.

"Mac and I are going out to that junkyard in Auburn. See if we can find a starter motor so we can finish up that car. You?"

"I need to prep for the teens' writing group tomorrow and meet with Jill. Then I promised the kids I'd take them to the park if they were good."

Ben looked up at the ceiling thoughtfully.

"Is something wrong?" I asked.

"No."

I waited for more, but that seemed to be it. I wasn't sure what he wanted from me, from our life together. Perhaps he himself didn't know.

After a few minutes, Ben stirred. He smiled then, his gaze coming to rest on my face, warm as the sunshine. He reached out and covered my hand with his, much larger and work-hardened, its knuckles reddened by the April wind, with sturdy blue veins and little golden hairs glinting in the light. His great strength that could lift a crankshaft or twist open a recalcitrant bolt was held in check as we sat there holding hands, and I knew everything was okay.

At the park I spread out a blanket beside one of the ponds and gave the boys their sandwiches. Bundled in heavy sweaters, they looked like roly-poly toys but it wasn't long before they were up and running around, begging me for bread to feed to the ducks. I leaned back, the sun warm on my face and watched them. Other families were walking beside the ponds, pausing to point out a fish or grab a toddler who wandered too close to the edge. Some children scampered up to Jeremy and Justin asking to share their bread. From behind me came the whir of bicycles on one of the paths and shouts, laughter, and the rhythmic screech of swings, from the play area.

It was somehow satisfying to have all these people around, to be relaxing on a blanket while the kids played, exactly like any other family out in the park on a Saturday afternoon. Normal.

When I folded up the blanket and took the kids over to the play area, we found Fay and Hamid already there. While the boys ran back and forth through the tunnel in the sandpit, I joined Fay on one of the benches.

She asked how my morris dancing was coming along.

"It's fine. I like the dancing, but the people, well, we don't have much in common," I said. "We have different ideas about what's important."

Fay said, "Maybe it's because we're mothers. We have these long-term commitments." She waved at the kids. "We think in decades. If they're still students, then everything's temporary for them. They're still waiting for life to start."

She asked about my workshops, and I told her about Arlene. Jill and I made her film, borrowing the video equipment from the library. Jill shamed them out of the $9,000 deposit we were supposed to pay by reminding them that they had bought the video equipment with a Model Cities grant that was intended for poor people.

"That Jill!" Fay said, shaking her head.

The film started with me interviewing Arlene and then went on to show old family photographs and an interview with her grandparents. Gardiner's story was something the gentle, elderly couple came back to again and again to prove that there was goodness in the world.

"Sounds great," Fay said. She wanted to join one of my writing classes but couldn't make the daytime classes. "What about starting a group in the evening?"

"Sure. Let me see if I can scare up enough people. Most of the women I've talked with aren't free in the evening. I guess Ben could watch the boys."

Fay started teasing me about having a boyfriend. "And where are your love poems? I want to see them."

"Maybe when we get the evening group started," I hedged. I wasn't sure what I felt about Ben living with me. His reticence sometimes seemed impenetrable. But I understood. There was a part of me that needed to stay in its own house, away from everyone, even Ben, even Jeremy and Justin.

We were distracted by the kids. Jeremy was trying to pull Hamid away to play in the sand, but the younger boy refused to go. Hamid threw his arms around Justin and said, "I'm playing with Justin."

Justin smiled, and the two of them ran back through the tunnel.

Jeremy threw a handful of sand after them, and I called him over to discipline him.

After he ran off again Fay said, "He's just lonely."

I shook my head. "I know, but it's no excuse." I didn't want to argue with her. "Hamid has gotten so big. He towers over Justin."

"He's huge," Fay said. "But then Justin's so tiny. Is he still on the lowest curve of the growth chart?"

"Yes. The doctor says we don't have to worry unless he actually falls off the chart."

"Did she say why he's so small?"

"Doesn't know. She swears it's nothing to do with his heart murmur, and that he'll grow out of that."

"He's so frail too," Fay said. "You should put him on a macrobiotic diet."

"I think he's holy enough already." I laughed and held up both hands. "I'm joking. I know it's more than spiritual."

"Does Jill still call him the Buddha Boy?"

"Sometimes. I think he's more like the Little Prince."

Fay looked over at the kids. Jeremy and Hamid were on all fours racing Matchbox cars against each other while Justin smiled down at them. "I can see that," Fay said.

Standing there so straight with his blond hair sticking up all over, Justin did seem as if he might have come from a distant star. The people at the day care center all adored him and called him the Love Bug. They liked Jeremy too, though he got on their nerves sometimes with his boundless energy and uncanny ability to get into scrapes.

"I'm just relieved they've both adjusted pretty well to day care," I said.

"I don't want to think about it," Fay said. "I'm never sending Hamid to school."

Despite what I said to Fay, leaving the boys at day care each morning wrenched my heart. If they cried, I felt guilty. If they didn't, I feared they didn't need me anymore. I loved teaching the workshops, but sometimes felt like a fraud. What qualified me to teach anything to anyone? I told myself that we were figuring it out together, my writing students and I. The groups ran themselves, with all of us doing the exercises and freewriting and sharing the results. Going to pick up the boys in the afternoon, I reviewed the day, obsessing over my failures but encouraged by any signs of progress.

Not only was the teaching rewarding, but the stipend from my grant was slightly more than my welfare check had been. One of the first things I did with the extra money was go to a sale at Marshall's and buy a work outfit. Three and a half years on welfare, and I had gotten nothing for myself beyond some new underwear and a pair of second-hand jeans from Goodwill.

A suit was too much, but I bought a grey wool skirt with matching vest, a pair of shoes and some stockings. Together with a white blouse from my high school days, they made up a reasonably formal outfit for days when I had to meet with the director of some program about starting another writing group. Stepping out of the door, looking all professional, made my confidence soar.

In May, an opportunity came up for Ben in Pennsylvania. He didn't mention it at first, but seemed even more quiet than usual, if that was possible.

One night when we were sitting on the couch, I asked him if there was something going on.

After thinking a moment, he described some land in Pennsylvania he'd heard about that he might be able to afford, maybe work out a rent-to-own deal.

"You know that's where I'm from," he said.

"Yes, I remember."

"It's a chance to have the kind of place I've always wanted."

"We talked about it that night," I said. "Remember? During the blizzard?"

Ben smiled. "Oh yes, *that* night."

I laughed.

He shifted in his seat and brushed something off his knee. He didn't look at me. "I've been thinking about it, and I've decided to move down there."

I stood up and walked over to door to the kitchen. We had only lived together a few months, but I'd come to rely on his steady good humor, the warm bulk of him at night. In the doorway, I turned around to look at him. "Oh" was all I could think of to say.

"You could come too," he said, coming to stand next to me. "I'd like that."

"Me too, but . . ." I wondered what he thought the boys and I would live on. What would I do without my group of friends who supported me in so many ways and the precarious financial balance I'd achieved with the help of Section 8 and food stamps? Plus the timing was wrong. "I've barely started the CETA grant and that's for a year. I made a commitment."

Ben looked thoughtful. "Well, maybe when your grant is over you can come join me."

I nodded.

So he packed his tools and few belongings into his beat-up VW and drove away. I moved back into the little bedroom where the light from the rising sun first crept in and the bells from the stone church on the corner rang at 6 a.m.

For someone so quiet, Ben left a big empty space behind. The boys mooned around, complaining of being bored. I washed the dishes at night and left them in the drainer to dry by themselves. I roamed the apartment at night after the boys were in bed, feeling as though I had mislaid something. I sat in the rocking chair in the sunset window, the floorboards creaking under me as I tried to lull myself to sleep.

Still wide-awake, I gave up on the rocking chair and stepped out onto the front porch. Salsa music drifted up from the street where some of my neighbors were working on a car. I thought about the house behind me. Not having Jill upstairs changed the whole feeling of my home. I looked out over Crystal Park where the new leaves shadowed the streetlights and felt keenly the difference. It wasn't my front porch. And the house behind me had strangers in it.

Of course, I was busy with the writing groups I was teaching and, through them I saw some of my friends regularly: Jill and I were working together on one group, and Fay was attending another. And I made a new friend, Emma, when Jill encouraged her to join one of my groups in order to exercise her hands.

Emma had a number of physical problems including hands that were permanently curled into claws. She had been an artist before the problems with her hands started, forcing her onto Supplemental Security Income (SSI), a program that supported people who were too disabled to work. Emma didn't think of herself as disabled. She had taken up weaving, still able to maneuver the shuttle, and always wore numerous scarves and shawls that she had made herself out of quirky mismatched yarn, shot through with unexpected textures and colors.

We talked about goals one day, and she said that she had a vision of how she wanted to be. "That's why I can do things; why I'm happy; why I'm sane." She added that much as she wanted to have long-term goals, she felt she could only handle short-term ones at this point, finish what was on the loom without worrying about what came next or whether her hands would get worse.

The boys liked her, and she them. She was one of those rare people who could talk with adults and children with equal ease. Jeremy said that she reminded him of Mrs. Tiggy-Winkle with her glasses, long brown hair and comfortable lap. She entered into the children's games, helping them make up long convoluted stories using characters Justin had created. He mimicked their facial expressions, like strict Mrs. McGillicuddy for whom he pinched together thumb and forefinger at either corner of his pursed lips, and Tomasio, a hero who stood with chest out and hands on hips.

One Saturday, we visited Emma, climbing the musty stairs to her studio apartment. Dark and stuffy in the May warmth, it was almost completely filled by the loom and boxes of yarn.

"I get old sweaters and things from Goodwill and unravel them," she said. "And often people give away yarn and knitting projects that they never finished."

"I have a couple of those," I said, laughing.

Sitting at the loom, she beckoned to the boys. "Do you want to try it?"

Jeremy immediately climbed onto her lap and she helped him work the shuttle between the threads.

"My turn!" Justin took his brother's place without the usual tussle. Emma's tranquility always kept the boys in check.

Watching them bent over the loom, I thought that the boys were right about Miss Tiggy-Winkle. Emma combined the common sense demonstrated by Beatrix Potter's character with the whimsical fancy that could dress a hedgehog in a mobcap and apron.

As we were leaving, she said, "I heard about Ben leaving."

"Yes. He moved to Pennsylvania."

She looked at me shrewdly over her glasses. "How are you doing?"

"Fine," I said. "Of course, it's hard not having him there to babysit when I go into Cambridge for morris practice."

"I could watch the boys."

At Emma's words, Jeremy and Justin started hopping around like jumping jacks, yelling "Yay! Emma! Emma!" I felt like jumping up and down myself but hugged her instead.

My nascent friendships with Cynthia and the other members of my morris team had become important to me, almost as important as the dancing itself.

I especially liked dancing across from Cynthia with her long black hair and upright posture. Her poise and effortless grace made me dance better. Although still happy working as an office temp to support her dancing habit, she knew that at some point she needed to finish college and have a real career. She was always coming up with new schemes that might build on her interest in movement.

During a break at practice, she turned to me and—as if no time had passed—continued a conversation started the week before. "So, one kind of job I could have that uses this . . ." She waved her hand around the clusters of women catching their breath, getting a drink of water, or chatting, ". . . would be to become a gym teacher."

I opened my mouth.

"I know what you're going to say," she went on, holding up a hand to stop me. "Gym teachers! Those iron-faced women who tortured us in high school. But it doesn't have to be that way. I was talking to a friend of mine, a guy I knew at college. He called me out of the blue and we talked for hours. Anyway, he's a gym teacher now and really likes it. You get to teach health classes and things like that too."

She paused and I cut in. "Sounds reasonable. What do you need, just teaching certification?"

"Yes. Of course it depends on the college and which of my old credits they'll accept, but mostly it's the education courses I need."

"With those kind of courses," I said, "it doesn't really matter what college you go to. They all count toward certification, so there's no point in paying an expensive school."

She nodded. "I hadn't thought of that. A state college might work. At least it would be cheap."

"Worcester State College has a good teaching program. If you wanted to go there for a semester, you'd be welcome to stay in my guest room."

She looked taken aback. It was the kind of thing my circle of friends always did for each other, like Walt and his band staying with me when they had a concert nearby.

"I'll think about it. Thanks. Actually, getting out of Cambridge for a while might be good for me." She looked around the room. "Guess we have to get started again."

I wondered what it would mean to me to bring my different worlds together and almost regretted my impulsive offer. The team wanted to come out to Worcester to spend a day dancing on the streets and in the park, but I wasn't sure how I would feel about that. There were people in Worcester I simply wasn't finished with yet, people like Emma and Fay and Sherry. Their friendship was important to me; I didn't want my dancing life to come between us.

Being pulled in so many directions—work, dancing, friends—left me exhausted. I wrote in my journal: *Where am I going to find the energy I need? I look at people and don't see them. I panic when someone wants to love me. I drift through the days and nights only half here.*

A few weeks later Cynthia came out to Worcester to talk to people at the college, and I took her on a tour of the city.

"People call it the armpit of New England," she said.

"Well, it has its down side, but there are some fun things."

Cynthia had said that she was interested in putting together a coffeetable book on neon signs, so I drove her around to see some of the wonderful neon signs that Worcester boasted, like the giant hot dog dripping mustard over Coney Island Hot Dogs.

"Coffeetable books are really big right now," she repeated as we drove around. "My brother's a photographer, so he'd help me. I saw this coffeetable book on diners, a big seller, with photos of diners and little paragraphs about them. Nothing to it."

"We'll go by some of the diners then, too, so you can see them."

"Worcester is the home of the diners."

"Yes, I know," I said.

"The first ones were manufactured here. They were made to look like train cars because that's how they started out."

"I know." The unstoppable flow of her words amused me.

"Oh, look! There's the Miss Worcester diner," Cynthia exclaimed, pointing to the yellow and blue diner nestled under the highway overpass. "Look, boys, do you see that?" She twisted around to look at Jeremy and Justin.

"I'm going to take you to the Top Hat, next," I said.

As we drove around, I told her about Ben, trying to describe his appeal. "It's not like we talked a lot or read the same books or anything," I said. "There was just this calm about him, some kind of ease. Nothing ruffled him."

"Oh, I get it," Cynthia said. "It's that competence, watching a man do something he's so good at he doesn't even have to think about what he's doing."

"And the kids. He was so comfortable with them."

"Listen," she said, "you need to get out more. You should go to camp this summer. You've been working; you deserve a vacation."

I didn't know how to explain that my world didn't include vacations.

"And," she went on, "You can get a scholarship. It won't cost you hardly anything."

Camp was Pinewoods, a rustic spot near the Miles Standish State Forest south of Boston. It was owned by the Conant family, who were active in the local dance organization, and they rented it out to various groups, mostly traditional dance and music organizations. For a large portion of the summer, it was rented by the Country Dance and Song Society, the national organization of which ours, the Boston Centre, was an affiliate. In addition, the Boston Centre itself sponsored two long weekends.

Driving to camp for the Boston Centre's Fourth of July weekend, I came close several times to turning around and heading back to Worcester. I had never been away from Jeremy and Justin for so long. I knew they'd be fine with Jill, but nonetheless felt bereft. Who was I if not their mother? And how would these Cambridge friends react to me without the cute blond tykes who came on every morris tour and danced around on the grass waving white handkerchiefs in the sunlight?

The narrow blacktop road was intimidating enough, but when I reached a dirt road I stopped and consulted the directions again. A moment ago, I had passed the little white church that looked like something out of a Christmas garden. A prolonged search of the pine trees and scrub oak that bordered the road finally revealed, tacked high on tree, a small weathered board with "Pinewoods" hand-lettered in green.

Rumbling over the corduroy road, I wondered if I had lost my mind. Here I was heading into the woods to spend a long weekend among people who all knew each other but were mostly strangers to me. I felt like Jack climbing the beanstalk that had magically sprouted in his mundane garden, not sure what awaited me at the top, what dangers, what treasures.

I turned down an even narrower dirt road whose deep ruts rocked my poor little VW. Eventually I came to a place where the road split and some people were milling around in front of a weather-beaten shed. One of them gave me a map with my cabin and a parking space marked on it.

My cabin was at the far edge of the map, sheltered by pine trees and a few steps from the water. As I carried my things inside, my fears were forgotten in the wave of nostalgia that swept over me. The soft sand under my feet, the lapping of gentle waves, the mingled scent of pine needles, wood and mildew took me back to childhood summers at the shore. I suddenly felt at home, some longing in me that I wasn't even aware of finally appeased.

I plopped my things down on a bed and consulted the hand-drawn map. The camp lay between two ponds and had two roads that met in a vee at the entrance. A path made up the third side of the triangle with the camphouse at the point near me and the dining hall at the far end. Scattered throughout were cabins and pavilions for dancing, as I discovered when I went exploring. Sunlight lay across the path under spreading fans of beech leaves. Wind shushed through the pine boughs and set sunlight dancing across a bank of emerald moss where glossy wintergreen leaves grew low and dark. Wild blueberry bushes grew right up against the path, and I helped myself to the tiny sweet berries.

I made one circuit of the roads but then returned to my cabin, afraid of meeting strangers with whom I might have to converse. At dinnertime, I arrived at the dining hall after most people were already seated, and the roar and bustle almost sent me scurrying back to my cabin. Then I spotted Cynthia and some other members of Muddy River and went to join them.

Arriving at the evening dance, I hung back but partners quickly appeared to lead me out onto the dance floor, men from other morris teams who recognized me and others who apparently wanted to make a stranger feel welcome. The bone-crunching giants I had feared were only in my imagination.

I didn't stay long at the party in the camphouse afterwards, not knowing what to say to anyone. When I saw these people at morris tours, I had the kids with me and could talk about them, but what could I talk about now? I felt lost without the kids and my role as their mother.

Back at my cabin, I sat on the steps listening to the whisper of the pines and waves lapping against the weed-fringed shore. I didn't want to reveal anything about myself. Surely if they knew about my life—the struggles and compromises and ugliness—they would reject me, and how could I bear to lose the dancing I loved? And yet, Cynthia hadn't been horrified when she came out to Worcester. It was all very confusing.

The next morning I woke at my usual early hour, way too soon for breakfast, and left my roommate—a woman I hadn't met before—sleeping. I walked out on the dock behind the camphouse and sat in a deck chair, watching the sun come up over the trees on the far side of the pond. I tried to marshal my thoughts, but they skittered away like spiders on the surface of the water, like the damselflies that flickered out from under your eye, one second bright blue and the next gone.

After breakfast, I was caught up in the heat and bustle of activity. The days were filled with dance and music classes where members of my team introduced me to everyone. Now at lunchtime I confidently approached the dining hall, surrounded by a group of friends. We all sat together at a long table, passing the bowls and platters of food, talking non-stop. Suddenly there was a lot to talk about: classes, different teachers, styles of dancing, jokes and stories.

The evenings were taken up with a combined contra and English Country dance. The contra dances I had been to in church halls had been hectic, sweaty affairs, fun in their own way. But in this pavilion with no walls, an island of light in the darkness, I felt that anything could happen.

Music swirled through the air as I smoothed my skirt. A man reached out his hand and led me onto the floor, an unfinished wooden floor that gave under my feet. From then on, I was lost in the sweet sensuality of physical contact: the clasp of my partner's hand, his strong arm behind me when it was time to swing, the air proud against my face as he led me down the set. And the touch that wasn't a touch: the wordless communication of a look—warm, eager, laughing.

By the last waltz I was hypnotized by the music and the smooth easy movements of the dances. A man swung me into the waltz, balancing me perfectly. As we twirled around the floor, sweet violins interweaving with the silver notes of the piano, I felt like Anna in *The King and I*, like Scarlett O'Hara at the ball, like no one but myself in my homemade cotton dress swept up in a magic circle of light among the dark pines.

Before I knew it, the distance I'd felt with the Cambridge folks had melted away.

I stuck pretty close to Cynthia, being the person I knew best. She and I planned all kinds of pranks. One night we laid a trail of Muddy River's green socks leading to the cabins on Women's Hill. Single men and women were segregated, with the men assigned to cabins on Men's Shore, so it was naughty of us to lure men up into forbidden territory at night. When they got there, they found women in sexy poses silhouetted against the curtains in Cynthia's cabin, paper cutouts that we had carefully positioned there, pinning them to the curtains. I felt myself getting sillier and more reckless as the weekend went on. I thought, *This is what I should have been doing in my teens.*

I skipped a few classes in order to have time to sit on the cabin porch by myself or walk in the woods. I could actually read a book without being interrupted by kids every couple of minutes. Pure bliss. But after a couple of days I became restless, feeling as if there were something I ought to be doing.

Still, I never missed an evening dance. Each one was like the coming out party I never had. I didn't lack for partners, being equally happy dancing with men and with women.

And I stayed for the parties after the evening dance. On the last night, waltzing in the camphouse, I caught my reflection in the window. For a second I wondered, *Who is that? That woman being waltzed around—how romantic.* Then I realized it was just me.

As Cynthia swept by in the arms of a gorgeous man, she sang out to me,

"Some enchanted evening . . ." Several men seemed to have developed crushes on me over the weekend, as I had on them. However, I did not take this seriously and when the moment to act arose, I let it pass into the darkness. We had been singing old Motown songs and it was about two-thirty in the morning and the unspoken invitation was there, but I let it go by.

The next morning, as I drove back to Worcester, thoroughly exhausted, I struggled to sort out the weekend. If the danger had been only in my imagination, the treasure at the top of the beanstalk most certainly was not. Yet I felt uneasy. The giddy sense of fun and unaccustomed freedom had fallen away, left behind under the pine trees. How did Jack and his mother explain the magic hen he brought back? What do you feed it? And where could you possibly sell golden eggs without being arrested as a thief?

I wasn't the same person who had driven this road a few days earlier. But I wasn't sure who I'd become. Nor whether I had perhaps lost more than I had gained. Tired and confused, I wondered who I was. My identity skipped and skittered between the tree shadows at camp and Worcester's crowded grey streets. Later I wrote in my journal: *There is so much that I want. I wish I could see it all a little bit clearer.*

Cynthia was intrigued by Worcester and decided to pursue the idea of taking education courses there. She signed up for courses at Worcester State College, staying with me during the week and returning to the Belmont apartment she shared with several other people for the weekends. I was a little conflicted about having her there. I'd worked so hard to keep my two lives separate. I wasn't sure what she would make of my life.

Although only three years younger than I, Cynthia sometimes seemed like a teenager: she watched a lot of tv, ate ice cream and cold spaghetti for breakfast, and left her dirty dishes on the table. She talked incessantly, relating the minutiae of her days, exploring endlessly the possible motivations behind each action or speech of another person. After Ben's reticence, I wasn't used to so much chatter, but her conversation always entertained and interested me. And she adored my boys.

At four, Jeremy radiated energy. He looked like an impish Christopher

Robin, with fine blond hair that curled a little at his neck and a determined chin. He was always busy, drawing pictures or peddling his hand-me-down tricycle determinedly up and down the sidewalk. He loved playing with Jill's boys who were six and nine, wrestling in the living room or building raceways for their Matchbox cars.

Justin was tiny, still barely clinging to the bottom curve of the growth chart. His friends Hamid and Nathan adored him, as did the women on my morris team. Imaginative, thoughtful of others, he sometimes seemed like a being from another dimension, a more advanced civilization. He could be wicked too. He often hid one or two of his library books. I wouldn't notice they were missing from our big stack of picture books until the overdue notices arrived. He finally admitted that he did it in order to get mail addressed to him.

Once when I asked the boys to clean up their room, Jeremy scowled and said, "What about Cynthia? Her room is messier than ours."

Cynthia looked around, surprised. "You're absolutely right. That's only fair. Come on, let's go."

An hour later, the kids were finished and went to peek in Cynthia's room to check on her progress. The room was still in chaos but her sock collection was flawlessly arranged in chromatic order, like a rainbow.

"You are such a perfectionist," I teased. "Typical Virgo."

"You're right," she said ruefully, looking around at the papers and clothes scattered around the room.

As I watched Cynthia prepare for each morris practice, researching the dances, taking copious notes, walking the separate track that each person in the set would have to follow, I began to understand why she was such a good teacher. I tried to emulate her in preparing for my writing workshops.

In the evenings, Cynthia helped with baths and bedtime. She had already learned that parental trick of continuing a conversation despite interruptions to settle a squabble or tie a shoelace. She loved playing with the boys, though she acted more like their older sister than a parent.

One night there came a knock at the back door I rarely locked and then Fay's voice. "Hi. Barbara? I have that book you wanted to borrow."

"We're in the living room," I called.

Fay appeared in the doorway and halted, looking around.

The kids having already gone down, the room presented a gentle mix of repose and industry. I was kneeling on the floor, Xacto knife in hand, working on the layout for the newsletter my Grafton Hill writing group put out. Cynthia was curled on the couch reading a book for school. The lamps cast a soft glow, and the sound of Bach's Partita #3 for Solo Violin played by Nathan Milstein filled the air.

"How lovely," Fay said hesitantly.

I stood up. "Come on in. You know Cynthia."

"Yes, hi." She held out the book to me. "I just wanted to drop this off."

"Thanks," I said. "Come sit down."

Cynthia set her book aside. "Won't you have a glass of wine with us? We were about to open a bottle."

"No," Fay said, shaking her head as if maybe her saying it wasn't enough. "If I sit down, I won't ever leave."

I walked her out. At the back door, I said, "Tired?"

Fay shook her head. "It's only . . . you both looked so peaceful. I might not want to go home." And then she was gone.

As I brought the bottle of wine and two glasses back into the living room with me, the record ended.

"What was that about?" Cynthia asked, getting up to turn it over. "Did I say something wrong?"

I shook my head. "It wasn't you." The elegant, intricate threads of the solo violin wove through the air as I poured the wine. I thought of Fay's house, the endless construction, the litter of tools, wood scraps and tarps that filled the hallway and crept into the corners of her rooms, the house that would never be finished because it had to be perfect.

That night I wrote in my journal: *Who am I? Where do I belong?* I didn't want to think about how my Worcester friends viewed the way my life was changing, between the brief relationship with Ben and my new friendships with the Cambridge folks. And my CETA job.

19

REACH OUT

Finding people to be in my classes was the hardest part of my job. Unlike teachers in a regular school, I had to go out and recruit students. I had learned to be assertive to defend my sons, but this outreach required a whole new level of boldness from me. I put up posters that Jill had designed for me. I consulted social service organizations like the Age Center of Worcester and the Girls' Club. I gave talks about creative writing at arts organizations and bookstores.

Mostly, though, I went around to neighborhood centers to drum up classes. Directors of the centers encouraged me to form classes there—they welcomed any free service they could offer their clients—and allotted me a metal table and chairs in one corner of the large busy room where usually day care was going on in another corner, a GED class was being held in the back, and intake workers were meeting with clients at desks scattered around the room.

Sometimes they gave me referrals to people in the neighborhood. A Hispanic woman I visited, Margie, had newborn twins and two daughters, one of whom was going to Head Start. Margie's twin 16-year-old brothers also lived with her. We sat around the kitchen table talking for a long time. She was interested in my classes but all her spare time was dedicated to getting a job so she could get off of welfare. I didn't say anything. We all wanted to get off of welfare, but I didn't see how Margie could hold down a job with six kids in the house, two of them newborns at that.

I visited several other women, including an extended French-Canadian family on Beacon Street: Jeanette, her teenaged daughter, her mother and her mother's sister. I enjoyed them immensely, the chaotic swirl of people trying to talk over each other, their evident concern for each other. Jeanette seemed to be the calm center. Friendly as she was, it didn't seem like the appropriate time to try to persuade her to join one of my classes. She clearly had too much going on and too many distractions to listen to my pitch.

I continued to do outreach even after the classes were organized, visiting people who had stopped coming, looking for new members. It was a never-ending task. I seemed to be living at a breakneck pace, racing through the fall, the windblown chill November days where everything was brown, even in the sun.

One group of teens met with me at St. John's Rectory. The basement room was pretty bleak, with a dirty beige rug, a few tables, and a corner apparently dedicated to collecting jumble sale items: bulging plastic bags drooping over cardboard cartons, a metal clothes rack with dresses and shirts hanging on it. The ten girls, a mix of black, white, and Hispanic, all from Doherty High, sat awkwardly in the rows of mismatched metal folding chairs.

I was introduced by Sister Michelle, who had assembled the group for me. The first thing I did was have the girls pull the chairs into a circle. They laughed at the idea but made the circle quickly, not letting Sister Michelle help, and ushering her to her seat as if it were a throne.

I began by talking about creative writing, how we can use the things that happen every day as a starting point for stories.

A heavyset girl who sat dead center in front of me was shaking her head.

I struggled to remember her name. "What is it, Lori?"

"No way. You're so wrong," she asserted, sitting up tall and spreading her arms wide. "Writing comes from the imagination and has nothing to do with real life. Like I'm going to write about being a princess and having ten boyfriends."

The other girls laughed, and she looked around at them grinning.

"And fairy tales," she went on. "You never have witches in gingerbread houses and stepmothers with poisoned apples in real life."

The girls laughed again. Sister Michelle opened her mouth to speak, but I looked at her and shook my head slightly.

"Those are good examples, Lori," I said. I went on to talk about metaphors and—suspecting that at least some of the girls came from broken homes—about stepmothers. When none of them said anything, I talked about how fairy tales have been passed down through oral tradition, and compared it to the game of Gossip or Telephone, where a sentence changes as it passes from one person to another.

"Yeah, I like that game," said another girl.

We played a couple of rounds, and then I asked them to tell me a story about something that happened to them that day. A few responded haltingly. Then a girl turned to the girl next to her and told her about being splashed by a car. After that, they all started talking, mostly about teachers, what Doherty High was like, and about a recent "rumble" at North High. It started with a white guy pinching a black guy's girl and ended up with blacks, whites and Chicanos fighting, people getting arrested en masse, and school administrators locked in their offices.

Sister Michelle looked a little hesitant, so I steered the discussion into character sketches and asked them to write a character sketch of a teacher for next time. I told them not to worry about grammar but just write as if it were a letter to a friend.

Having gotten over their shyness and with Lori as a ringleader, the girls liked to talk, but were reluctant to write. Sometimes I brought in something to read to them. In later sessions, I tried other techniques such as writing down what they said and giving it to them to use as a jumping-off point. I brought in a tape recorder, but they laughed and refused to let me use it.

I used some of my funding to buy journals for them, plain old spiral notebooks, but they were delighted and eagerly discussed strategies for keeping them secret from brothers and sisters.

Patty, a quiet and reserved girl who consistently refused to write anything, came in late that day and accepted a journal without enthusiasm.

"Is something wrong?" I asked.

She looked up at me, her brown eyes narrowed.

Lori leaned over to Patty and said, "She doesn't know."

Patty glanced at Lori and then back at me. Finally she said, "We were burned out this week."

I waited expectantly.

Patty sighed. "It was like a nightmare. People were screaming and it was dark. I woke up and couldn't breathe." She went on in a monotone, telling about the terror of that night, trying to get out of the house and then to find the rest of her family, her father finally staggering out of the smoke carrying her crippled sister. "The stink was the worst. Going back to pick through and see if we could save anything."

Lori told me later that our class was the only time Patty ever talked about the fire. I felt like I'd taken a giant step if she trusted me enough to talk, even if she still refused to write.

Another day our topic was colors, and we talked about what our favorite colors were. We wrote some collaborative poems, each contributing a line, and then talked about what colors we associated with ourselves.

Lori said that she was greyish-black on the outside—"Tough, ya see? like a rock."—but inside she was pink. She went on to write a detailed description of her bedroom, the room she wanted, not the one she shared with her sisters. Her ideal room was painted pink with white woodwork. Pink curtains hung in the windows and green plants sat on the windowsills. The canopy bed had a pink bedspread and sat on a pink shag rug. Even the white desk and bureau had pink knobs. There was a big closet full of clothes and a bookcase large enough to fit in a lot of books.

Listening to Lori read her piece made me sad about what she had to keep secret. Yet I understood the importance of being tough.

Often I wished my students had someone better than me to teach them, someone who knew what she was doing. I knew enough about writing itself, but was less confident about the way I'd chosen to teach it. The syllabus I'd put together looked great on paper but wasn't playing out quite the way I expected in the dingy church basements and neighborhood centers.

When I poured out my concerns to Jill, she suggested that all teachers probably felt like that, most barely staying a few steps ahead of their students. In her own art classes, she found she had to be flexible and stay open to the students.

I spoke with Jill almost every day. If we didn't run across each other in our travels—we taught classes in the some of the same neighborhood centers—then we'd meet for coffee at Friendly's or talk on the phone.

"It's not a question of literacy," I said to her one day in March when we met outside Main South and ducked into the coffee shop on the corner. "They all know how to read and write just fine. Well, their grammar's a little rough sometimes, but that's nothing. I can't get them to do it."

Jill opened two plastic cream containers and poured them in her coffee. "What do you mean?"

"I thought the only problem would be getting them to talk to me, to join in the group. But sometimes it's hard to get them to stop talking and write something."

"You could try not talking. Going directly into the assignment."

"I guess. The talking was meant to get them warmed up, but it's so much easier than writing. They'll do anything to keep from writing," I said.

Jill smiled ruefully. "I'm the same way. I procrastinate like crazy. I'll even clean the house to put off working on an art project."

She had me there. I hadn't thought of it that way. "You're right. I do that too. Are you having the same problem?"

"Slopping paint around is a lot less scary than picking up a pencil and exposing yourself. Once we decide on the design for a mural there's not much they can do to put off painting it."

I nodded. "I guess it is different."

"How's Emma doing?" Jill asked.

Emma had asked to join one of my groups in order to be prompted to write more often, as a form of exercise for her twisted hands. She said it was also a good way to communicate with other people and talked about having a newspaper column or radio show. After some discussion, she selected the group of elderly women from the Age Center.

I said to Jill, "Emma's gotten to be friends with this one woman, Maria, despite the age difference. But one day this woman named Miriam showed up and immediately turned the meeting into a counseling session for Emma."

"That's ridiculous," Jill said.

"I know. I tried to get Miriam to stop telling Emma what to do, but she said, 'I can because I'm special. I'm a gypsy, and I was born with a caul. That gives me the right to tell people what to do. I have a sixth sense to guide me.'"

Jill stared at me and then burst out laughing. "You meet the strangest people."

"I ended the meeting fast. And Miriam hasn't come since." I leaned back against the wall, reflecting back on my failure to control the group. I was discouraged too that the groups were still so small that I was having to do outreach all the time just to keep them going.

"You're not that desperate for people, then, I guess," Jill said.

"I am. I'll do anything to keep people. Emma's group? I spent an hour after class addressing Easter cards for one of the women whose arthritis was bothering her. And one of the women in the Green Island group broke her leg, so I've been going to her house to meet with her and take her some of her poetry that I'd typed up because she wants to try to publish it. One time I went over right after she got the cast and couldn't move around easily, so I mopped her kitchen floor for her."

"That was a kind thing to do."

I waved Jill's words away. "The last time I went over, she wasn't living there anymore. Turns out she'd moved and gotten a second job so she didn't have time to write anymore." Again I was sure that it was my fault the woman had dropped out, that I had not been a good enough teacher.

"People are going to do what they have to do," Jill said. "Anyway, what's the worst that can happen? They aren't paying anything for the classes, so at most they are wasting some time. I figure whatever little bit they get out of our classes is something they didn't have before."

I thought about the poem I had written the day before, joining my class in their exercise of writing down whatever images came to mind and then putting them together like a collage, trying to find the pattern that linked them. My horses and ice skaters had suddenly come together into a poem, but looking at it later I realized that all the images were of helplessness, the horses trapped in a burning barn, the skater caught under the ice.

Jill drank the last of her coffee and started putting on her coat. "Where are you off to next?"

"I have to go see Marsha," I said.

Marsha was part of my group at Green Island Neighborhood Center. One day, when she was the only one to show up for class, she sat at the table with me, slumping forward, her shoulders collapsed inward, and her hair falling around her face. She fingered the pad of paper I'd given her, pushing it this way and that.

"See, this is the thing," she began. A short woman, she wore a heavy sweater that billowed around her.

"Yes?" I said encouragingly.

She hesitated. "I want to write because . . ." She looked down, noticed that she was fidgeting with the pad and put her hands in her lap.

"Maybe we should just start with freewriting," I suggested. "If you want, you can explore your reasons for writing, but you don't have to."

She hooked her shoulder-length dark hair behind her ears and looked up at me. One corner of her mouth quirked up. "Okay."

As we worked together that day, she finally opened up a little. "I'm not used to talking. I have ideas and opinions, but no one wants to listen to me." She lived with her mother and brother in an apartment up Bell Hill.

"How is that?" I asked.

"Well, you know, I want to move out, get my own place." She was nearly thirty and worked part-time at a Cumberland Farms, so it was a real possibility. I offered to help, maybe driving her around to look at apartments, as I had recently done for Emma.

Over the next few weeks, Marsha did the freewriting and the exercises we worked on in group, writing steadily in her rounded backwards-leaning script, but completed none of the home assignments. One day, I gave her a spiral-bound notebook and encouraged her to keep a journal of a trip she was taking, driving her mother to Virginia.

I shared some examples in a collection I had, *Revelations: Diaries of Women.* "You don't have to do anything like these," I assured her. "I only wanted to give you some ideas. It's your journal. You can do whatever you want."

She was delighted with the journal, writing her name on the cover. Then she told me a little about her family, admitting shyly, "My mother treats me like I'm still a little girl. She bosses me around all the time."

"It must be nice to have someone else clean and cook, though," I said, ever the Pollyanna.

"Oh, I have chores." Marsha looked away. "It's really my brother."

"You don't get along with him?"

"I stay away from him."

I leaned forward. "What do you mean? Are you afraid of him?"

She looked down at her clasped hands and nodded her head.

I felt my stomach drop. I was merely a writing teacher, not a psychiatrist or social worker. "Is he abusive? Does he hurt you?"

She looked up at me. "No. Not yet. But he wants me to leave. He wants to have the place to himself, and my mother to wait on him."

"But what does he do?"

"He has a gun," she said.

"Does he threaten you with it?"

"It's not like that. I mean, he doesn't point it at me and tell me to get out or anything."

"Then what?"

"Well, like last night when I got home from work and went to get ready for bed? He was out, but on my pillow there was a trail of bullets pointing to the hollow where my head was, you know, that it left when I was sleeping."

I was horrified. "Marsha, you have to get out of there."

"I know. It's just, well, scary."

"Believe me, getting an apartment by yourself is nowhere near as scary as someone leaving bullets on your pillow."

She did write in the journal while on the trip to Virginia and thought that it helped her to be more assertive, even if only in carving out time alone to write in it. Her next project was an essay about her brother's planned visit to Lebanon, where their parents were from. "It won't be what he thinks," she said.

"Write it out, all of it, the dangers you suspect he'll confront," I advised.

During the summer, Marsha found an apartment and moved out. She started looking for some kind of training program so she could qualify for a better job. At first she was joyful and excited about making a new life for herself, but then she showed up for group one week with her hair in her face and her shoulders hunched up.

It was only the two of us that day. It took a little prodding but eventually she told me that one of her neighbors was beating his children. "He does it right outside on the sidewalk," she said. "He hits them across their faces; pulls down their pants, the boy and the girl both, and beats them bloody with his belt."

"How old are the kids?" I asked.

"They're just babies. Four and five, maybe." Marsha's face was flushed and her eyes wet. "I don't know what to do. I can't say anything to him."

"No, that would be too dangerous," I agreed. "But you have to report him to Child Protective Services."

"What if they take the children away? That's what they do, isn't it?"

"Sometimes. If that's the best thing for the kids," I said. For all my fears about having my own children taken away—since being on welfare automatically made me an unfit mother by some people's definition—still I knew that in some cases it was the right thing to do.

"What if he gets back at me somehow?" Marsha asked.

"How would he know it was you?"

"That's true." Marsha seemed energized by her decision and we were able to get on with the lesson.

Jill and I both had groups at another neighborhood center up on Grafton Hill. Jill's group was working on an art project while I was helping some teenagers put out the community newsletter. I was the editor, taking over from a woman whose temporary job had ended, but I had only agreed to do it on the condition that it was part of one of my groups. I planned to have the students come up with the story ideas, research them, and write them up. Sometimes that happened, but more often I ended up writing the articles. It was hard to keep the teens involved, especially since I never knew who would show up on a given day.

A man from the printers taught me how to do layout, a matter of pasting up storyboards with the printed articles, photos, captions, and ads. I spent many long evenings kneeling on the living room floor, Xacto knife in hand. Jill helped with advice about graphic design.

Jill was waiting for me one day as I finished a session. Only one girl had shown up, a slender, serious twelve-year-old dressed in shorts and a tee shirt revealing long delicate arms and legs. She raised a hand in farewell as she trotted down the corridor ahead of us, clutching a bulky pocket folder with her other arm. Jill looked at me enquiringly.

"That's Tina. She's off to collect more ads for the paper," I said, walking out with Jill into the August sun, the heavy metal door clanging shut behind us.

"Is she the one you had to give a talking to?"

"About responsibility? Yes. Since then she's shown up for every meeting and done whatever I've asked her to do," I said. "It's astonishing. She's so young."

As we stood by our cars, I told Jill about the day that I'd driven Tina around to some advertising prospects. We stopped by Tina's house first to pick up her folder of forms, and she asked me to come inside with her, telling me we had to be quiet.

As we stepped into the living room, Tina glided over to the door to the front room. Before she gently pulled it closed, I saw in the shadows of the drawn curtains, a figure sprawled across a bed. The living room had a red beanbag chair that had been mended with masking tape, a tv on a plastic milk crate, and a plastic laundry basket overflowing with clothes.

"Shh," Tina said. "Wait here." She went into her bedroom to retrieve her folder.

Later in the car she explained that her mom worked nights and slept during the day.

"But who stays with you?" I asked.

"No one." Tina looked at me sideways. "I'm not a child. I know what to do. I finish my homework, watch some tv and go to bed."

I looked at her sitting there, so calm, so still. "Are you ever, I don't know, afraid to be there alone?"

"No. My mom locks the door when she leaves."

"She locks you in?"

"Yes. It's for my safety."

I was horrified. I thought of my own boys, how I hung over them at night after they were asleep, pulling up Jeremy's blankets—he always kicked them off, even when he was a baby—and rearranging Justin's stuffed animals so they were out of his way.

"How could any mother lock her daughter in and go off to work?" I asked Jill. "Leave this vulnerable girl alone? What if there was a fire or an intruder?"

Jill looked at me without speaking.

"Do you think I should report her?" I asked. "Tina's twelve, which is pretty old and she's so self-sufficient, but something about her seems so fragile."

Jill took a deep breath. "Sometimes I'm not home when Richard and Michael get home from school. I can't be, not with how crazy this job is."

"But that's only for a little while, no more than an hour or two," I protested. "And the woman downstairs listens for them."

"You send your kids off to day care every day," Jill went on remorselessly. "Some people would say that's neglect of the first order. They'd say, 'Why did you bother to have kids anyway if you were just going to warehouse them over on Edward Street?'"

"That's not the same."

Jill relented, dropping her eyes and rubbing her forehead with one hand. "We do what we have to do. We do the best we can. Given what we have. Have you seen Richard's room?"

I nodded. Jill's oldest son, finally given a room of his own, had made it a monument to order: everything in place, put away, even his bed made. His Legos were in their bins and his drawings for Dungeons and Dragons neatly filed.

"I wish I could be the mother he wants," Jill said. I thought of the clutter on every surface in her apartment, the table where I had to push aside papers and bills to set down a coffee mug, the stovetop with pots jostling jars of paintbrushes, the sink stacked with dishes. "But I am who I am. I do my best."

"We all do," I said sadly, thinking of all I had failed to do for my kids. "You're right. Tina's mom too." I felt like I would never understand the rules. None of the novels I'd read had prepared me for this world.

Jill said, "But the fact that you're worried about her . . ."

"I know. I care too much."

"I wouldn't say that." Jill paused. "But, well, it's not all up to you."

One Saturday morning not long after that, I was at the kitchen table long after the sun was up, reading the paper while I finished my coffee. Justin was still in his high chair acting out some story with two pieces of banana peel he pretended were people, jiggling them up and down and using different voices for them.

Jeremy pulled at my arm. "Come on, you said we could go to the park."

"Stop. You're going to spill my coffee," I said without looking at him. "Hold on a second."

I was mesmerized by the front page story of another fire, this time on Bell Hill. It was one of those double buildings, two triple-deckers stuck together, six apartments. Four people had died, two adults, two children. *Another landlord not wanting to de-lead his building*, I thought.

The phone rang and Jeremy, dancing with impatience, answered it. "Yes, she's here, but not for long," he cautioned, giving me the evil eye.

I took the phone. "Hello."

It was Marsha, the young writer from my class who had escaped her abusive brother. Marsha's voice was choked with tears. "Did you see the paper?"

"What's wrong? Is something wrong?" I asked. Justin laid down his banana peels and even Jeremy stood still, both of them looking at me with round eyes.

"Did you see about the fire?"

"Yes," I said. "I was reading about . . ."

"It was him," Marsha whispered.

"Who? I don't understand."

"That man who beat his kids. They just arrested him, right outside. He was yelling that they took away his kids. He thought someone in that building reported him." Marsha paused. "It was me, but he thought it was them, and now they're dead. What if he finds out it was me?"

What have I done? I thought. My sense of responsibility felt like a stone in my chest. I vowed never again to interfere with someone's life.

20
MOUNTAINS

Our CETA grants ran out early in 1979. Exactly as the CETA program had promised, Jill stepped into a job as a social worker at a halfway house where she had been teaching art therapy workshops. It was a different story for me.

Although still overwhelmed by the result of my personal advice to Marsha, I was determined to continue teaching the writing workshops that I had worked so hard to start. The CETA grant had not only "trained" me to teach by giving me the opportunity to try my hand at it, but had also whetted my appetite for the work. Teaching seemed like gardening: preparing the ground, planting seeds that might magically sprout, and nurturing the shoots while they became something quite special.

I had expected to find a way to continue to get paid for my workshops, but I was wrong. The neighborhood centers and other groups could not scare up any funding for me. Once in a while I was invited to give readings around town or to lead a writing workshop but there was no pay involved. Fay and I applied for some grants, including a Massachusetts Arts and Humanities grant, but neither of us was successful. I thought about writing to Ben but I hadn't heard from him since he left and wasn't sure if he was at the same address.

I didn't know what else to do, so I went back to welfare.

It was the easiest thing to do, even with the frustration and humiliation of having to deal with the welfare office. When my first check didn't arrive, I headed back to the office with Justin while Jeremy was at school.

After the familiar wait on the cold metal chairs, I finally saw a social worker, a woman in her 30s who was flipping through the papers in a manila folder. She looked up and greeted me and then went back to the papers.

When she finally picked up my file, she found that my hiring letter and request for reinstatement were missing. Anticipating a problem like this, I had brought my copies.

She was apologetic about the mix-up. Handing the papers back to me after copying them, she said, "I can't say when you'll get a check, but at least it will be for the whole month."

"And in the meantime?"

"Well, let's hope it comes soon. If not, come back and we can talk about Emergency Assistance."

It took several weeks for the process finally to grind out a check. Luckily Cynthia was still living with me and was able to lend me some money. This was the life I knew, arguments with the welfare office and all. I slid back into it as if I'd never been gone.

I began reading fantasy and science fiction by authors like Ursula LeGuin and Tolkien, losing myself in enchanted woods and heroes' halls, struggles of ordinary beings against evil wizards and dark magic. It seemed so easy in a book: the magic cloak turned up at just the right moment or the unexpected ally arrived to save the day.

I drifted. The snow that buried the park across the street began to melt, the top surface unchanged, only the trickle of water from underneath and the barely noticeable shrinking to indicate the change.

I took up writing again, continuing to work with some of the women I'd met during my job, but I missed the satisfaction of being paid for my work. I wrote in my journal: *All my work energy is gone.* If I wasn't going to be able to pursue this career of teaching writing in Worcester, then I wasn't sure what kind of work I would do or where I would go.

I considered leaving Worcester, though I wasn't sure how I would manage without the supportive community I had established. The sad truth was that day after day went by and I did the same things. It was hard to imagine making a change.

One cold morning I was jolted awake at dawn by a loud crash. Disoriented, I looked around the small room. Were the kids hurt? Maybe the house was collapsing, starting a slow tumble down the hill to the park.

Terrified, I rushed into the kitchen. The dim light revealed dark shapes all over the floor, like detritus from an eruption, silent now but for a trickle of dust. I crunched across the floor and turned on the light. The kitchen was a mess. The fiberglass panels of the drop ceiling had become saturated with water and fallen, along with chunks of the plaster above them. Remembering Jill's experience at West Street, I realized that there must be a slow leak in the pipes above the ceiling.

I checked to make sure the boys were still asleep and glanced at the closed door to the guest room, where Cynthia and her boyfriend of the moment slept. A dancing friend, he had come out from Cambridge to spend the weekend with her.

I lifted the sodden fiberglass panels one at a time, carried them into the bathroom and propped them in the tub to drain. Then I got out the broom and dustpan and started to sweep up the damp plaster.

The door to the guest room cracked open, and Cynthia's boyfriend appeared wearing only pants.

"What happened? Oh, the ceiling," he said, looking up.

"Yes, a leak somewhere. I'll go down and wake up the landlord in a little bit. There doesn't seem to be any water dripping now." I kept on sweeping.

"Do you want help?"

"No, I'm almost done. Thanks."

He looked at me for a long moment and then said, "You're amazing. The ceiling falls and you just start cleaning it up. Anybody else would be fussing and wringing their hands and complaining about their bad luck. But not you. You just clean it up."

I laughed. "Well, someone has to." It didn't seem like such a big deal.

He grinned back. "I think you must be the strongest person I know."

Startled, I stopped sweeping to stare at him. "Me? No."

He waved his hand and retreated to the bedroom, shutting the door behind him.

If only he could see the real me, fumbling, exhausted, groping my way forward and scrabbling up an endless cliff, rocks and scree slipping out from under my feet. It wasn't that I was too strong or confident to cry over fallen plaster; it was just that crying wouldn't clean up the mess.

I tried to set aside the hopelessness that threatened to overwhelm me. As spring inched closer, I started waking up at five to hear birds singing and smell the mud and thaw.

Cynthia was still there, finishing up her second semester courses. She listened to my travails and reassured me every day that somewhere a job was waiting for me.

On the back of an old envelope I made a list of possible jobs divided into those I could do at home and those outside. Determined to be thorough, I pondered them one at a time. What investment would be needed, in terms of training or funds? Which would provide enough money to support my kids? It was a daunting prospect. Nothing would be easy.

Not sure of what else I could do to find a job, I continued to read the want ads, but they only reminded me that I wasn't qualified to do anything. I had little work experience. I didn't have professional clothes, other than my one grey outfit, or the money to buy them. I got as far as applying for a few jobs— waitressing, retail—but was always turned down.

When even a Friendly's that had advertised for waitresses wouldn't hire me—"How long has it been since you held a real job? Are you kidding? Quit wasting my time!"—I gave up and lay on the couch reading my fantasy novels. *What did you expect?* I told myself. *No one wants a welfare mother, and that's all you are.*

In April, Jill suggested that we go to a fortune teller she had heard about. *Why not?* I thought.

We packed the four boys in the backseat of my VW and drove west on Route 9 in the pale spring sunshine. Following directions that Jill read off to me, I wove through a rather barren suburb of new-looking ranch houses. The one where the fortune teller lived had aluminum siding a cream color like the door and a grassy yard without even a bush.

My mother and her Roland Park friends would have turned up their noses at these identical houses set on sterile lawns. But I was swept by an intense wave of longing. What I could do with so much space! With a yard where the dirt wasn't mixed with broken glass, lead paint dust and soot, or trampled hard as concrete.

The woman who opened the door was big, taller than me and Jill, with a middle-aged heaviness. She wore an aqua pantsuit with a matching flowered blouse. Her hair was a brassy color and had an odd immovability about it. Her large features were accentuated by bright red lipstick and heavy mascara.

"There you are. I'm Gladys. Come in. Don't mind my stories," she said breezily, waving at the large television glowing in the corner. The curtains were drawn so the room was dim and very small. It felt claustrophobic, and I was nervous about having four small boys in a room crowded with knick-knacks. But the boys sat in a row on the brown and orange plaid couch, completely subdued. I sat on the matching chair while Gladys ushered Jill into another room and closed the door behind them. The boys huddled together and watched the soap opera silently.

After about ten minutes Jill emerged and it was my turn. I went into another small room, crowded with a disproportionately large maple table and chairs. Gladys sat down and started shuffling a desk of playing cards. Half-expecting her to deal a gin rummy hand, I sat down across from her and watched as one at a time she snapped the cards down on the table in bewildering patterns, sometimes tapping them with her long red nails.

As she laid them out, she described what they meant in a plain, matter-of-fact tone.

"Well, see, here this card with this one means you'll have a daughter."

"No way," I said. "No more kids for me."

"Yeah, sure, they can be a pain, but there's no doubt about it. A girl on your lap. It's your daughter."

I thought: *Well, we'll just see about that.*

"And this here," she said, tapping the card with her nail, "this means you're going to move. And soon."

"Huh," I said. "I like my apartment."

"No, a big move, far away. South."

"I would never move south," I said. "Well, maybe Connecticut, but no further south than that."

"Oh, yeah." She nodded her head and snapped down two more cards. "Much further south. Maryland. Maybe Virginia."

"Maryland!" I said. "Never in a million years. Nothing could make me live there again. Maybe you're seeing me visiting there. I do that once or twice a year."

"No, this isn't a visit. You're going to live there for many years."

That'll be the day, I thought, but listened to the rest of her predictions. I asked her about a job, a career, but she didn't see anything in the cards about that. Soon we were all getting in the car and waving to Gladys who stood in the doorway, a cheerful smile on her face but already turning back to her stories.

Jill and I compared notes on the way home. Jill thought what Gladys had to say about her was pretty accurate, but for me, a more unlikely fortune teller I couldn't imagine, and her predictions were not at all what I expected. Way off base.

"You never know," said Jill, laughing, and then turned to hush the boys who seemed to be making up for lost time thrashing around in the back seat and hollering at each other.

One day near the end of May, the phone rang as I was chopping kale and onions for lentil stew. I reached over to the phone and heard my mother's voice.

"I'm selling the house, and you have to come help me," she said.

I took a breath, but she went on before I could speak.

"This is a big job, packing 23 years worth of stuff. And your father! He won't let me throw anything away, all his precious boxes and books that he hasn't looked at in years. We'll have to find a way to 'lose' some of them during the move."

I cut in, "You're asking me to come down to Baltimore and help you move?"

She took a deep breath. "Yes. Could you please come help me? I need you. It's not like anyone else is being much use."

Remembering how my brother used to call her the Martyr Mother, I coughed to cover up my laugh. "Sure. Okay. But not till next week." I would have to wait until my next welfare check came to have gas money for the trip to Baltimore, but that little necessity would never have occurred to her.

As I hung up the phone, there came a loud thump from the living room. Wearing a superhero cape he had rigged up from a towel, Jeremy flew into the room. "Whoosh! Was that Jill? Are Richard and Michael coming over?"

"No," I said, picking up my disappointed boy. "Come on, then, Superman; let's make some play dough."

"Justin!" he yelled. "Play dough." He squirmed to get down and ran to get the bowl. "I'm going to help."

Justin, four to Jeremy's almost-six, came trailing into the kitchen holding his stuffed cat. He slept with a bedful of stuffed animals while Jeremy preferred to sleep with an eighteen-inch red plastic lobster.

Justin leaned against my leg while I pushed the chopping board to one side and mixed flour, salt and water in the bowl. It had been an odd conversation. My mother actually asked for my help rather than demanding it! Other than the time I had gone down to help two years earlier when she had her gall bladder out, my visits had been brief, usually a few days at Christmas. I thought, *Maybe this is what the fortune teller meant about going to Maryland!*

Roland Park in June, if it isn't too hot, is pure heaven. There are flowers everywhere, and a depth of greenery that buries you, layers of leaves that stretch up and up. But I had little time to enjoy it. Things had changed at home.

With her children grown, and over my father's protests, my mother had gotten a job as a real estate agent. When I walked in the door, she walked out, saying she had an open house.

"What do you want me to do?" I asked.

"You decide," she said. "I'm too busy."

Of course I knew how to pack up a house—it wasn't hard to establish a routine and show my siblings how to mark the boxes so they would be easy to sort later—but I was shocked that she would leave it up to me. When I was growing up, she was always telling us to think for ourselves but never actually letting us.

I decided I liked this new version of my mother. If only she had gotten a job earlier, back when we were kids. But back in the fifties, it was expected that women would stay home with their children. No wonder she hadn't wanted me to bring my babies home where my siblings could fall in love with them. She equated having children with giving up the idea of having a rewarding and useful life.

Of course, she still didn't ask about my life, much less offer to help. She saw only what she wanted to see, resolutely ignoring what she didn't want to know. A lifetime of secrets, of wearing long-sleeved blouses to cover the bruises, had created the public face she still turned towards me.

Although most of my time was spent packing, I did occasionally manage to take the boys out walking around the neighborhood, showing them the places where I had played my solitary childhood games. The boys climbed the tulip tree next door in Mimi's yard, the first tree I ever climbed. We walked the few blocks to the library to get a new pile of picture books, and across the street to the pharmacy and grocery store where people still knew my name even after so many years. We walked around the outside of my old elementary school.

I had grown up loathing Roland Park's inhabitants for their snobbishness and hypocrisy, but my years in Worcester had taught me to take people one at a time and judge them for themselves, so I found ways to talk with and enjoy the people I encountered in Roland Park. Several times a week I visited Dodie and Libby, a couple of my mother's friends, finding common ground despite the difference in our ages and circumstances.

Living among such people wouldn't be so bad, I thought, *especially if it meant a better life for my boys.*

One couple on our street, only three years senior to me, lived in a huge white house with almost an acre of beautifully landscaped yard, partially fenced in for their two preschoolers who were already put down for the prep schools their parents had attended. He ran a business that he had inherited from his parents while she did volunteer work and took care of the children. I sometimes stopped in to chat with them while my boys went off to play with their kids.

"Have you ever been to Bermuda," the woman asked me.

I blinked. "No."

She told me that her husband took her there every year for their anniversary, and this year he had outdone himself by having a stretch limo pick them up at the house and take them to the airport.

He smiled at her, his eyes warm. "You deserve it."

The two of them went on to extol the joys of escaping dreary February and luxuriating on Bermuda's balmy shores. I didn't have much to add to the conversation.

Knowing they had grown up in Roland Park, I asked if they had ever considered living anywhere else.

The woman drew back in surprise. "But I have. I went away to college, you know."

Then they started talking about improvements they wanted to make to the house. They complained at length about being too poor to put in both the pool and the foundation extension topped by a deck this year, and how inconvenient it was to have to wait till next year to do the pool if they decided on the deck.

I thought about my life back home in Worcester, balancing the purchase of dish soap or trash bags against paying off the electric bill, the nightmare panic when the car needed a new starter motor.

I remembered one of the boys' favorite stories, the story of the fisherman and his wife, where the man caught a magic fish who offered to grant his wishes in return for its freedom. There are many fairy tales about magic fish, but this was the one from Grimm where the wife is never satisfied with what the fish has given them and asks for more and more until the fish, in disgust, takes everything away, leaving the couple with only the simple life they had in the beginning.

It seemed very sad, to be unable to appreciate what you had. I was often guilty of the same thing, dreaming of traveling to places like England and Morocco, instead of simply enjoying my circle of friends and two smart, healthy children. But listening to this couple bemoan their poverty did help me understand something that had been puzzling me: if even these ostentatiously wealthy people thought of themselves as poor, no wonder so many wealthy people begrudged the few pennies of their income tax that went to keep women and children from starving. How could they understand what it meant to do without even something so simple as trash bags or a pad of paper because food stamps didn't cover it? They probably didn't even realize that their own entitlements, such as the tax refund for their mortgage interest, were more money than a welfare mother saw in a year.

As we walked home, the kids told me about the mountains of toys overflowing from the kids' rooms into the playrooms. "They never even play with them," Jeremy said with disgust.

Justin swung my hand. "I miss Hamid and Nathan. When are we going home?"

Even if I wanted Roland Park for my children, it was as out of my reach as it had ever been. Loved and hated, feared and craved, something in its layers of green and its entangling vines sent me racing back to the comfortable clarity of New England.

We got back to Worcester in the beginning of July, the weather unusually hot. The apartment had been shut up while we were gone, since Cynthia had moved back to the Boston area, abandoning the idea of teaching after two semesters of education courses.

I missed her company and the games that we had played. Back in May I had found a beat-up croquet set at Goodwill and Cynthia and I had held garden parties in the park across the street, dressing up in long skirts with hats to shield our delicate complexions. We had served iced tea, cucumber sandwiches and strawberries. She had shown me that it was possible to combine my two lives, Worcester and Cambridge, welfare and dancing.

When I went to Pinewoods for Fourth of July weekend, leaving the boys with Jill, I took the croquet set along. One night shortly before dinner, Cynthia and I held a garden party on Women's Hill and invited the whole camp. Admittedly the croquet set was hardly used and the iced tea we provided was supplemented by G&T's contributed by others, but we had fun swanning around in our white dresses and flirting with the men, some of whom added a tux jacket to their shorts and tee shirts for the occasion.

On the last night, my roommate left for the dance and I stayed on the porch alone. I wrote in my journal: *I'm too tired to know exactly what's real; I have to cut out all peripheral vision because the periphery has widened to a margin beyond reality.* I closed the book and sat on while the darkness deepened, looking out at the tree-fringed lake, listening to the frogs and the wind in the pines. Then I heard, faintly, from across the water, a piano, the gentle notes sifting through the trees. I waited until the piece ended and then got up and went to the dance.

Just as in the previous summer, the quiet reflection and carefree fun I had at Pinewoods disappeared once I got back to Worcester. Back to my same old dilemma. I had liked working. I wanted to work. Having a job had transformed my mother, somehow released that tightly-wound spring inside of her. But I didn't know what else I could do to find a job.

The summer heat sapped my strength. Sometimes I would sit on the stoop at Gates Street and look up from the want ads and wonder what I thought I was doing. Would I ever be able to get a job? I felt the weight of the house behind me, of the long years on welfare heavy on my shoulders.

So far I had come up with three employment schemes: being an auto mechanic, teaching creative writing, and my old dream of getting an advanced degree to teach in a college. Ben had made it clear that the first would be difficult for a woman and not pay very much; I could not find a way to fund the second; and the third seemed unrealistic. I felt like I was trying to climb a mountain only to find each path petering out or blocked by rocks.

Tired of chasing phantoms, discouraged, I wondered if I should instead be trying to figure out a way to stay on welfare. Welfare was the life I knew. And our life wasn't so bad. The days slipped by like watermelon seeds, too fast between my fingers. Every morning the boys and I got up early to work in the garden I'd planted in a community lot. On the way home, dirty and sweaty, we stopped at Bell Pond for a swim. After lunch, I needed to rest on the couch while the boys took a nap, but in the late afternoon we usually went across the street to Crystal Park where they could run around and play on the slide and jungle gym.

Giving up began to seem like a real option. The desperation to get off of welfare that had haunted me since the moment I decided to go on it had dimmed, worn away by the repetition of days. My life with its falling ceilings and recalcitrant social workers had become routine. I could barely imagine a different one.

It was not an easy life as some people would understand it; certainly nothing like my parents' lives, wrapped in the cotton batting that a steady and sufficient income provides. It was more like that path up the mountainside, the mud occasionally slippery after a rain but mostly okay. I had to keep going, hold my sons' hands and ignore the steep plunge of the cliff falling off to the side and no guardrail to catch us, only the flimsy rope connecting us to our community of friends, struggling as we were on the same path.

July slipped away, and still I did nothing.

I cursed my laziness, but my friend Emma comforted me, saying that it was hard to change. We saw a lot of our Mrs. Tiggy-Winkle that summer.

One day she and I walked the boys up to the top of the hill in Crystal Park, the park across the street, and sat on the ground under a copper beech while the boys played on the tall red slide that curled around and dumped them screaming out onto the ground. I had brought the newspaper with me, but left it lying on the ground. Emma and I looked to the south, watching the cloud galleons move slowly across the sky, seeming to catch on the steeple of the smoke-stained stone church. From beyond the church came the sound of a train.

Emma said, "Sometimes we have to be pushed out of our safe ruts." She held up her hands, bent like an eagle's claws . "If it weren't for these I never would have started weaving."

Her courage in the face of such a terrible handicap shamed me. How could I despair so, when I still had my health and my boys?

"The important thing is not to give up. There's always a way through." She leaned back against the tree. "Like my weaving. I see the pattern in my head before I start, but I never know how it will work out. I have to push through to find out."

"Your pieces are so cool," I said. "Unpredictable. The colors you pick are so unexpected and yet they work."

Emma raised her arms and looked up, her face and arms speckled with the light that filtered through the beech leaves. "Look at those colors. Who would have thought to put copper and grey against that blue?"

Justin picked himself up from the bottom of the slide and came racing towards us. "Emma, come push me on the swing." He got a stranglehold around her neck.

As she stood up awkwardly, Justin released her neck and began to drag on her arm to get her to move faster.

Left alone, I picked up the paper and turned to the want ads. Absorbed, circling anything that seemed remotely possible, I didn't look up until I heard Jeremy and Justin yelling Hamid's name. Their friend was running up the hill, his mother trailing behind him, her electric hair catching the sunlight.

While Hamid joined my boys at the slide, Fay sat down next to me, her fizzy energy subsiding. She looked over at the ads I'd circled and snorted. "Why are you knocking yourself out to get a job?"

Joining us, Emma said, "She can't stay on welfare forever."

"You're lucky. You don't have to worry," Fay responded.

Emma looked down.

"One of my friends is trying to get SSI like Emma," Fay said. "That lasts forever."

"Is she really disabled?" I asked.

"Oh, they all think she's crazy because she doesn't pluck her eyebrows and wear makeup. If she can get herself declared insane, then she'll qualify."

I couldn't help frowning.

"What?" Fay said. "The system is stacked against us. Even if we are able to get jobs, we'll only be paid half what a man is. Maybe we have the right to take what we can. Arts aren't supported. Hell, even teaching's not supported. You can't make enough to live on. And why? Because it's a woman's job."

I said, "Well, once Justin and Hamid are in school, you and I will have to find something."

"It's so frustrating," Fay said. "There's not enough time for everything now: Hamid, the house, the food co-op, writing. How can I get a job?"

Emma said. "You'll find a way, both of you. It might not be the path you expect but there's always a way."

"Maybe if I become a teacher," Fay said. "At least I'd get the summers off."

When we got home I dug out the envelope with the list of jobs I had made and sat down at the kitchen table. The boys were in the front room looking at picture books.

The air was sluggish with late-afternoon heat. No breeze stirred the curtains at the windows next to me. Feeling almost drugged by the thick air, I was tempted to go lie down on the couch with a glass of iced tea.

Instead, I pushed the newspaper with its useless want ads to one side and picked up the list of possible jobs with their pros and cons. My eyes tried to skim over the words, but I forced myself to go back and think through each one.

What about teaching children, as Fay had suggested? It was not even on the list.

I remembered running into Sherry a few days earlier. Suddenly there she had been, walking down Pleasant Street towards me, with her multi-colored eyes and gentle smile. She was still living out in Charlton with a boyfriend, but—like Fay—wanted to teach and had started working toward an Early Childhood Education degree.

I considered the idea of becoming a teacher myself. I had discounted the idea because my mother had always insisted that I would be an elementary school teacher when I grew up. But teaching had one great advantage: my work day would coincide with the kids' school day.

The night I decided to go on welfare came back to me, the way I sat with baby Jeremy on my lap weighing pros and cons. Back then, the two things that made any budget impossible were day care and medical expenses. Surely teachers got medical benefits. And day care wouldn't be an issue, especially if I could teach at the same school where the boys went.

What would it take to get certified? I tapped the eraser end of the pencil against the table. I had taken some education courses while in college to placate my mother, but had no idea how many courses were required or what they were.

Suddenly, preparing for a teaching career seemed like an overwhelming and almost impossible task. I looked out of the window, where the leaves of the maple tree seemed to droop in the still air.

Jill's decision to just do the next thing came back to me. That seemed like good advice, as did Emma's to keep trying.

I supposed I could at least go talk with someone at Worcester State College about what courses I still needed and if there was any way to get some financial help to pay for them, even though the thought of going to talk with a professor seemed like one more phantom path that would lead nowhere.

In the fall, Jeremy and Justin started school at Freeland Street School, a block beyond the park, Jeremy in first grade and Justin in a morning pre-school program.

Justin enjoyed making macaroni necklaces and painting huge blue and red pictures, but Jeremy was terribly unhappy at the school. He had been reading since he was three, but his teacher refused to believe that he could read and forced him to do consonant-sound worksheets for hours.

Ms. Johnson was about my age, big-boned with wavy blond hair. She wore tight dresses that stretched across her stomach, but they were in bright colors that I thought the children must enjoy. I tried to talk with her, offered to stay sometimes and help with the class, but she had a way of looking through me, as if I didn't exist.

She had taken a dislike to Jeremy the first day of school when he'd pointed out a misspelled word on the board. She took it as a personal criticism. She even made fun of him in front of the class for—as she said—pretending he could read.

I didn't know what to do. Jeremy came home from school every day and drew pictures of large faces with tears rolling down them. He printed across the bottom of each one: Im so sad.

I tried to comfort him, but he wriggled off my lap. I proposed trips to the library or the park, but he would only lie on his bed facing the wall, hugging his lobster.

The principal wouldn't consider moving him to the other first grade class. If I wanted to send him to a different school, we would have to move to that district, and what if we ran into the same problems? I could take them out of school and teach them myself, but then how could I get a job?

I felt baffled at every turn. I didn't know what to do.

One night I was sitting on Jeremy's bed watching him put on his pajamas. Justin was already dressed and curled up next to me sorting through a stack of books, choosing one for me to read to them.

"*One Fish, Two Fish,*" Justin said holding it up.

"No," said Jeremy. "We read that one every night."

"You can each pick a book," I said absent-mindedly.

Jeremy had been unhappy all evening, ever since he'd gotten home from school. He'd had a long timeout after trying to punch a hole in the wall of his room.

His frustration was understandable. I didn't know how to protect him. Helpless in the face of his misery, I said, "Jeremy, come sit on my lap."

"I can sit by myself," he said and arranged himself next to me, arms folded across his little chest, eyebrows drawn together in a scowl.

"I want to," Justin said, starting to crawl onto my lap.

Suddenly I felt Jeremy tense up next to me.

"What's that?" he said, taking my arm and pointing to the wall.

Looking up, I saw a strange light. A light that was moving. I got up and went through the door into the front room, the boys trailing after me. The front windows were lit up with an eerie orange light that I had never seen before, and we ran to the windows over the couch to see what it was.

It was my nightmare come true. A house on the other side of the park was burning, not just a flame here and there, but the whole house a torch in the darkness. People were already gathered outside. I went to call 911, but they said they already had a truck on the way.

So I knelt on the couch, the boys standing on either side, leaning against me, clutching me with one hand and the back of the couch with the other, their eyes bright in the strange light. They didn't make a sound.

We watched the house burn, the fire's brilliance dimming the streetlights and making the stars disappear. Even so far away from the fire, the air we breathed seemed thin and oxygen-starved.

It wasn't fair. Other people lived lives that were safe, where they could breathe freely and not fear cruel teachers or the ceiling falling or the house being burned down around them, where every decision didn't have life or death consequences. We skirted danger every day. I was the first to acknowledge that I'd made some pretty stupid decisions in my life, but I had always tried to put the kids first. And none of my choices—so far—had damaged them. Yet here they stood, excited and afraid.

When the firemen finally arrived, they stood around helplessly for a while before turning to spray the neighboring houses. People still stood in groups watching, more people arriving all the time.

Then came the terrifying crash of the roof falling in. The flames leapt higher than the treetops. The walls turned to light, becoming undulating sheets of molten gold, mere ghosts of a shape, before crumbling.

Everything changed in that moment. The despair and depression that had hung like weights around my neck vanished. I thought: *I will do whatever it takes to get out of this. I will not allow my children to grow up to this.*

21

Nursery Rhymes

That same autumn of 1979, I enrolled at Worcester State College. The professor with whom I'd spoken, Dr. Osborne, had walked me through the teacher certification requirements and helped me figure out what I was missing. I was astonished to discover that, if I didn't go for Early Childhood Education but was willing instead to teach in secondary schools, I only needed two courses and student teaching. I had no idea that I was so close. Getting certified—which had seemed an almost impossible task when I first considered it—now looked like a breeze.

Dr. Osborne understood my desire to get certified as quickly as possible, so that I could get a job teaching. When we discovered that the courses I needed weren't being offered that year, he took pity on me and offered to teach them to me as independent study courses.

Overwhelmed that a professor would go so far out of his way, I vowed to work harder on my schoolwork than I ever had before. After I finished these courses, all I would need was student teaching. However, Dr. Osborne warned me that it might be too late to set up a student teaching assignment for the spring semester.

Gloria offered to sit for the boys while I met with Dr. Osborne. While grateful for her offer, I hated to impose on her. She seemed to have enough to cope with already now that she had a new baby.

The previous spring, Gloria and Wayne had invited me over to their house to help with the birth of their third child. When we lived together on West Street in that rickety grey house, their son Nathan had stayed with me when Chanté, their second child, was born on Thanksgiving day. Gloria and Wayne's house was grey as well but a single family home. They were still in the process of fixing it up: some of the walls were partially demolished, and there was not much furniture.

They had decided on a home birth with a midwife in attendance, partly for financial reasons and partly for control. At home they could ensure that the lighting and music were conducive to the mood they wanted to create. They could also be sure that no unwanted drugs could be imposed on Gloria, as they had been during Chanté's birth. Natural childbirth was still new and had not been fully embraced by Worcester's hospitals.

When I got to the house, there were about a dozen people, chatting and carrying plates of food between the kitchen and living room. The bedroom was a bit chaotic, with piles of clothes jumbled against the wall, a stereo in the corner playing easy rock, and friends wandering in and out. The children—mine and theirs, along with some others—ran up the stairs, bringing their excited voices into the bedroom and then trailing off downstairs as they raced around. The double bed—just a mattress and box spring without a frame—took up most of the room, its head pushed up against the center of the far wall. Gloria lay back against a pile of pillows, her face twisted and pale.

I sat on the bed next to her, and we talked in between her labor pains.

"Could you press on my back with the next contraction?" she asked. "Wayne won't push down hard enough. I think he's afraid of hurting me."

I was surprised. She was always so reluctant to accept any help from me.

The midwife passed through the room and said, "That's a good idea. It should help."

Gloria rolled on her side. When she gasped in pain, I pressed hard on her back and felt the shudders of her contraction through my fingertips.

We were connected, not only by my hands on her back but by all we had been through together. She was like my sister. I thought of my own family's distance and of Gloria's brother and sister who had rejected her after all the sacrifices she made to save them from abusive parents by taking custody of them while she herself was still in high school. None of that mattered. We had created our own family here, supporting each other through difficult times and celebrating good times such as this child's birth.

I could hear Wayne's voice, even over the music and the buzz of conversation from downstairs. He sounded excited and proud.

"Wayne can't decide whether to be the host or the father," Gloria said. "Stay with me."

"Of course."

The midwife called Wayne when the baby started crowning. He held one of Gloria's hands and I held the other. When I saw the wriggly little boy come sliding out, it felt like a miracle, like my own sons' births.

Now, five months later, it seemed forever since I'd seen Gloria. When Justin begged me to find a time for him to play with Nathan, I called her to see when we could get together. Gloria asked if we would mind coming to her house, since it was hard for her to get away. A baby was hard enough to mobilize without wrangling a two- and four-year-old as well.

So the boys and I walked the few blocks to their house. I kept a careful watch while Jeremy ran ahead to the end of the block and back again. Justin held my hand and scuffed happily through the leaves.

The paint was peeling badly on the big grey house. Gloria was apologetic when she let us in.

"I still haven't finished the wall," she said as we discarded coats and gloves by the door, "but come into the kitchen."

The hole in the wall where she had started to knock it down had the same tangled nest of wires hanging from it. The paper on what was left of the wall was stained with damp and smelled musty, under the usual odor of garbage and dirty diapers.

"You haven't turned your heat on yet?" I asked as I followed Gloria, admiring the dark beauty and stately posture that had Jeremy convinced that she was a countess, despite the tight clothing that my mother would have said made her look cheap.

"No." She smiled back over her shoulder. "Trying to save money. Are you cold?"

"We're fine," I said as the four children ran past us, Nathan yelling at the others to keep up. They dashed to the kitchen to see the baby and then pounded towards the stairs. "They don't slow down long enough to feel cold."

In the kitchen, she offered me a cup of tea. She glanced at the sink full of dirty dishes and said, "I can wash a mug."

I declined but asked why she didn't use the dishwasher. "I'd kill for a dishwasher," I said. "Washing dishes is the chore I hate the most. I wait till they're all dirty before I can force myself to tackle them. That's why I only have a few dishes: if I had more, I'd never wash them."

"I can't bring myself to use it. All that hot water, so wasteful," she said picking up the baby and handing him to me.

It seemed to me that the dishwasher would also help with her kids' persistent colds but I didn't say anything more about it. I held the baby propped on my crossed knee, his little fists curled and batting at the air. His mouth pursed and relaxed as he examined me with big dark eyes.

"He's beautiful, Gloria," I said. "You must be so happy." At her skeptical look, I added, "And tired. Is Wayne helping much?"

"Wayne's gone." My shock must have shown since she shook her head and went on quickly. "Not like that. He goes away sometimes. You know he lost that last job."

I remembered how short of money they'd been in the summer, even with his paycheck. "Will he be back soon?"

"I don't know for certain, but, yes, it had better be soon."

"Did he go looking for work?"

"That or to get his head together."

"I don't understand how he can just leave you and the kids. What are you living on?"

"We're okay. We still have rice and beans from the last bulk food order. I haven't paid the phone bill for a couple of months, but they won't turn it off, not with little kids in the house."

"Can I help?" I asked. "I can lend you something if you like."

"No, we're okay. Don't worry about it."

But I did worry. Gloria was already stick-thin and the children sniffly. She probably had little if any heating oil in the tank.

It wasn't the first time Gloria and Wayne had had money problems in the two and a half years I had known them. In fact they always seemed to be struggling to pay off debts accumulated from the last jobless stretch or emergency expense.

I knew that it did not take much to push someone over the edge into poverty: a few missed paychecks, a bout of ill health.

Gloria always refused help. Food stamps or any kind of public assistance were out of the question. She would never let me lend her money—which was probably a good thing because she'd never be able to pay me back—and acted insulted when I tried to give her gifts of food. The most I could do was have them over for a meal, and that not very often since she couldn't reciprocate.

I admired her independent spirit and the proud lift of her chin. She stayed true to herself throughout her toughest times. But I feared for the children.

The baby started to fuss, so I lifted him to my shoulder and patted his back. "Sometimes I miss having a baby around," I said. "He's so sweet."

"He's quieter than the other two," she agreed.

Finally there was a light at the end of the tunnel for me: these two courses, student teaching, and then I'd have a job and be off welfare at last.

In addition to my schoolwork, I had new responsibilities with the morris team, having volunteered in a moment of madness to be squire, the person who handles administrative things like running team meetings and setting up performances. On our team, no one wanted to be squire. As the internal split widened between those who wanted to practice hard in order to perform well and those who only came to practice to socialize, the meetings became vituperative. Arguments multiplied, and it was up to the squire to act as referee.

There seemed to be no way to bridge the gap between the two sides. To complicate matters, we had determined from the start that the team's decisions should be made by consensus rather than majority vote. Ever the peacemaker,

I hoped to find a way to run meetings so that we could reach a reasonable agreement on the issues that were tearing the team apart.

For the past four years, dancing had been my escape from the drudgery and disappointments of my life, so having it become yet another angry battle left me feeling betrayed. My only other escape was reading. Jill had her artwork and the company of her artist friends. I reminded myself that we were lucky. Many of the women I had worked with during my CETA grant had no such escape.

As it grew colder I continued to study. There were days when I loved November best, all the colorful nonsense of autumn foliage over, the trees stripped bare and the park across the street reduced to shades of brown and grey. The water in Crystal Pond was still, unruffled by children and dogs playing around its edges. Everything seemed clear somehow, open.

Then the snow came. The frozen landscape outside my windows reflected the bleak winter light, unchanging as day after day went by.

One morning Gloria called and asked if I could watch her kids while she went for a job interview. "It'll only be a couple of hours," she said.

"Sure," I said, privately wondering how on earth any job could pay enough for child care much less leave anything over. I offered to come get them, but she insisted on bringing them to my place.

Always thin, her face looked gaunt, her cheeks flushed and patchy with red, perhaps from the cold. She was excited and barely stayed to kiss the children goodbye before sailing out the back door.

We had a quiet morning. After feeding Nathan and Chanté a second breakfast of scrambled eggs and toast, hoping Gloria wouldn't be angry at me for assuming they'd be hungry, I made play dough to occupy the children.

Then I bundled them up and we walked over to get Justin from pre-school. I put the baby in the stroller Gloria had left and got Nathan and Chanté to hold onto either side. On the way home, Justin and Nathan ran ahead while Chanté walked with me.

After lunch and a rest that was mostly giggling and surreptitious movements, with the occasional squawk of a toy quickly stilled, I let them get up and play until it was time to walk over and get Jeremy.

He was one of the last ones out, walking with his head down, kicking at pebbles. When he saw Nathan and Chanté, he tried to swallow his unhappiness. On the way home he held Chanté's hand so she could stumble after Nathan and Justin, her chubby legs unsteady at that speed but her eyes crinkled up with joy. I walked behind. It felt very familiar to be pushing a stroller and thinking about nothing but children.

I gave them a snack and let them watch Mr. Rogers and Sesame Street. I still hadn't heard from Gloria. Annoyed that she hadn't let me know she would be late, I called the house, but there was no answer.

I fed the children dinner. Still no answer at the house. I began to worry something had happened to her, so I started calling around. No one had seen Gloria. Calling the police was out of the question; no one I knew would voluntarily bring themselves to the attention of the authorities.

Not knowing what else to do, I told Nathan and Chanté that they were spending the night and put them down together in the double bed in the guest room. I put the baby in a cardboard box padded with a quilt in my room. At first—angry and worried—I had trouble falling asleep, but finally exhaustion from the kid-filled day overwhelmed me.

I heard Nathan and Chanté moving around in the night but assumed they just had to pee. In the morning, though, I was shocked to find their bed littered with empty cookie wrappers, a cereal box, and some apple cores. Nathan was already up and in the boys' room, but Chanté, looking a little sick, sat woefully in the middle of the mess.

"Don't be mad," she said, her little mouth turned down at the corners and trembling a little.

"I'm not," I said, "but please don't take food without asking. Now I'll have to go to the store again."

I got all the children dressed, and we walked Jeremy and Justin over to school. As the morning wore away, I continued to worry about Gloria. Finally, as we were leaving to go pick up Justin, the phone rang.

It was Wayne. "Gloria is in the hospital," he said abruptly. "Can you keep the kids for a while?"

"Sure. What's wrong? Is it serious?"

"I can't talk now. I'll call you later."

It was a week before I found out more.

Wayne came over one night after dinner and stood in the kitchen, shifting from one foot to the other. Nathan and Chanté came to hug him, but then went back to playing with my boys.

Wayne pushed his glasses up and then brushed his hair off his forehead. It flopped back immediately.

I said, "What hospital is she in? Can I take the kids to see her?"

He looked at me blankly. "No. It's the state hospital. She had a nervous breakdown."

Apparently, there had been no job interview. Feeling that she was losing control, she had brought the kids to me so they at least would be safe. According to the note she left, Gloria thought I would be a better mother for them than she could be.

I wanted to curl up in a ball and howl. How could she have thought that? I was always so aware of my own inadequacies and mistakes that I thought they must be obvious to everyone else. Had I done something to make her feel that way?

I took refuge in practical matters. Since I would have to keep the kids for some time and Wayne didn't have any money, I suggested that I arrange for them to go through foster care. It was only a formality. There was no question about their living with anyone else; their being classified as foster children simply meant that I could get some financial help. Wayne agreed.

He called Nathan and Chanté into the kitchen and explained carefully that their mother was sick and they'd have to stay with me for a while.

Their solemn faces didn't change. "Okay," Nathan said finally. "We like staying with Jeremy and Justin." Chanté nodded, her fingers in her mouth.

"Good," Wayne said. Then he went on to explain that he and Gloria were getting a divorce but they both still loved the children.

This was news to me too, but I was unable to talk with him about it because he made his escape soon after that. All four kids were very quiet so I suggested that they 'camp out' for the night. I pulled the double bed mattress into the boys' room and rigged up a sheet over it, Jeremy helping.

The four children slept together on the mattress, curled up in quilts. I heard their voices late in the night as I walked through the kitchen to get to the bathroom.

Jeremy was talking. "It's okay. Divorce isn't so bad."

"But what will happen to us?" Chanté's small voice.

"You'll live with your mom and your dad will visit," Jeremy said. "You'll see. It won't be much different. Look at us. Justin and I are fine. Your parents still love you."

"Is it my fault?" Nathan asked, just above a whisper. "I tried to help."

"No, of course not. It's between them. It has nothing to do with you. I know you helped your mom all the time."

I stood in the kitchen listening. Although it drove his teacher crazy, I was grateful for Jeremy's self-assurance at that moment. I was so proud of him: six years old, fighting his endless battle at school, yet able to say the right things to comfort these children.

Although I was horrified that he needed to act like a parent, I knew it was better coming from him; they'd believe him in a way they never would a grown-up. Unlike my boys who treated adults as peers, Nathan and Chanté were shy around grown-ups, even me, as though childhood's world were some secret place where adults could not go.

A social worker friend of Jill's did the paperwork so the three of them became my foster children.

"Don't expect the money any time soon," she cautioned me. "The office is so mixed up you probably won't get any until the kids have gone back to their parents."

Nathan, with his sad eyes, enjoyed having his beloved Justin to play with every day. Too, he was glad to have Jeremy around, someone else to be the big brother so he could shuck off that responsibility for a while.

I found that with five kids to care for—one six-year-old, two four-year-olds, a two-year-old, and a baby—I began to run the household with military precision. Every minute was devoted to the children.

I scheduled everything tightly. The weekly menus never varied. Oatmeal most mornings, that was the rule. Scrambled eggs on Wednesday and pancakes on Saturday. Lunches were peanut butter and honey sandwiches on the bread I made twice a week. I still had some applesauce I'd made after a trip to the U-Pick orchard. The weekly dinner menu was fixed too, beans, spaghetti, more beans, macaroni and cheese. Treats like fresh fruit were out, as I stretched the food stamps to feed three extra children.

All toys had to be cleaned up before every meal; and bedtimes were rigidly enforced. There was no getting out of naptime either. They didn't have to sleep, merely be quiet for one precious hour. Suddenly I began to understand my mother's rigid control of her six children's lives.

One book each before naptime and bedtime. Sometimes Jeremy helped me out by reading some of the bedtime books, on those nights when I was stunned with exhaustion and could only sit on the couch, holding Chanté while the boys snuggled against me.

One night, books finished, Chanté stayed on my lap while the boys went off for one last pee before bedtime. Heavy and logy with incipient sleep, she turned her head to look up at me and asked if I had any daughters.

I explained that Jeremy and Justin were my sons, so, no, I did not have any daughters.

She reached up a chubby hand to pat my cheek. "Don't worry, Bah-bwa. I'll be your daw-der."

Jeremy had made friends with a boy in his class who lived next door. Both of them could already read and were bored by Ms. Johnson's lessons, but only Jeremy with his outspoken rebellion drew her ire. The boy's mother joined me in trying to pressure the school to do something about their teacher.

I tried everything I could think of: I met with his teacher and with the principal, but they stonewalled me. Ms. Johnson said she didn't know what I was talking about. The principal insisted that he had to support his teachers.

On our weekly trip to the library, Jeremy got out five books on spiders. He wrote and illustrated a paper on spiders based on his research, hoping to convince Ms. Johnson that he really could read. But she refused to look at it, saying I'd done it for him.

Finally I got the Central Office to do an I.Q. test. When the results came back showing Jeremy to have a high I.Q. after all, high enough to justify his reading skills, I met with the teacher and the principal.

"How was I supposed to know?" Ms. Johnson complained. "Who would expect to find a genius in a neighborhood like this one, full of welfare mothers and Puerto Ricans?"

Barely containing my fury at this blatant prejudice, I looked at the principal, but his expression of mild boredom hadn't changed.

Although the principal didn't seem to see anything wrong with the teacher's attitude, he did agree to let Jeremy go to a Gifted and Talented program one afternoon a week.

This was not much of an improvement for Jeremy, as he still had to suffer Ms. Johnson's treatment the rest of the time. She took to standing him up in front of the class and asking, "Now what does our little genius have to teach us today?" No wonder he was angry. I fumed helplessly every time I watched him trudge through the school door, his shoulders drooping.

No word reached me from Wayne or Gloria. There was never an answer at the house, and the people at the hospital would only say that Gloria was improving. I settled in for the long haul.

It was thanks to my friends that I was still able to meet with Dr. Osborne occasionally. He was understanding about my situation. I managed to finish the semester and reflected that not being able to find a student teaching slot for the spring semester had turned out to be a blessing in disguise. There was no way I could have taught in a classroom fulltime and still taken care of five children.

"You're like the little old woman who lived in a shoe," Jill teased me.

"It's not funny," I said with an exaggerated groan.

Since Jill was working, she couldn't help much with child care but provided moral support in late-night phone calls. Sometimes Richard and Michael, now twelve and nine, would come over when they weren't in school. Michael, with that mischievous gleam in his eye, devised wicked games for the children to play, but I could trust steady, serious Richard to keep things from getting out of hand. While they watched the children, I could go in my room and shut the door for a little while, or sit at the kitchen table watching water drip off the icicles that hung from the roof.

Emma gave me a break sometimes, too. She never seemed to lose patience with the kids and would enter into their games. If it wasn't too cold, she took them across the street to play in the snow in Crystal Park. Alone, I sat in my grandmother's rocking chair where I had nursed both my sons, giving Gloria's baby a bottle. He looked up at me with impenetrable dark eyes as he sucked on the nipple. I stroked his cheek. It felt natural to have a baby in my arms.

"Hush," I said, though he hadn't fussed. "Everything's going to be okay."

As it was, I barely made it through each day. It was like slogging through mud. The four kids were certainly old enough to dress themselves but there was always something for me to adjust: rebuttoning Justin's shirt, combing Chanté's hair, finding a belt for Nathan and making sure he threaded it through every loop.

Monday and Wednesday were art days, when I would mix up play dough or some powdered tempera, and let them have at it. Tuesday and Thursday were music days when they could get out kazoos and pot lids and be a marching band, or put on music and dance around. I felt sorry for my landlord's family downstairs. Saturday was library day, so Jeremy could come with us.

Every day was laundry day, with the drying rack permanently set up in the sunset window and more clothes hanging on the line, frozen solid. And no more letting the dishes slide for a day or two; I had to wash them twice a day. My hands were always red, with little cracks across the knuckles.

The social worker had been right about the foster care payments being delayed. When my car gave up the ghost, I was reduced to walking everywhere with my cloud of children, wrestling the stroller through snowy patches that dragged on the wheels. It took a whole day just to go to the grocery store.

Crazy time was late afternoon. After watching Mr. Rogers and Sesame Street, the kids had a lot of pent-up energy. Nathan screamed with delight as Jeremy wrestled with him. When the boys got rough, Chanté came to find me and stood close by.

"We're the girls," she said.

Later, when I gave the baby a bottle, she stood next to me holding onto the back of the rocking chair. "That's my brother," she said.

"Yes, Sugar Pie," I said. "Don't worry. Everything's going to be okay."

Sometimes at night after all the children were in bed, I set the laundry rack to one side and pulled the rocking chair back into the sunset window. With the lights out, too tired to read or even think, I listened to the floor creaking under the rocker and looked out at the snow covering the park, its icy surface glittering in the moonlight.

Late afternoon and the sun was already gone. Justin, Nathan and Chanté had finally settled down in front of Sesame Street. Jeremy was lying on his bed, sullenly kicking the wall.

I moved through the apartment, stirring the spaghetti sauce for dinner, taping the afternoon's paintings on the kitchen wall, flipping the hats and mittens I had put to dry on top of the space heater in the small front room, hushing the baby in the playpen in the large front room, checking the laundry on the drying rack in the sunset window, glancing out at the iced-over pond.

The phone rang.

I went back to the kitchen, scooping up the baby as I went to stop his fussing. Jiggling him on my hip, I picked up the phone. "Hello?"

"Hello."

He didn't have to say anymore. I knew who it was. Almost five years since I had last heard it, and the sound of his voice was as much a part of me as ever.

"Lewis."

"Yes." He paused and then went on with an odd formality. "Jill told me about

Gloria being in the hospital and you having all the kids."

"Mm-hmm. It's a madhouse around here." The baby started to fuss again so, propping the phone up with my shoulder, I turned him around so he faced away from me, hanging over my arm.

Lewis said, "I thought that might be the case. I thought, if it was okay with you, that I might be able to help."

"What did you have in mind?" Keeping the phone on my shoulder I reached over to stir the spaghetti sauce.

"That's up to you."

I didn't know what to say. I'd stood on my own too long to go back to hiding behind him, but the sweet rushing sound in my ears was the same as it had ever been, pulling me along with its song, overwhelming rational thought.

"Are you still there?" he asked.

"Yes." The baby was pulling on the cord so I moved the phone to my other ear. "I don't know. I mean, yes, of course. Thank you. Anything you want to do to help out would be great."

"Jill said you needed a car."

"That's right."

"Well, I have one that you can have. It's nothing fancy but it runs. It's pretty reliable."

Lewis always seemed to have cars around that he was in the process of restoring. "That would be great. Thanks."

Jeremy trailed into the kitchen. "Who's on the phone? When is dinner?"

"Wait a minute," I said to Jeremy. "I have to go, Lewis. Would you like to come over sometime? For dinner? Or coffee?"

"How about if I bring the car over one night this week? I need to clean it out."

I stiffened. One of our areas of disagreement had been our different definitions of when the house or car was clean enough. Maybe, though, he was trying to be conciliatory. It was hard to tell from his emotionless tone of voice.

"Okay. We'll be here."

Jeremy was pulling on me trying to attract my attention. The baby was reaching out to him and wriggling. The sauce needed stirring again.

"Well, goodbye," I said.

"Goodbye."

I was nervous about seeing him again. I planned to dress up, or at least think about what to wear, but before I knew it he was knocking at the door, and me still in my old jeans and tee shirt. When I opened the door, it was as if no time at all had passed, and I knew everything would be fine. He looked the same as ever, with his strong compact body and that quirky smile that turned my knees to water.

Justin, Nathan and Chanté hung back, hidden behind the bedroom door, giggling and squirming, but Jeremy, always the bold one, marched right up to Lewis and said, "Who are you?"

"Now, Jeremy . . ." I began.

He looked down at Jeremy and, without smiling, said, "I'm Lewis."

Jeremy eyed him for a moment and then said, "All right." He turned and walked back to the bedroom saying, "It's okay, guys. It's just Lewis." The other children peeped from behind the door.

Lewis raised one eyebrow at me. I could only shrug.

I had coffee ready, knowing that he could never get enough of it. His initial stiffness melted quickly as we sat over our mugs, talking as we had back in the beginning, politics mostly, agreeing about so much: *The City Manager's office . . . That bunch of crooks . . . Foster care.* Meanwhile, the children raced around screaming, excited at having a stranger in the house.

Lewis gave me a rueful grin and said, "I guess I should give in and play with them for a while."

The boys were delighted that he was willing to get down on the floor and wrestle with them and strong enough to swing even Jeremy up to the ceiling. Chanté hid in the kitchen with me while the boys rough-housed, but when Lewis came back in and sat down, she smiled at him before going to play with the boys.

We talked like old friends who hadn't seen each other for a while. When other emotions started to creep in, I ignored them and moved on to a safer topic. I was not going to go down that road again, not today, not a chance, no way. Lewis seemed to feel the same. There was no point in arguing about the past. No point in succumbing to the old attraction.

After a while he took us down to see the car. It was a 1966 Dodge Polara, a huge vehicle with a V-8 engine and a hood that you could launch jets off of. Lewis had added the ram's head hood ornament from our old Dodge truck.

"It seemed to fit," he said, glancing at me.

Something long frozen seemed to thaw inside of me. "That was thoughtful. You're right. It's perfect."

"It's an aircraft carrier," Jeremy said.

Lewis quirked an eyebrow at me. I knew he was questioning Jeremy's knowledge of military craft, so I shrugged.

"Well, I'd better get going. Here are the keys," he said.

I thanked him again and watched as he unhitched his truck from the Polara and drove away, not sure if it would be another five years before I heard from him again. And not sure whether that would be a good thing or not.

Having a car alleviated much of the difficulty that lumbered my days and drained my energy. The gas mileage was appalling, but I didn't care—I was just so grateful to have a car big enough to fit all five kids easily.

Once I had the car and Emma's offer to babysit, I started going to morris practice again, but the endless sniping kept it from being the relief I'd hoped for. Their complaints seemed so trivial. Compared to worrying about Gloria and struggling to keep things together for the children's sake, fighting about whether practice should start on time or not seemed ridiculous.

In the spring I got word that Gloria was finally getting better. Wayne had disappeared again; no one knew where. Having no means of support, Gloria had given in and applied for welfare. I was glad that she hadn't let her prejudice against handouts prevent her from getting aid.

The social worker who had handled the foster care came to our house.

"No money yet?" she asked.

I shook my head. We were sitting at my kitchen table, the sun falling weakly over the clean wooden surface. With all the children's activities, I must have scrubbed it twenty times a day.

She said, "It won't be long now. Listen, there's something I want to talk with you about."

I waited. She looked out the window. Finally I said, "What is it?"

"Don't answer me now," she said, leveling a look at me. "It's only that we don't think Gloria is competent to take the children."

Disbelief had me running my hand through my hair. "But she's being discharged. She's all better." Then I thought: *Nathan and Chanté, and my darling baby.* My heart went out to them. "What will happen to the children?"

"We'd like you to consider adopting them."

It was some time before I realized my mouth was hanging open. I shut it.

22
DECISIONS

"We'd never find anyone else to adopt all three of them," the social worker said. "I don't want to break them up, so if you won't take them, the next best choice is to give them back to their mother."

I still couldn't say anything.

"Just think about it," she said, collecting her coat.

It was an intolerable choice for me. I didn't want to be part of the system that intimidated poor women by threatening to take their children away; I had seen enough of that myself. On the other hand, they were my children now, my daughter, my sons. I thought of Chanté patting my cheek, the baby's weight in my arms.

Or was I being selfish, unwilling to stay on welfare for three more long years, until the baby was old enough for day care? I could feel the tunnel close in around me and that elusive teaching job slip further away. When would it be my turn?

I remembered my touchstone: *the kids come first*. But which kids? Jeremy and Justin had been good about sacrificing our private family life to help out our friends, but they would suffer if the situation became permanent. With five children to support, I would never be able to provide them with the better life I had been working toward since the night of the fire.

Would Nathan, Chanté, and the baby really be better off with me? Certainly I loved them, but how could I replace the parents they had known all their lives? The children liked staying with us, but they did not consider it permanent, more of an extended vacation. Nathan often asked about his parents, and sometimes we walked past their house so he could be sure they weren't there. No, I was positive they belonged with their mother. I couldn't believe she would allow any harm to come to them.

And keeping them would be a betrayal, because I had promised Wayne that foster care was merely a formality. I remembered my own fear of having my children taken away. If her children were removed from her care, surely Gloria would spiral downwards and find no way back. I simply could not do that to Gloria.

And they would fight me for the children. I had fought and fought for so long, but how could I fight against my own? I would be starting a civil war within the community I had worked so hard to foster, forcing people to choose sides, setting friend against friend.

I turned the social worker down. I told her that I thought the best thing for the children was to be with their mother and that she—I believed—would take good care of them.

The day Gloria came to pick up the kids was warm and sunny. Jill's son Richard had taken the four kids around the corner to Monaghan's drugstore to get a Milky Way to split between them for a treat. The baby was asleep in my room.

After refusing my offer of tea, Gloria stood in my kitchen, very straight as always, her dark hair tied back and her face very pale. "There's no way to thank you for taking care of the kids all this time. Oh, I can't wait to see them," she said, her eyes bright. "Do you think they'll be long?"

I assured her that they would only be a minute. I told her that they'd been good, no problem aside from those early episodes of pigging out in the night.

The light in her eyes faded. "That's because they were starving." She went on to explain that she had run out of money weeks before, with no word from Wayne. She had stopped eating first, even though it meant that her milk dried up. The day she scrambled the last egg, Nathan had given his share to Chanté because she loved eggs so much. On the final morning, Gloria had split the handful of lentils—the last bit of food in the house—between the children and then brought them to me.

I was shocked. For the first time—and too late—I doubted my decision. I hadn't known she had let them go hungry for weeks because she was too proud to accept help from friends or the government. If she had set aside her pride and applied for food stamps or emergency assistance, things never would have reached the point of her children coming to live with me while she struggled to regain her ability to function in the world.

I almost hated her in that moment, when I realized she might indeed hurt the kids. I almost took a step back away from her.

I looked past her at the kitchen table where the honey jar caught and held the sunlight, golden light that fell too across the basket of oranges, the jar of daffodils and the table I had just scrubbed for maybe the tenth time already that day, its cleanliness a slap in the face to her. I had succeeded where she had failed, not only with my own children but with hers on top as well. But her failure meant that I had failed too. What kind of support network had I helped to build if she couldn't come to me for help? It seemed a rejection of the community we had created, the one I was so proud of. And a rejection of my own first principle, the one I thought we shared, that the kids come first. I was almost afraid of her, this stranger with her unfathomable conduct.

I knew then that I should have kept the kids, despite the weariness of the inevitable fight with Gloria and all the years afterwards of struggling to raise five children.

I started to speak, but at that moment the kids came clattering up the steps and burst in the back door.

Gloria turned swiftly towards them. Nathan ran to his mother, his face crumpling. But Chanté came to me, hiding behind me, holding onto my leg. I put my hand on her shoulder. It was all I could do not to grip her to me and refuse to let her go.

With all the rumpus, the baby woke and started to cry. Not letting go of my pants, Chanté followed me into my room as I went to pick him up. The baby was quickly soothed but when I went to hand him to Gloria, he screamed and reached out for me.

Stone-faced, she held the struggling baby.

Nathan came over and took Chanté's hand. "Come on," he said. "We're going home."

On the receiving end of Chanté's panicked look, I said, "Don't worry. We'll visit soon."

At the door, Gloria turned, her face hard, the baby in her arms still crying and reaching out for me. "No," she said. "You'll understand that we can't see you for a while." She looked at the baby, at Chanté who had her fingers in her mouth, and then back at me. "Don't come around."

She shut the door behind her.

I stood there, my arms empty at my sides. Then I started to cry.

Richard, Jeremy and Justin stared at me for a minute and then crowded around, patting my arms and back, murmuring, "It's okay. It's okay."

I stopped crying and hugged them, one at a time. Richard suggested he take Jeremy and Justin across the street to Crystal Park for a little while. After they left, I stood in the kitchen looking around. I didn't know what to do next.

Summer came and Worcester sweltered under the relentless sun. The garden I had planted dried up and died. I pulled up the spindly brown tomato plants and broke off the straws that had been beanstalks. There seemed no point in replanting.

Fay invited us out to the farm in Oxford for a picnic. I took my big straw hat but Fay gloried in the hot sun, shaking her long hair out as though washing it in light. She and I wandered through the garden she had planted and compared notes on our gardening failures.

She asked me about different kinds of mulch and if I thought another strain of beans would work better next year. A little surprised still that anyone would come to me for advice, I responded, finding that I knew more about mulch and beans than I had realized.

We found a shady spot to spread out our blanket and watched Hamid and my boys running around. I had splurged on a jar of bubble soap, something you couldn't buy with food stamps, but it was worth it to see how much fun they had with it, taking turns to blow bubbles while the other two chased them.

Eventually they collapsed onto the blanket and we feasted on bread and peanut butter and bananas. By the time I got my boys home, they were hot and cranky so I gave them a bath and put them down early.

After they fell asleep, I stood in their room in the long summer twilight watching them breathe. Justin's hair stuck in damp curls to his forehead, so I pulled back his light summer blanket leaving just the sheet.

The responsibility for protecting them and shaping their lives weighed on me. I tried to make decisions but fumbled or rushed through them. My past decisions too were beyond my ability to evaluate. Did I do the right thing taking up with Lewis? So much had turned out wrong but I had these two boys. They appeared so small when they were asleep. But even as I held and hefted it, their precious childhood seemed to slip from my hands.

I didn't know what to do about schools for next year. Nothing was resolved. After being abused by Mrs. Johnson all year, Jeremy had turned from a loving, generous child into a sullen, angry boy. I hated to send him back to Freeland Street and hated even more the chance that Justin might get a teacher like Ms. Johnson. But what could I do?

Committed as I was to public schools and the opportunity to meet all kinds of people, I found that the city school system would not let my kids transfer to a different school unless I moved to that district. With Jill accompanying me, I had visited almost every school in town, even the private ones that I could never in a million years afford, but none seemed much better than Freeland Street.

A college preparatory school told me that it was too late to apply for a scholarship for the coming year. Knowing that you didn't need to be certified to teach in a private school, I described my teaching experience and training, but not only did they have no openings for teachers, they didn't offer free tuition to the children of their teachers.

Jill and I went to a couple of Catholic schools, but conversations with students and parents revealed the same mix of good and bad teachers that I had found at Freeland Street. And I had no way to pay the tuition.

The final straw was a private school run by the Seventh Day Adventists. I picked up a science textbook in a fifth grade classroom and it opened to a unit on Noah's Ark—this was for Science class, not Religion. I joked that the Geography and History textbooks must have units on the Garden of Eden and Moses parting the Red Sea, but the look on our guide's face told me that it wasn't a joke. I gave up after that.

I was in despair. How could I send Jeremy and Justin to Freeland Street to be tormented for another year? I tried to remember Miss Smith's great lesson to me: that everyone has something good inside, something to teach me. But the reality was that I had to protect my children. I just didn't know how. I began to consider keeping them out of school.

Dr. Osborne failed to find a student teaching slot for me for the fall—too few slots for the number of student teachers he said, but I heard a rumor through a friend of Fay's that the Worcester Public Schools would never allow me teach because I was a welfare mom. I watched my chances of getting off of welfare recede.

The morris team was on hiatus for the summer, but I wasn't sure I would go back in the fall. I could not bear their bickering any longer.

To my surprise, Lewis continued to call and visit occasionally. Although my old feelings for him still rumbled beneath the surface, I was wary of starting up a relationship with him again.

We drank coffee together, talked, played with the children. I felt comfortable with him; I knew him so well. Even after all these years. The boys treated him like any other friend who came to visit, anyone that is who didn't mind a couple of ruffians jumping on him and bearing him down to the floor for a bout of rough-housing.

Gloria relented after a month or so, allowing me to visit the children now and then. I still felt a little awkward, though the children clearly did not, running off together as soon as we arrived. They seemed happy and well-cared for, their clothes clean.

Gloria and I went into the kitchen, where the baby lay in a carseat on the floor by the table, waving his arms and smiling. I yearned to pick him up, but was afraid to ask. Every word and gesture had to be weighed, so that Gloria wouldn't think I was criticizing her.

We sat at the table. I couldn't help but look around, notice the pile of dirty dishes in the sink, the rancid-smelling bag of garbage by the door, the stickiness of the floor under my feet. I found myself thinking like a social worker on a home visit. I hungered after my decision, believing I had made a terrible mistake, but there was no way to rectify it now.

In early July my mother called to tell me that my father had been diagnosed with cancer, a low-grade malignancy that supposedly was operable. However, there was some concern since he had already had one heart attack. To my surprise, she went on, "I want you and the boys to come live with us. Could you move back to Baltimore, just for a little bit? Your father and I won't know what to do with ourselves if you don't."

Astonished, I recalled how, back when I was pregnant with Justin, she had turned me away, saying that I had made my bed and could lie in it. But five years had passed since then. Things change. People change.

With my youngest sibling away at college, my mother was panicking at the idea of being alone. More than simply an empty nest, she now had to face the idea that my father might die, leaving her for the first time in her life completely alone in the house. The children and I could ease her over the hump of her fear and my father's illness.

And it would be a good thing for us, too. If we went to Baltimore—just for a year or two—the boys could go to the public school in Roland Park which was famous for its gifted and talented program. A year or two at Roland Park Public would heal Jeremy's wounds and give them both a good start. Even better, the school had a full-day kindergarten, unlike Worcester's morning-only class. With Justin in school all day, I wouldn't have to worry about child care, that perennial stumbling block.

Here—finally—was the answer to our school dilemma. A few years at a good school would give me the breathing room I needed to finish my teaching certification and find the right school for my boys.

I contacted Towson University in Baltimore. They assured me that I could student teach in the fall, even though school was starting in a little over a month.

With the summer drought hanging on, the pond in Crystal Park began to shrink, its edges pulling in and the sour-smelling water dark with algae. I walked around the pond and up the hill weighing my options.

I didn't know anyone in Baltimore. All my carefully stored-up knowledge of Worcester—shortcuts, the best bagel shop, the right junkyard for parts for my car—would be useless there. But I wouldn't be there for long, only a couple of years. My Worcester friends were making their own way out, as I was: Jill with her job at the halfway house, Sherry in school, and Fay looking into teaching.

What difference would it really make? I would be following the same path whether I stayed in Worcester or went to Baltimore. I had, after all, only been waiting for the kids to be in school so that I could afford to get a job—in that sense, nothing had changed since the day I went on welfare; I still couldn't get a job that would pay for both child care and our living expenses.

In Maryland, it would still be on me to succeed; my parents would not help me. They insisted that as soon as my student teaching was over in December and I got a job—a sure thing given how desperate the city was for certified teachers—I had to start paying room and board. It would be a bit of a struggle in the fall, until I got a job, but we could do it.

I could not have gone back before, while my mother barred the way. However, now that my siblings were gone, I could no longer infect them with my wild ways. My parents had come to see me as an adult, someone independent of them. But it was more than that. My parents were different people from who they had been five years earlier.

My mother—born to run things—was happy in her job as a real estate agent. Feeling that she was finally making use of her abilities, she filled her days with work, scheduling open houses, meeting clients, putting in her time at the office.

And my father had lost his angry edge. He seemed determined to be a better grandfather than he had been a father. I remembered how he had searched all over to find a Snoopy train for Justin.

It was too late for me to learn to love them. But I could set aside the ogres of my childhood and deal with the people they had become. True, moving in with them after being on my own for so long would be difficult. But the benefits for everyone were overwhelming, and it would only be for a year or two.

Cynthia didn't think I should go. "You are only going because they need your help. But it's yourself you should be thinking of. You don't owe them anything."

I found it hard to explain. It wasn't about my parents. It was about the kids. *The kids come first.* In the end, the choice was obvious. I had to do what was best for my boys.

I steeled myself against second guessing. Just go, I told myself.

At the welfare office, where I went to cut off my checks, I was seen right away for once. The social worker, who had loosened his tie and unbuttoned his collar button, wearily handed me a form. "Sign here."

I looked around the musty office, metal fans clacking from every corner. This place had been the enemy I had fought over and over, the benefactor who had kept us alive. Like a parent almost. This was the environment that I knew. I felt as though I was leaving home.

I signed the form and handed it back.

"Good luck," the man said, sliding the form into my file. He smiled, and his face briefly lightened. "I have a feeling that you're going to make it," he said.

Packing was easy. I gave away as much as I could and dropped the rest at Goodwill. Erica, my old neighbor from Newbury Street, arranged to move into the apartment, so I left the appliances for her.

Lewis gave me a small trailer he had built and welded a hitch for it onto the Polara. "Think you can fit everything into that?" he asked.

I promised to bring the boys up to see him the following summer.

"I don't want to hold you back," he said. "Do what you have to."

He opened his arms, and I stepped into them. We stayed like that for a long time.

The old attraction was still there. If I remained in Worcester, perhaps we would get together again. All the more reason for going.

I didn't want to make a big deal out of saying goodbye to our friends. After all, it was only for a year, maybe two.

Muddy River threw me a goodbye party, setting aside the tensions of the last year to crowd around and wish me well. They had made me a card out of a photograph of us dancing on the sidewalk in front of the museum, me in the set across from Cynthia.

Later Cynthia said, "What about dancing?"

"There's no morris team in Baltimore," I said thankfully. I had been so worn down by the fighting on the morris team that I wasn't sure I ever wanted to be on a team again.

"But you have to dance. Dancing is your life."

"There's a weekly contra dance I can go to if I get desperate. And I'll be back soon." I hoped the team dynamics would settle down before I returned.

She made me promise to come back for the Marlboro Ale in the spring. I knew Cynthia would stay in touch with us. In fact, we started getting cards and letters from her even before we left.

We visited Gloria and the children, giving them the furniture from the boys' room and the toys we weren't taking. Nathan immediately ran off with Justin, while Jeremy sat with me. Standing behind her mother's chair, Chanté had two fingers in her mouth.

Gloria rattled on about an argument she was having with the welfare office, but I wasn't listening to her. Finally, a thin wail came from the playpen.

"May I?" I asked.

"Be my guest," said Gloria, with a generous sweep of her hand.

I picked up the baby and shushed him. Holding him, I returned to my chair. I saw that Chanté now had a third finger in her mouth. My eyes burned, but there was nothing I could do.

Our farewell visits with Emma and Fay were sad, but not as traumatic as the one with Gloria. Hamid demanded that I leave Justin behind with him, but gave up with a scowl when Justin said he had to go with me.

Jeremy and Justin were a bit shell-shocked by this point. Jeremy kept asking, "When exactly are we coming back?"

Saying goodbye to Jill was the worst.

Richard and Michael were like my own sons, but they were big guys now. They wouldn't forget us while we were gone. They carried my boys off to their bedrooms where they had piled some of their toys that they wanted to pass on, leaving me and Jill in her whirlwind-tossed living room.

I looked at her helplessly. I didn't know what I was going to do without her, even for a year. No one else would ever understand what my life in Worcester had been like. Who but Jill had been in the trenches with me? She had steadied me through every crisis and helped me find my way when I was lost. If I had realized it would be this hard, I never would have decided to go.

"Jill," I said, but then couldn't say anything else.

She hugged me hard. "We will always be friends," she said. "Write to me."

The boys and I left at 6 a.m. on August 4th. I steered the aircraft carrier and its little black trailer down Cambridge Street. It was a month short of the ten-year anniversary of my arrival in Worcester to go to Clark University. I felt no sense of triumph or uplift; I had survived but that was all. And I still had a hard road in front of me.

As I dismantled my Worcester life, I began to feel like a dust-bowl Okie from a Steinbeck novel, pulling up stakes because times had gotten too hard, saying goodbye to everyone, and striking out for someplace better.

EPILOGUE

Some changes are deliberate, only made after much weighing of pros and cons, while some are decided in an instant. Still others are the merest accident: the garden party Cynthia and I threw on Women's Hill has become a tradition at Pinewoods, faithfully held every Fourth of July weekend for more than twenty-five years by people who do not remember when or how it started. Whether well-thought-out or just a summer afternoon's whimsy, the changes I've decided upon have rarely had the results I expected.

I stayed in Baltimore and taught in the city schools. When teaching still did not lift us out of poverty, I took night classes and became first an electronics technician and then an engineer.

Sitting in my car in a poor section of Baltimore, all these years after leaving Worcester, with the doors locked and the air conditioner running, I could have passed for any affluent tourist who had gotten lost trying to find the Inner Harbor. I had not forgotten the past, but neither had I made a point of telling my new friends and co-workers about my life on welfare.

It seemed useless to me to try to challenge the stereotypes I heard voiced around me by people whose only experience of welfare was what they heard on television or read in the paper. But to remain silent was doing a disservice to all the brave women I had known who lived in poverty.

It wasn't laziness or greed that brought the people I knew to welfare; some bad choices, perhaps, but mostly circumstances and the near impossibility for single mothers of finding a job that would cover living expenses, child care and medical needs. Even I, with my privileged upbringing of good education, health care, and positive role models, found myself needing the temporary assistance of welfare. And it was temporary, not only for me, but for the vast majority of recipients.

Nearly all of the women I knew were desperate to work even when it didn't make sense, when they had more income on welfare. They tried to work despite the many obstacles in their way: child care costs, lack of job skills, unreliable transportation. Not only did they not have appropriate clothes to wear, but also in many cases they didn't even know what the appropriate clothes would be. Some people, such as Amy, that heavy-set woman who sat on the porch on Newbury Street and tried to feed my kids marshmallow sandwiches, were too dysfunctional or disabled to work. Amy did finally get a job but was only able to keep it while she had the support of her mother. When her mother died, Amy had to go into assisted living.

I didn't feel guilty accepting welfare. I knew that the minimal investment that society made to keep us alive would be paid back thousands of times over as I, and soon my children, became taxpayers. That has happened. I may be the only person who actually enjoys April 15th. Although I don't agree with everything my taxes support, I am grateful to be working and paying taxes. I welcome the opportunity to contribute to maintaining our civic life.

Welfare, as it was administered in the 1970s, worked for me exactly as it was supposed to, keeping me and my children alive until we could get back on our feet. However, I understood how it could become a trap. I found it difficult to believe that I would escape and take my place as a worker again. For me, it was the CETA grant that snapped me out of my funk of hopelessness and taught me to believe that I could succeed. Although I started with many advantages, the main factors that helped me get off of welfare are things that could be provided to every parent of young children living in poverty: training, housing assistance, medical care, and day care assistance.

Recently Cynthia asked me if I could have had a perfect childhood, what that would have been like.

Without thinking, I blurted, "But I did have a perfect childhood."

I surprised myself, but after some thought realized that it was true. My childhood made me who I was. If nothing else, it taught me to stand alone, an emotional self-reliance that I needed later. And, as it turned out, I didn't have to stand completely alone; I had a community of friends and teachers and random strangers who helped me.

My decision to set aside the past and relate to my parents as the individuals they had become turned out to be a good one. Forgiving them would have been too hard. Instead, I recognized that they had faced their own challenges—my father coming from a blue-collar rowhouse background to become a doctor, my mother giving up the working life she loved to care for six children—and had done the best they could. Eventually my parents adjusted to their empty nest and remained secure in their prosperous world. My mother loved working right up until the day ill health forced her to retire. Saved from my pernicious influence, my siblings all stepped into successful, middle-class lives.

Cynthia and I are still close. She lives in Baltimore these days, where she works as an occupational therapist.

Thanks to her, I dance even now. Dancing was a great gift to me, on so many levels: not only opening to me the community of friends and the transcendent experience of the dance itself, but also breaking the isolation of being in one socio-economic class, giving me a different perspective from the one I saw every day from my front stoop.

I didn't realize that all these years later, many of these people would still be my friends: Cynthia, my teammates on Muddy River, Shag, Tony, and the dancers from the other teams. I didn't realize that those teams would split and reproduce until there were hundreds of morris teams across the U.S. I also didn't know that I was doing the best possible thing to help myself get off of welfare: associating with people who themselves worked and never doubted that I too would be working as soon as my kids were old enough for day care. My friends' support and encouragement helped give me the confidence to leave welfare behind and enter the workforce.

Jeremy and Justin grew up dancing. They still dance, just as they are still a part of this community that we created. It has welcomed them with open arms, the way it welcomed me all those years ago.

Christine has remained a close friend. She still lives in Washington state where she is Vice President for Enrollment Management for a university and Executive Director of the University Center, which promotes higher education opportunities in technology and the sciences. Of my other friends from Western Maryland, Jim and Charlie both continue to play music when not busy with their jobs and families. Music also remains a big part of Walt's life. In addition to performing with his band, he has started a visionary program aimed at using music to bring people together.

Some of the people I knew in Worcester have not been as lucky. Amy died a couple of years ago, in her mid-forties, from kidney failure or diabetes or some other complication of excessive weight. She was comforted at the end by getting her wish to have her beloved son, Teddie, come to live with her for a little while.

Recently I heard that Arlene too had passed. I thought of her bright, open face and her gap-toothed grin, her ambitious plans. Constrained by children and poverty, she still found a way to make art out of her life, in that half-buried apartment on Wall Street.

Sad, wishing I hadn't lost touch with her, I pulled out the film we made and watched it. I saw again the exotic fish swimming through the air of mystery and fun that she had created, the animals on the walls, the story of her grandfather's grandfather and the townspeople who saved him. Arlene fulfilled her goal of graduating from high school and even went on to get a nursing degree. I don't know what happened to the book about her family. I doubt she finished it, since she had so much to tell and, as it turned out, so little time.

My friendship with Gloria never recovered, and eventually I lost touch with her and the children who had almost been mine. My other Worcester friends are doing well: Sherry works as a massage therapist, while her daughter Rora has children of her own and is going to school. Fay became a special education teacher for the Worcester Public Schools. She also has become a successful painter who shows and sells her work frequently. Emma is still disabled but her volunteer efforts have made her known and beloved throughout Worcester.

I wasn't the only one shipwrecked in a strange and hostile world. Welfare worked for us the way it was supposed to: it kept us and our children alive during a difficult time.

Jill said we would always be friends, and she was right. We talk on the phone and visit regularly. She is still working as a social worker in Worcester and doing her amazing and inventive artwork. Richard became a software engineer. His wife is a teacher, and we are all in love with their extraordinary daughter. After struggling with an injury on the job, Michael has gone back to college.

I see Lewis now and then, most recently at Kevin's wedding and before that, at Jeremy's wedding. Our lives have gone in different directions, but he seems to be doing well.

My boys, too, are doing well. Both Jeremy and Justin have been working since their teens. Both are married and own their own homes, living lives even my mother approves of, balancing their professional careers and their love of the arts.

In my memory, it was always summer when we lived on Newbury Street and always winter when we lived on West Street.

I went by West Street one Saturday afternoon not long ago. The big houses of Becker Junior College were still well-kept, freshly painted and the shrubs manicured. Other houses on the street appeared to have been restored, and resembled the college's houses, though still divided into apartments. Elm Park Community School was unchanged, with neatly clipped fields behind chain-link fencing and boys playing basketball on the courts by the building. Across the street, the neighbor's house looked better than ever, with wrought iron grates on the windows and a new SUV out front.

Our old house, however, was boarded up. No shrubs softened the brick foundation. White paint peeled off into the small yard, its straggly grass choked by plantain and clover. The front door and a random assortment of windows were boarded over with sheets of plywood. With so many houses being restored, the fact that this one, our house, had been left to fall apart was troubling. It was as though the house had died once we were gone, as though we had skated the edge of what was possible, and it had collapsed behind us.

At the time, I did not recognize how tenuous our safety net was. I was lucky enough to catch the momentum generated by the activities of the Welfare Rights movement. Benefits had been standardized, and emergency assistance was available to cover things like furniture and appliances. Jill and I lived in Massachusetts where the welfare allotment was one of the highest in the nation. We managed to get Section 8 housing assistance and the grants from CETA that enabled us to work.

Things are very different today for welfare recipients. Soon after I left welfare, the cocaine epidemic of the 1980s sent drug use and crime rates soaring. Social services have been cut drastically, reducing welfare allotments across the country. Poorly funded transportation systems make it harder than ever to get to work, while housing and medical costs have skyrocketed. Add to these obstacles the effects of the Welfare Reform Act, and escaping poverty becomes a nearly insurmountable challenge.

My parents liked to say that I had battled my way out of poverty; I had pulled myself up by my bootstraps. But it wasn't true. Many people reached out their hands to help me, not just my friends, but the professor at Worcester State College who helped me get certified to teach, the friend of Jill's who helped us get the CETA grants, the dance organizations who gave me (and later my sons) scholarships to camp, the old man who taught us how to garden back on Newbury Street.

He showed me that believing you can do it is the first step in getting up off that stoop. Even though I felt the drag of the familiar and the difficulty of reinventing your life when I tried to escape poverty, I barely tasted the hopelessness that many of the women I'd known on welfare expressed. Because I entered welfare with advantages of education and health and experience that enabled me to see another future, I'll never know what that blind alley feels like any more than I will ever know what it feels like to be dark-skinned in a world that's far from color-blind.

But I have to try. Every day, I need to be reminded of what Miss Smith taught me back in college: pay attention. Driving down Monroe Street, even I who knew better felt how easy it would be to see the people on those stoops through the lens of a stereotype instead of recognizing that each person had his or her own story, his or her own reason for sitting there.

It's too easy to accept the voices around us as our opinions, too easy to rely on stereotypes instead of opening ourselves to the new and unexpected.

It's too easy to be insulated, too easy to forget, to look at what we have and think it was somehow earned instead of given.

Anyone can be poor anytime; we are only an accident, a divorce away from poverty. Once you've slipped into poverty, all the hard work in the world may not be enough to get you out. So much is outside your control. You have what you're born with, the luck that falls into your hands, and the help that comes out of nowhere.

And when the fight is over, you forget how hard it was, like childbirth. It's easy to get soft. It's easy to drive down Monroe Street, blind to the lives of the people sitting on stoops there, the decisions and trade-offs they've had to make. In the end, I'm only a tourist in their world, but I owe it to them to remember to see them as individuals, valuable human beings without whom my life would be the poorer.

The End

"Poverty is no sin"

George Herbert

ACKNOWLEDGMENTS

Working on this memoir has brought home to me the maxim that people remember the past differently. I have tried to be as accurate as possible, plundering my journals and my own and others' memories. All the people in this book are real, though some names have been changed. There are no composite characters, and the sequence of events is as faithful as fallible memory can make it. Any errors are mine alone.

I am more grateful than I can say to all those, whether mentioned by name or not, who helped me when I needed it. In writing this book, I must thank Marita Golden and Jewell Parker Rhodes for their ideas and encouragement; the talented writers in my critique group—Johanna Zackarias, Patricia Meisol, Stephanie Citron, and Christel Cothran—for their skilled and patient editing; Ruby Pratka for editing assistance; and the members of the Compound Book Club for celebrating every small achievement. I also want to thank the friends described in this book for all that they have given me, and Jeremy and Justin for their love and support.

The future of publishing...today!

Apprentice House is the country's only campus-based, student-staffed book publishing company. Directed by professors and industry professionals, it is a nonprofit activity of the Communication Department at Loyola University Maryland.

Using state-of-the-art technology and an experiential learning model of education, Apprentice House publishes books in untraditional ways. This dual responsibility as publishers and educators creates an unprecedented collaborative environment among faculty and students, while teaching tomorrow's editors, designers, and marketers.

Outside of class, progress on book projects is carried forth by the AH Book Publishing Club, a co-curricular campus organization supported by Loyola University Maryland's Office of Student Activities.

Student Project Team for *Innocent: Confessions of a Welfare Mother:*
       Rebekah Alavi, '10

Eclectic and provocative, Apprentice House titles intend to entertain as well as spark dialogue on a variety of topics. Financial contributions to sustain the press's work are welcomed. Contributions are tax deductible to the fullest extent allowed by the IRS.

To learn more about Apprentice House books or to obtain submission guidelines, please visit www.ApprenticeHouse.com.

Apprentice House
Communication Department
Loyola University Maryland
4501 N. Charles Street
Baltimore, MD 21210
Ph: 410-617-5265 • Fax: 410-617-2198
info@apprenticehouse.com
www.apprenticehouse.com

CPSIA information can be obtained at www.ICGtesting.com
Printed in the USA
LVOW132000290712

292063LV00010B/11/P